MORAMONA

MORAMONA

THE MORMONS IN HAWAII

R. LANIER BRITSCH

MORMONS IN THE PACIFIC SERIES

Published by
The Institute for Polynesian Studies
Laie, Hawaii

In association with
Polynesian Cultural Center
Brigham Young University–Hawaii

Published and distributed by
The Institute for Polynesian Studies
Brigham Young University–Hawaii
Laie, Hawaii 96762

Third printing 1998

ISBN 0–939154–46–3

Portions of this book appeared in slightly
different form in *Unto the Islands of the Sea:
A History of the Latter-day Saints in the Pacific,*
© 1986 by Deseret Book Company.

Library of Congress Cataloging-in-Publication Data

Britsch, R. Lanier.
Moramona : the Mormons in Hawaii / R. Lanier Britsch.
p. cm. — (Mormons in the Pacific series)
Includes bibliographical references.
ISBN 0–939154–46–3 (alk. paper).
1. Mormon Church—Hawaii—History. 2. Church of Jesus Christ of Latter-day Saints—Hawaii—History. 3. Hawaii—Church history.
I. Title. II. Series.
BX8615.H3B77 1989 89–37402
289.3'969—dc20 CIP

This book is printed on acid-free paper and meets
the guidelines for permanence and durability
of the Council on Library Resources

Book Design by Roger Eggers

To Hawaii

No alien land in all the world has any deep, strong charm for me but that one; no other land could so longingly and so beseechingly haunt me sleeping and waking, through half a life-time, as that one has done. Other things leave me, but it abides; other things change, but it remains the same. For me its balmy airs are always blowing, its summer seas flashing in the sun; the pulsing of its surf-beat is in my ear; I can see its garlanded crags, its leaping cascades, its plumy palms drowsing by the shore; its remote summits floating like islands above the cloud wrack; I can feel the spirit of its woodland solitudes; I can hear the splash of its brooks; in my nostrils still lives the breath of flowers that perished twenty years ago.

—Mark Twain
1889

CONTENTS

PART V
1950–1987 FULFILLMENT IN THE CONTEMPORARY WORLD

ILLUSTRATIONS

TABLES

PREFACE

A WORD of explanation is in order to justify yet another volume on Hawaiian missionary history. The history of Protestant missions, and to a lesser degree, the Roman Catholic missions in Hawaii, is well known. Both preceded The Church of Jesus Christ of Latter-day Saints in the islands and laid much groundwork upon which the Mormons built. Yet the history of the Mormon missions to Hawaii is also important and has never been published in book form. A few articles, stories, autobiographies, and theses exist on the subject, but this volume is the first to attempt a complete account of the history of the Latter-day Saints. Thousands of Mormon missionaries have served in Hawaii since 1850, and a large number of Hawaii's peoples have affiliated themselves with the Church. They have settled local "Zions," farmed Church-owned plantations, established schools, and built hundreds of chapels and a temple.

Moramona will doubtless have greatest appeal to Latter-day Saints, but it is hoped that others will also find it of interest. Thus an attempt has been made to explain concepts and terminology perhaps unfamiliar to non-Mormons (see appendix B).

The scope of this work is somewhat narrow. I see no need to write another political or economic history of the islands, and thus I have included few details concerning either topic. While I may be criticized for not including much familiar material, its familiarity justifies its exclusion.

It will be noticed that missionary journals, diaries, and autobiographies have been used extensively, as has the Manuscript History of the Hawaiian Mission and other mission records. These and many other records and documents were collected or created under the direction of Andrew Jenson two years before he was officially called as assistant Church historian in 1897, a position he held for forty-four years. On 29 May 1895 Jenson arrived in Hawaii on one of the early stops of a multination trip to most of the Mormon missions. His purpose was twofold—to gather historical information and records and to help establish better record-keeping practices in the missions. During his stay, which lasted until 26 July 1895, he visited most of the mission branches, saw many of the scenic and historic sights of the country, and interviewed many Hawaiian Saints about the early years of the mission. Fortunately these records, and others he acquired following this visit, have been preserved for use by later historians.

Although critics may find the use of native Mormon documents and sources lacking, such materials are almost nonexistent. There is unquestionably some "white missionary" bias and this is regrettable. But it is difficult to avoid because even local Hawaii newspapers, if in English, were almost always written and published by Caucasians. This of course is relevant for the earlier portion of the book, primarily to 1919. The emphasis since that time is upon institutional growth.

Moramona, the title of this book, means Mormon. It is the spelling used in the Hawaiian-language editions of the Book of Mormon. Purists may note that authentic Hawaiian has no "R" sound, but whether spelled "Moramona," "Molemona," or "Moremona" (the latter two given by Pukui and Elbert in their *Hawaiian Dictionary,* rev. ed. [Honolulu, 1986]), all are but loan words from English.

I'm pleased to acknowledge the generosity of the Islands Foundation of the Polynesian Cultural Center for funding this book. I have likewise appreciated the encouragement and support of Institute for Polynesian Studies Director Jerry Loveland and IPS Editor Dale Robertson. Sharlene Rohter and Pam Kelley, technical editors, have been as thorough and helpful as editors can be. I'm thankful for their painstaking efforts to make this book readable and to Ron Safsten for photo help to make it visually pleasing. Many individuals have read parts of the manuscript and contributed suggestions for its improvement. To my father, Ralph A. Britsch, emeritus professor of Humanities and Comparative Literature, Brigham Young University, I express my aloha and mahalo for the hours he spent teaching me how to write and correcting this and other manuscripts. In spite of our efforts to produce a book without flaws, I'm sure we have fallen short. I accept the responsibility for whatever shortcomings will surely surface.

As always, I appreciate the support of my family. My wife, JoAnn, has been of great help, having listened to the first draft of every word and page.

MORAMONA

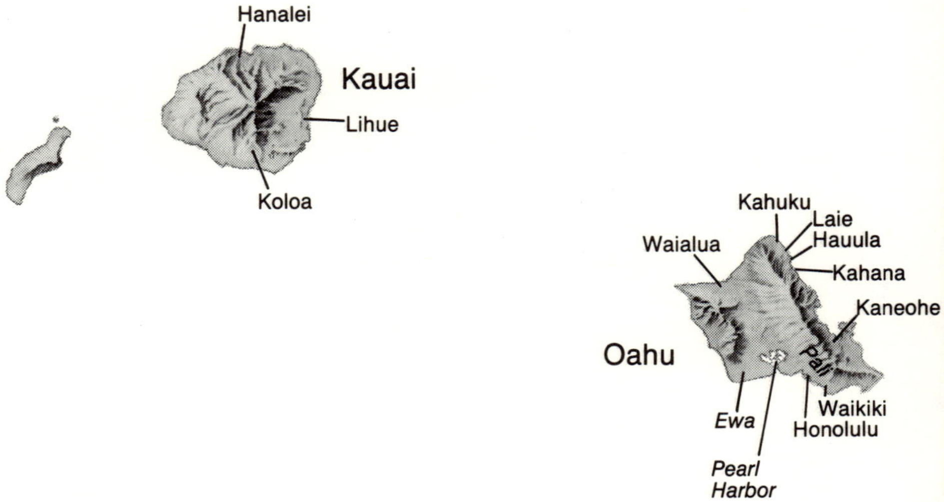
Hanalei
Kauai
Lihue
Koloa
Kahuku
Laie
Hauula
Waialua
Kahana
Kaneohe
Oahu
Pali
Waikiki
Honolulu
Ewa
Pearl Harbor

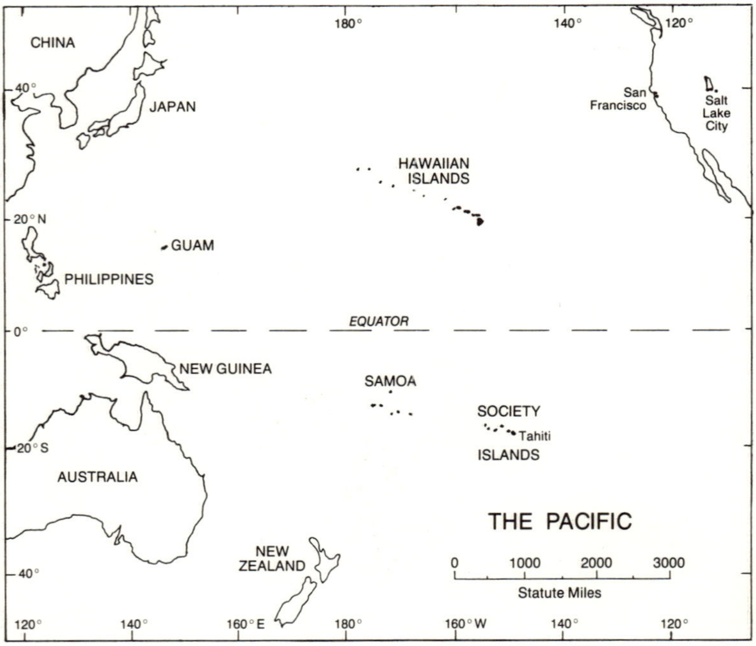
CHINA
JAPAN
180°
140°
120°
40°
San Francisco
Salt Lake City
HAWAIIAN ISLANDS
20° N
GUAM
PHILIPPINES
0°
EQUATOR
NEW GUINEA
SAMOA
SOCIETY ISLANDS
Tahiti
20° S
AUSTRALIA
THE PACIFIC
NEW ZEALAND
0 1000 2000 3000
Statute Miles
40°
120°
140°
160° E
180°
160° W
140°
120°

THE HAWAIIAN ISLANDS

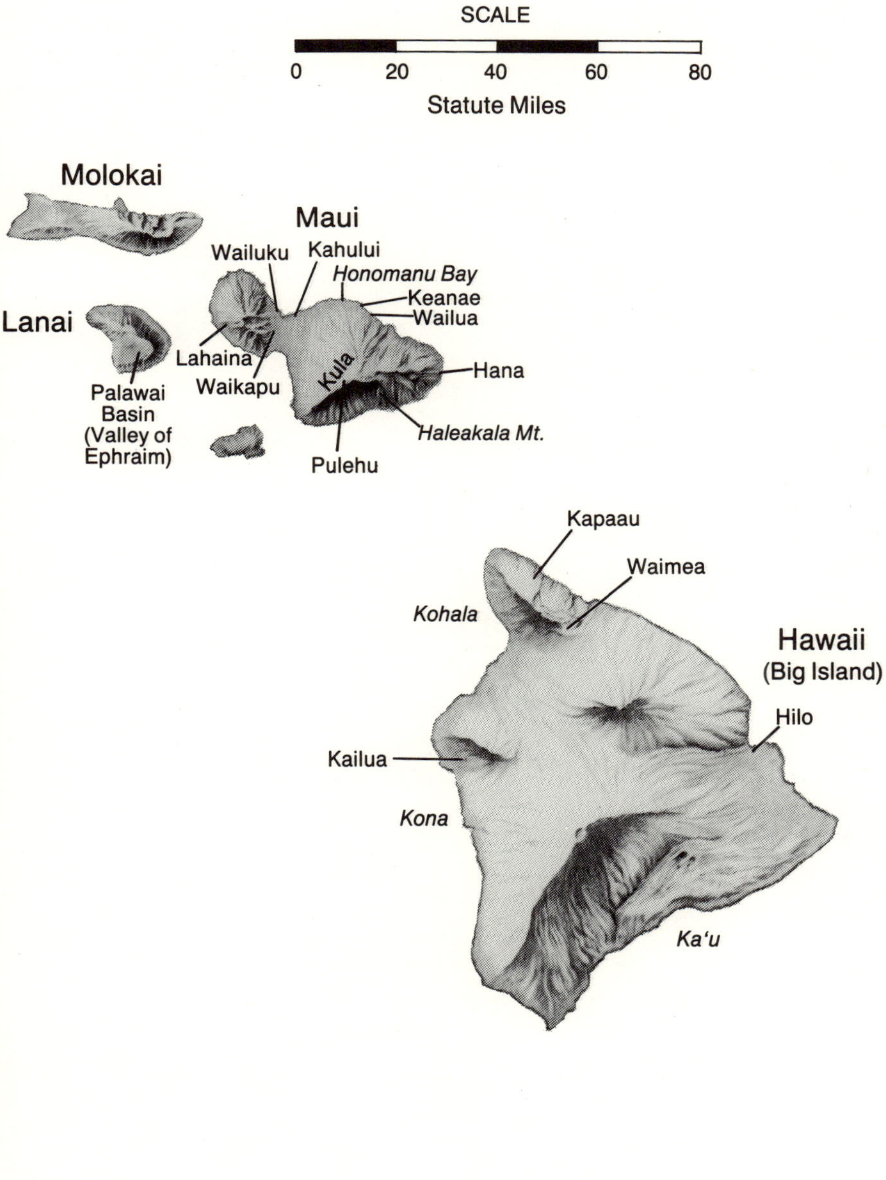

–PART I–

1850–1864

FROM A
PROMISING BEGINNING
TO A
DISAPPOINTING SETBACK

–1–

THE BEGINNING

THE CABINS and homes of Great Salt Lake City were still new and much remained to be done when in 1850 President Brigham Young sent a group of Mormon elders to California as gold-mining missionaries. Their purpose was to obtain money to strengthen Zion. It is among these men that the story of the Latter-day Saints (LDS) in the Sandwich Islands—Hawaii—has its beginning.

President Young had not been quickly enticed by the prospect of the great wealth to be obtained by mining. In fact he once told his people, "If you Elders of Israel want to go to the gold mines, go and be damned!"[1] But the financial obligations of some of the Mormon pioneers, particularly of the elderly, were brought to his attention and the prospect of clearing these debts convinced him that a few well-chosen men should go to California in search of gold.

The chill of fall had come upon the hills of northern California when Elder Charles C. Rich, a Mormon apostle, rode into a little mining camp called Slap Jack Bar on 24 September 1850. Here, on the middle fork of the American River, the group of gold-mining elders had staked their claims and were digging for the precious yellow metal. Apostle Rich, Brigham Young's personal representative to all the Latter-day Saints in the Pacific Coast area, did not take long to come to the point: he wanted some of the Saints at Slap Jack Bar to fill missions to the Sandwich Islands. His plan had much to recommend it, for the cost of living in California during the gold rush was high (some successful miners sent their dirty laundry to Honolulu to be washed because it was cheaper than having it done in California), and no mining could be done during the winter months. Hence the idea to send some of the idle gold miners to the Sandwich Islands for the winter was appealing.

The next morning Rich's suggestion became a firm call to missionary service. He selected and set apart eight men—that is, gave them special blessings—to fill missions and preach the restored gospel in Hawaii.

Among those called was Henry William Bigler, who had been at Sutter's Mill when gold was discovered in January 1848. In fact, his journal is one of the most accurate records of the beginning of the California gold rush. The others were George Q. Cannon, who later served in the First Presidency of the LDS Church, John Dixon, William Farrer, James Hawkins, James Keeler, Thomas Morris, and Thomas Whittle.[2] In addition, Hiram Clark, who had filled two previous missions to Great Britain, and Hiram Blackwell were called from other mining camps. The fifty-five-year-old Clark was appointed president of the mission. The miners remained in the gold fields for a few days, then journeyed to Sacramento on horseback and to San Francisco by riverboat where on 15 November 1850 they embarked for the islands. After a rough voyage they arrived in Honolulu on 12 December.

Steerage passage in a mid-nineteenth-century vessel was the worst of sailing accommodations. The dirt, grime, and foul smells of the *Imaum of Muscat* were probably difficult to escape even after landing in Honolulu. But the purpose of their long voyage was clearly in their minds as the little band of missionaries first set foot in the strange new land. As they walked the streets of Honolulu that Thursday evening they felt mixed emotions of disappointment and exaltation. The Hawaiian people appeared strange to them and their language seemed like little more than an incomprehensible babble. But the verdant greenery that adorned the hills around the city and flourished so profusely everywhere they walked provided a visual loveliness and sensory grandeur that the miners from Utah had never before experienced. Before sleep fell upon them that night they laid plans for a special service to dedicate themselves to the Lord and to seek God's blessing for the success of their venture. When sleep came, memories of the uncomfortable voyage were behind them. Only tomorrow seemed important.

In the early morning of 13 December the elders walked up Nuuanu Valley to the beautiful King's Falls. As the new arrivals viewed the paradise-like surroundings, the sensuous feeling of the Hawaii morning must have been almost overwhelming. At the falls they bathed, their first real bath in a month, and then hiked another mile up the valley. In a secluded place about a thousand feet above sea level, in an area now called Pacific Heights, they built a stone altar about three feet high and three feet around. Together they sang hymns and prayed. After sharing their feelings about their mission, they knelt together as President Clark offered a prayer dedicating Hawaii to the preaching of the gospel. Clark asked the Lord to "open the way that we might be enabled to preach the Gospel on these islands . . . have his Spirit . . . to guide us . . . preserve us from the adversary and from every evil, and that the honest in heart might embrace the truth."[3]

The next step was to learn as much as possible about the people they wanted to teach. The missionaries assumed that they had been sent to the islands to preach the gospel only to white people; but surveying the situation later in the day they realized that very few whites were available for proselyting. Since there was obviously not enough work to be done among the *haole*s (whites) in and around Honolulu, the missionaries decided to divide into pairs and go to other islands to preach. It was decided that Blackwell and Hawkins would go to the "Big Island," Hawaii; Cannon, Keeler, and Bigler to Maui; Dixon and Farrer to Kauai; and that Clark, Morris, and Whittle would remain in Honolulu. President Clark, concerned about the safety of the elders, visited British Consul General William Miller, who told him the laws of the kingdom would provide protection for the new missionary force. With this assurance they set sail for other islands of the chain. Thus began the dissemination of the message of Mormonism among the people of the Sandwich Islands.

THE MORMON MESSAGE

The elders[4] from the mining camps of California had sailed over twenty-three hundred miles to deliver a message. What was it? Other Christian missionaries in the islands, Protestants and Catholics, puzzled over the need for these Mormons to do a job they believed they had already done.

The Mormon message differed from the teachings of traditional Protestant or Catholic Christianity. The ten elders came to Hawaii to tell the people that the ancient gospel of Jesus Christ had been restored through an American prophet, Joseph Smith. To accept Mormonism was not only to accept the divinity of Jesus Christ, but also to accept new revelation through contemporary prophets. The missionaries saw little distinction between the Hawaiians and mainstream Christians: both required the saving ordinances of salvation as performed by men who had the authority or priesthood, as restored through Joseph Smith.

The Mormon story begins in the spring of 1820 with Joseph Smith, a fourteen-year-old New York farm boy. While reading his Bible, as was his custom, he was moved by the unequivocal promise of the Apostle James: "If any of you lack wisdom, let him ask of God, that giveth to all men liberally, and upbraideth not; and it shall be given him. But let him ask in faith, nothing wavering. For he that wavereth is like a wave of the sea driven with the wind and tossed."[5]

Deeply impressed by this scripture, young Joseph repaired to a secluded spot in a grove near his father's farm. There he asked God for wisdom, specifically for the wisdom to know which church was right. After a struggle with the powers of darkness and a fervent prayer for deliverance, he beheld a pillar of light. Of this experience he later wrote: "It no sooner appeared than I found myself delivered from the enemy which held me bound. When the light rested upon me I saw two Personages, whose brightness and glory defy all description, standing above me in the air. One of them spake unto me, calling me by name and said, pointing to the other—'This is My Beloved Son, Hear Him!' "[6]

In his vision Joseph Smith was instructed not to join any existing church because there had been a universal apostasy from the original church of Jesus Christ. He was told that there would be a restoration of the pristine church and that if he were faithful he would be an instrument in the Lord's hand in reestablishing the truths, principles, and ordinances necessary for the salvation of all of God's children. Three years later a heavenly messenger, Moroni, directed the fledgling prophet to the location of a set of ancient, gold-colored metal plates that contained the record of earlier inhabitants of the American continent. In 1827 Joseph Smith was given possession of these plates and, through the gift of God's power, he translated a portion of their contents, which was later published as "The Book of Mormon." This book, which recounts the ministrations of Jesus Christ among the people of the Americas, soon gave the followers of Joseph Smith the nickname, "Mormon."

On 6 April 1830 Joseph Smith and a group of fellow believers legally organized the church that was later named The Church of Jesus Christ of Latter-day Saints. From 1830 when the Book of Mormon was first published, missionaries of the Church began to fan out across the eastern United States and Canada. Their message was that the heavens had been opened after many centuries of silence following the death of the original apostles of Jesus Christ.

Mormons always held the doctrines of "Mormonism" to be in harmony with the teachings of the King James Bible. Yet members of established Protestant and Catholic churches frequently found the doctrines of the new sect to be in opposition to the traditions of mainstream Christianity. For example, Joseph Smith taught that the Holy Trinity consisted literally of personages—divine people. God the Father and Jesus Christ possessed bodies of flesh and bone, and the Holy Ghost was a personage of spirit. This theomorphic concept of deity, which the world found revolutionary, was based on Joseph Smith's direct encounter with the Father and Son.

Another break from mainstream Christianity came over the issue of continuous revelation. The Prophet Joseph based everything he did on his visionary experience. The Bible, he maintained, was not sufficient to meet the needs of all people at all times: the God of Heaven was not to be limited in his relationships with man to writings from the distant time of Christ and the apostles.

These and many other doctrinal differences between the teachings of Joseph Smith and the concepts of traditional Christianity attracted many followers but also antagonized people and helped create enemies for the new church. Equally important, the political and economic implications of Mormon community building antagonized even more people and fueled persecution, driving them from place to place in the early years after the founding of the Church.

During the 1830s the members of the Church, or "Saints" as they were called, began to gather together. This process culminated in the establishment of a Zion community at Nauvoo, Illinois. Here, in June 1844, Joseph Smith was shot and killed by a mob while he was held prisoner in Carthage Jail a few miles from Nauvoo. After the martyrdom of the Prophet, Brigham Young, who had been president of the Church's Quorum of Twelve Apostles, became president of the Church. Young is best known as the leader of the Mormon exodus into the wilderness of Western America and as the founder of the new Zion communities in Utah and its surrounding territories in the Mountain West. Only three years after he led the Saints into Great Salt Lake Valley on 24 July 1847, the first LDS missionaries were called to the Sandwich Islands.

HAWAII BEFORE 1850

In 1850 the city of Honolulu was a fairly large urban center by the standards of the time, with a population of about eleven thousand people.[7] Most of them were native Hawaiians, but over a thousand were Caucasians. These missionaries must have felt surprise and wonderment as they wandered the streets and observed the people with their unusual mix of native and Western ways. For example, it was not uncommon to see Hawaiians dressed in costumes combining formal Western-style clothing with native garb. Although the influence of Euramerican customs was apparent in dress and manners, the missionaries were shocked by evidence of drunkenness and prostitution. Some were quick to criticize the work of previous British and American governmental servants and missionaries. Why, they asked, were so many Hawaiians living in filth and degradation? Is this what happens when Christians take control of supposedly benighted peoples?

Their concern was understandable, but there was much the first Latter-day Saints in the Sandwich Islands did not know about the land and people. Revolutionary changes had taken place in the islands during the previous seventy-two years.

The islands were discovered for the Western world in 1778 by the great English navigator Captain James Cook, who named them after the Earl of Sandwich, first lord of the Admiralty. Cook was greeted with reverence as a Hawaiian god, Lono. But a year later, when the mortal nature of his crew had become all too evident, Cook was killed in an altercation at Kealakekua Bay on the Kona coast of the Big Island. Both whites and Hawaiians were shocked at the turn of events that brought about Cook's death, an outcome no one had wanted. But despite the incident, regular contacts between the Hawaiians and the people they called haoles were firmly established.

During the next three quarters of a century, the indigenous culture was almost completely destroyed. A new way of life—social, political, religious, and aesthetic—was foisted upon the Hawaiians that they were almost incapable of comprehending or assimilating.

The approximately three hundred thousand people discovered by Cook were organized in a tribal system ruled by *alii* (chiefs and nobles) and *kahuna*s (priests). These men controlled relatively small, autonomous parts of the islands. Their rule was absolute, and capital punishment for even small misdeeds was not unusual. Tight restrictions, *kapu*s or taboos, were placed on personal relationships (for instance, common men could not interact freely with alii); on eating habits (only certain foods could be eaten by women and commoners); and on land and water use. Kapu rules had become so rigid by the time of Cook's arrival that the common people literally could hardly walk during some seasons of the year.

The Hawaiian gods were numerous and difficult for Westerners to comprehend. Religious traditions centered on the powerful kahunas (who were viewed with awe by Hawaiians) and on idol worship. *Heiau*s (temples) made of lava rock and posts were adorned with idols. Although the Hawaiian religion was officially abandoned in 1819, kahunaism died hard. Even in this century aspects of the ancient religion live on.

Cook's discovery excited and thrilled the maritime communities of the world. Soon sailors from all parts of the globe were frequenting the ports of Honolulu and Lahaina. At the same time, changes were taking place in the islands' political structure. Even before Cook arrived they were politically disunified. Frequent wars plagued the common people as their chiefs struggled for supremacy over one another. Finally, in the 1790s, Kamehameha I emerged as the first king of the islands. He was a man of magnificent stature, both physically and intellectually. His power base was the Kona coast region of the Big Island. After years of bitter warfare, Kamehameha I (r. 1795–1819) conquered all the islands by 1795 (except Kauai and Niihau, which were ceded to him in 1810). Kamehameha was a powerful ruler whose people respected him, as did most of the foreigners who came to his ports. During his reign he instituted many changes, and sailors unfortunately introduced many others. Numerous plants and animals were brought to Hawaii during this era, but many diseases were also introduced that ultimately caused the Hawaiian population to drop from three hundred thousand to only forty-four thousand people in the 1870s.

By the time Kamehameha I died in 1819, Hawaii was the permanent residence of over two hundred foreigners and a temporary residence for the many visitors arriving by ship. Among these people were some of the most debauched in the world. The saying that sailors hung their consciences on Cape Horn as they entered the Pacific Ocean was all too true. Dishonesty and malice of every kind were common. In addition to disease and social upheaval, sailors introduced liquor. When the first Protestant missionaries arrived in 1820 they found drunkenness a very serious problem. Missionaries reported seeing whole villages—men, women, and children—drunk.

The total effect of the Hawaiian encounter with the outside world was one of physical, moral, and especially psychological destruction. Ships, guns, and elaborate tools of iron and steel convinced the Hawaiians that their way of life was inferior to that found elsewhere. The immediate result was a sort of national shock as well as a sense of defeat. Neither chiefs nor common people found it possible to understand and adjust to the new way of life with its combination of local traditions and foreign accretions. Strange ideas and styles developed that were neither their own nor foreign. The past was gone, and the present was baffling.

As foreigners became more common in the islands their behavior caused Hawaiians, both the alii and the common people, to question their religious traditions and kapus. Kamehameha I had not wanted to change the old ways, but when Kamehameha II (Liholiho) came to the throne, he decided to bring an end to the ancient customs. In November 1819 Liholiho ordered the destruction of the heiaus and idols and called for the abolition of the kapu system.

Although there was some native resistance to change, especially from the kahunas, many of the common people and the alii were happy to see the old system disappear. But Liholiho did not realize that he was destroying not only a group of gods and the traditions surrounding the kapu, but also what remained of the Hawaiian value system. His action created a spiritual vacuum that confused most Hawaiians and set their lives aimlessly adrift.

CONTRIBUTIONS OF THE PROTESTANT MISSIONARIES

Only two weeks before Liholiho's drastic act, the first contingent of Protestant missionaries had set sail from Boston on the brig *Thaddeus.* Five months later, when they arrived at the island of Hawaii, they found that Kamehameha I was dead, Liholiho was king, and the kapus, heiaus, and idols had been destroyed. The missionaries believed that God had prepared the way before them.

The accomplishments of the Protestant missionaries in Hawaii are well known. Historians have lauded their work, and novelists have romanticized it. But there have also been many critics of the missionary enterprise. The usual criticism has been that the missionaries destroyed the Hawaiian way of life. In truth the Hawaiian life-style was well on the way to destruction before the missionaries ever arrived—the result of forty-two years of contact with foreigners. Much had been lost, and little had been replaced. When the missionaries came, they brought the more wholesome aspects of Western civilization. Many seamen and resident whites resented the intrusion of morality and fought bitterly, sometimes with cannon and rifle, for the continuation of debauchery. The missionaries were at times misguided or poorly informed, but most cannot be accused of any sins greater than those caused by overzealousness and misinformation.

Some critics have called the Protestant missionaries "pie-in-the-sky" preachers with nothing to offer but the promise of eternal bliss; however, the first group of missionaries included not only two ordained ministers but also two schoolteachers, a printer, a doctor, and a successful farmer. They wanted to teach not only Christianity but also the arts of civilization. They were remarkably successful at both; their aims were high and so were their achievements. The story of these missionaries of the American Board of Commissioners for Foreign Missions is well documented in histories and in the journals of the missionaries themselves. Especially famous are the Reverend Hiram Bingham and Dr. Gerrit P. Judd, but others were as devoted and diligent—ability and nobleness of purpose were not in short supply among these early workers.

The greatest accomplishment of the Protestant missionaries was the almost complete Christianization of the islands. The first few years of proselyting were slow and difficult, but by 1853 almost fifty-seven thousand people (of a total population of around eighty-four thousand) claimed to be Christian, although not all had been baptized. By that time the Catholics were well established, and the Latter-day Saints were making some headway. The missionaries' success was the result of their conversion of the Hawaiian nobility. The chiefs received considerable attention from the missionaries, and when they espoused the new faith the commoners, who were still subservient, easily followed suit.

It was fortunate for the people of Hawaii that the missionaries were concerned with education. By 1850 schools were so widespread and successful that most Hawaiians could read and write. In the minds of the Hawaiians, religious instruction *(pule)* and reading and writing *(palapala)* were an inseparable pair. The desire to learn was first felt among adults and later among the young. By 1824 there were about two thousand pupils in mission schools. Already some of the schools were led by Hawaiians who had quickly mastered the basic skills. Education became so popular that seven years later there were over fifty thousand students and more than eleven hundred schools. Almost 40 percent of the population attended school. In 1840 the Hawaiian government formally recognized its responsibility for education by passing a law that required common schools in every area. A department of public instruction was organized in 1846. Although most education was at the elementary level, a few high schools flourished even before 1850.

Closely associated with schools were publishing and translating. From the outset the ministers recognized the need in both areas. They published the first printed Hawaiian work, a spelling book, in 1822, and their translation of the New Testament was completed and printed in 1832. The entire Bible was translated and in print by 1839, and translation continued at a rapid pace. By 1842 two mission presses were operating, one at Lahaina and another in Honolulu. By the end of 1842 nearly a hundred million pages in the Hawaiian language—Bibles, textbooks, tracts, and two newspapers—had been printed. Both the literacy of the Hawaiians and the availability of the scriptures facilitated the work of the Latter-day Saints when they arrived.

Some Protestant missionaries left the mission and entered government service. These missionaries-turned-government-advisors had a democratizing influence on the government. Before that time laws had been created according to the whims of the king, but as a result of their advice, a code of laws was published in 1839. A constitution followed in 1840 that called for a representative assembly elected by the common people. This body was coequal with the council of chiefs, which included the king and prime minister. A supreme court was also established.

These advances notwithstanding, Hawaii suffered through a very difficult decade from 1840 to 1850. International competition to control Hawaii became heated, and Great Britain even seized the islands for a brief period. However, by 1850 the Hawaiian kingdom was a financially solvent, independent nation. Of special importance was the establishment of complete religious freedom.

It was into this setting that the first LDS missionaries brought the new American religion. The groundwork laid by the Protestant missionaries made the work of the Latter-day Saints much easier than it would have been; it was unnecessary to Christianize and educate the Hawaiians, translate the Bible, establish a sound government, and prepare the people for a higher standard of living. The unification of the islands under Kamehameha I, as well as the destruction of the heiaus, pagan gods, and kapus, worked for the benefit of Protestants, Roman Catholics, and Latter-day Saints alike.

The Sandwich Islands of 1850 constituted a very cosmopolitan nation. Honolulu was the center of cultural and artistic affairs. The haole residents were not content to live in traditional Hawaiian fashion and many of them constructed large, beautiful homes, usually following the styles of the eastern seaboard of the United States. During the 1840s and early 1850s a library, theater, and amateur music society were created. Newspapers were published regularly. Protestant missionaries were to a large degree responsible for raising the cultural standards of the people, but many businessmen and government representatives also brought a wholesome influence to Honolulu and the rest of Hawaii.

The California gold rush was a partial cause of Hawaii's prosperous condition in 1850. California-bound vessels frequently stopped at Honolulu or Lahaina en route from the east coast of North America. Such ships brought added wealth to residents of the islands. All in all, the Honolulu that the first group of Latter-day Saints saw was a unique combination of Polynesian and Western, old and new, debauched and puritanical, illiterate and educated, primitive and civilized ways of life. The Hawaiian people found this combination difficult to live with. Most foreigners found the islands a paradise.

–2–

THE ESTABLISHMENT OF THE SANDWICH ISLANDS MISSION

WITHIN a few days of their arrival in Honolulu the LDS missionaries dispersed to separate regions. Not all the elders began preaching and performing missionary labor immediately. For some unknown reason President Hiram Clark advised Elder Thomas Morris to go to work at a profession, and almost immediately upon his arrival he took employment with British consul William Miller.[1] President Clark and Thomas Whittle arranged to preach in a free room in the market area of town. They placed a notice of their meeting in the *Polynesian,* a weekly newspaper, but it attracted little attention. In short, the work got off to a slow start on Oahu.

On Kauai the work hardly fared better. After an uncomfortable voyage, William Farrer and John Dixon arrived at the island of Kauai on 21 December 1850. During a brief layover at Nawiliwili they taught a small group of haoles; then two days later they sailed on to Koloa, the site of the first successful sugar plantation in the islands. There they found little response to their message; in fact, they sensed a degree of antagonism. The elders worked at setting up meetings with the small white population at the plantation, but after three weeks they had not succeeded in stirring interest. Farrer began studying the native tongue, but was making little progress for want of a teacher.[2] Some rather discouraging letters from President Clark and others led Farrer and Dixon to decide that Farrer should go to Honolulu to find out what the other elders were planning to do.

Farrer arrived in Honolulu on 28 January. When he reported that he was achieving nothing among the whites, he found that Clark and Whittle were similarly discouraged. Hardly a month after their arrival some of the men were talking about going home. In fact, according to Farrer, Clark said that he "did not think it was any use for those of the brethren who were going home in the spring to stay any longer."[3]

Seven days later Elders Cannon and Dixon arrived in Honolulu from Maui and Kauai. Cannon had been much surprised to receive Clark's letter, informing him that Whittle was returning to North America and that Clark wanted Cannon to be his companion and clerk. Cannon did not like this because matters were moving in a positive direction on Maui. The elders there, realizing that there were few whites to teach, had made up their minds to learn the language and teach the Hawaiians. Cannon, who was twenty-three years old, took charge of the trio and lead the effort to learn the native language. The spirit and leadership that would later call him as an apostle and finally as counselor to three presidents of the Church was already evident in his behavior.

Lahaina, a wide-open whaling port, was also the largest town on Maui. Today it is a tourist village with little remaining of the grog shops and lusty sailors but memories. Soon after their arrival on 19 December, the elders—Cannon, James Keeler, and Henry William Bigler—visited Mr. Bunker, the U.S. consular representative at Lahaina. Bunker offered to help them establish themselves and introduced them to the governor of Maui, a *hapa haole* (part-white) named James Young. They asked Young for permission to use the then uninhabited royal palace for religious services, but he did not grant their request.

The Sunday after their arrival the missionaries asked the Reverend Mr. Taylor, who ministered at the Bethel Chapel, for permission to use his facilities. Taylor granted their request, but at the end of their afternoon service it was evident that if any good were to be done they would have to appeal to a larger population than the available whites. "Preaching to them with the hope of convincing them of the truth seemed a hopeless labor," wrote Cannon some years later.

At this point one of the most important decisions concerning the mission in Hawaii was made. Cannon recounts the event this way:

> The question arose directly, "Shall we confine our labors to the white people?" It is true that we had not been particularly told to preach to the natives of the islands, but we were in their midst, had full authority to declare unto them the message of salvation, and if we did not declare unto them, some other Elders would have to come and do so, in order to fulfill the command of God to his servants.
>
> For my part I felt it to be my duty to warn all men, white and red; and no sooner did I learn the condition of the population than I made up my mind to acquire the language, preach the gospel to the natives and to the whites whenever I could obtain an opportunity, and thus fill my mission. I felt resolved to stay there, master the language and warn the people of those islands, if I had to do it alone; for I felt that I could not do otherwise

> and be free from condemnation; the spirit of it was upon me. Elders Bigler and Keeler felt the same.[4]

Cannon, Bigler, and Keeler had begun studying the language within two days of their arrival. They found the local people friendly and willing to help. In only three weeks Cannon had begun to understand the language. Although he did not boast complete mastery, he could understand most of what was said, and speaking ability followed relatively quickly.

At the end of three weeks the Maui missionaries were almost destitute and found it necessary to leave the small native house they had rented. Their only recourse seemed to be to split up and go in different directions. Strangers were more likely to help them individually than if they were together. Just when they were parting, a kind old Hawaiian lady named Nalimanui, who had been their neighbor and laundry lady, offered her own room to them. They were touched and blessed her for her kindness, which enabled them to remain together longer.

Cannon made further progress in the Hawaiian language during the short time he stayed with Nalimanui. He also had some powerful spiritual experiences; as he later related, he heard the Lord's voice "more than once as one man speaks with another, encouraging me and showing me the work which should be done among this people if I would follow the dictates of His Spirit."[5] The future of the Hawaiian people and the Church would be greatly affected by these revelations.

Latter-day Saints believe that the Hawaiian people and all other Polynesians are heirs to the blessings promised to the posterity of Abraham. This doctrine originated through George Q. Cannon, who while at Lahaina, Maui, had a revelation in which the Lord spoke to him telling him that the Hawaiians were of the House of Israel. From this time on Cannon and his associates began to preach that the Hawaiian people were an offshoot branch of Israel through the posterity of Lehi, a Book of Mormon prophet. (See p. 116.)

It was at this point that Cannon received his instructions from President Clark to come to Honolulu. But after Cannon explained what had transpired on Maui, it was apparent that it would be better for him to return there.[6]

The following day, probably 29 January 1851, Elder Dixon decided to return home with Elder Whittle. According to Cannon, Whittle had been told by Charles C. Rich that he should fill a short mission and then return. The others don't seem to have had such instructions. They were supposed to stay at least through the winter—and longer if the Holy Spirit so moved them.

Young Cannon was disgusted with the talk of going home and told the elders so, saying he would feel condemned if he left Hawaii at that point. "The Lord," said Cannon, "would hold me accountable for not doing my duty to that people." Farrer, excited by the spirit of the Maui elders, decided to go to Maui to be Bigler's companion.[7]

Cannon and Farrer arrived back on Maui on 30 January, only four days before Hiram Blackwell's visit on his way to Honolulu from Hawaii. On the Big Island matters were no better and possibly worse than in Honolulu and Kauai. Elders Blackwell and James Hawkins worked briefly in Hilo and then moved up the coast toward Kohala. There were so few haoles to teach that Blackwell decided he had done his duty. On 1 February he sailed from Hilo, stopping off at Lahaina a day later. The missionaries there were surprised that he had left his assigned area. Blackwell had worked at the Hawaiian language a little but said he thought it would take at least a year to learn it, and even then he doubted whether the Hawaiians would accept the gospel because "the people were so degraded." He was even considering going home. He had wanted "Brother" Hawkins to come with him, but Hawkins preferred to stay where he had been sent until he received other directions.[8] Blackwell sailed on to Honolulu, later deciding to return home with Dixon and Whittle. President Clark released all three and they sailed from Hawaii at the end of February. Hawkins stayed on the Big Island learning the language. He worked alone there for a number of months, especially in and around Waimea.[9]

On 10 February 1851, President Clark baptized a sixteen-year-old boy. The young man, who spoke English fairly well, was the first native Hawaiian to be baptized into the Church in the islands. At about the same time Clark baptized a man named Blake, a printer. Blake had resided for a time in the Marquesas Islands northeast of the Society Islands group. In mid-February Clark also became acquainted with Brother Clifford, who had been baptized in the Society Islands by Elder Addison Pratt.[10] Together they discussed the possibility of mission work in the Marquesas Islands, and they finally decided that Blake would accompany Clark there. Blake would take along a small box of printer's type, and they could publish material concerning the gospel.

Greatly excited by this plan, President Clark proceeded to Maui, intending to convince the elders there to accompany him. He arrived on 20 February and immediately laid out his plans before the Maui elders. They found the idea improper but hesitated to say so since he was president of the mission. Clark discerned their true feelings and did not persist, suggesting instead that he go without them, and then, if he succeeded, they could join him there.

Clark left his field of duty on 27 February 1851. He sailed that day for Tahiti, intending to go from there to the Marquesas group. He never reached the Marquesas, but instead went to Tubuai, where Addison Pratt, one of the first three Mormon missionaries in the Pacific, and the Society Islands Mission were established. He did not get along well with the Saints there and spent some time working on a schooner, finally returning to California where he later took his own life.[11]

Dixon, Blackwell, and Whittle left Hawaii at about the same time, and Morris sailed in April. Thus hardly more than four months after the Sandwich Islands Mission opened, half the original ten missionaries had left the field. Considering the nature of their original call, which was to spend only the winter in Hawaii and open a mission, four of the elders deserve little reproach for leaving. However, it was difficult for the remaining elders to understand the actions of President Clark. During a visit to Hawaii in 1900 Cannon remarked that the five elders who left the mission field early all died soon after returning home, while the five elders who stayed to fulfill their missions lived to be old men. His belief in the judgment of Divine Providence is obvious.

SPREADING THE GOSPEL ON MAUI AND OAHU

The efforts of George Q. Cannon were the first to bear fruit in Hawaii. He left his companions at Lahaina for the first time on 4 March 1851. The weather was bad, but during the next three days he made his way over a rough road through beautiful scenery to Wailuku. He recorded that as he traveled, he felt he would meet someone who would be interested in his message and would be willing to provide for his needs. A series of unusual incidents brought him into contact with a Hawaiian judge named Jonatana H. Napela, a man of considerable influence in the area. Cannon stayed with Napela for several days and spoke to him and several of his friends about the restored gospel. These men were much interested in the differences between Protestantism and Mormonism.

Cannon returned to Lahaina after a few days but was eager to get back to his new friends in Wailuku. When he returned to Wailuku he found that the Reverend Mr. Daniel Conde, whom Cannon had encountered during his first visit, was even more upset with the Mormon threat than before. Cannon reported that Conde "used all his influence against me among his congregation, and one Sunday he came out in public and delivered a most abusive discourse against the Prophet Joseph Smith and our principles, in which he gave an entirely false statement of the cause of his death, and also warned the people against me."[12] Cannon was present on this occasion and understood what was said in Hawaiian. Conde did not expect this and was embarrassed when Cannon asked him to change his position and correct the lies he had spoken. Conde, of course, refused to do so, believing he had spoken the truth. The two men discussed matters for more than half an hour as many intelligent Hawaiians listened. The result was a new arousal of interest in Mormonism.

Napela's continued study of Mormonism after this confrontation brought Conde's wrath down upon him. Conde threatened to have Napela's judgeship taken away if he persisted in his interest. Napela was not concerned, but Cannon, who had been staying with Napela while in Wailuku, decided it would be wiser to go to another area for a while and let matters settle down at Wailuku.

He chose to go to an area called Kula, "the country near the base of a mountain." The mountain, in this case, was Haleakala, a 10,025-foot extinct volcano of renowned beauty. Napela had recommended the area because he had friends there who could take care of Cannon. At a place near modern Pulehu Cannon stayed with a man called Pake, who was in charge of Napela's interests there. Kula was especially important to Hawaii's economy at this time because Irish potatoes were grown there for export to California for sale to the gold miners. This trade was dropping even while Cannon was there.

From 13 May, the day of his move to Kula, Cannon worked diligently to spread the gospel, traveling from village to village. On 15 June friends of Napela completed a Hawaiian-style hut constructed especially for use as a meetinghouse. Cannon held meetings that Sunday both in the morning and afternoon.[13] During the following week he was joined at Kula by Elder Keeler, whom he hadn't seen for two months. Both men were elated with their progress and the prospects for conversions, and on the next Sunday matters began to move at a rapid pace as four people were baptized. A week later six more were baptized, and within a few more days the membership in Kula had grown to nineteen. Among the new converts were a man named Kaleohano, Cannon's host, and Pake, the friend from his first arrival.

Elder Keeler, who was gaining courage faster than linguistic facility, continued on around the island attempting to teach the gospel. Three weeks into July he came back to Kula and asked Cannon to come with him to Keanae. The people there had listened to Keeler, but he was not able to express himself fully and needed help. Cannon accompanied him, and, while traveling, enjoyed the incomparably beautiful scenery of the islands. They were joined by newly converted Saints excited about the gospel. Cannon wrote:

> Our arrival at Keanae created great excitement. The people had been watching for us, and seeing us approach from a long distance, had gathered to meet us. Had we been princes they could not have treated us with greater consideration and honor. We obtained the Calvinistic meeting-house the afternoon of our arrival, and there was a large attendance to hear the preaching.
>
> This was on Wednesday, and from that time until Monday we were constantly speaking, baptizing, confirming and counseling the people. During that time there were upwards of one hundred and thirty baptized. The Spirit of the Lord was powerfully poured out, and all rejoiced; I never enjoyed myself so well before in my life.[14]

Cannon's companions admired his speaking ability, a gift that was later recognized by most members of the Church, not only in Hawaii but in Utah and everywhere he went.

At the end of July Cannon returned to Kula, where on 6 August he organized the first branch of the Church in Hawaii. The site was the village of Kealahou. Two teachers and three deacons were ordained in the priesthood, and one of the teachers, Kaleohano, was appointed clerk of the branch.[15]

Cannon was not at Kula long for he wanted to get back to Keanae to perform similar work. Within two weeks he had organized four branches in the Keanae area: the Keanae, Wailua, Waianu, and Honomanu branches. This extraordinary event, the organizing of four branches at one time, took place on 19 August at a meeting of all the Saints from the area. The day before, Sunday, Cannon and Keeler had administered the sacrament to 190 members of the Church and then baptized fifteen more people.[16]

Cannon's success was largely the result of two factors: his fine oratorical skills, which he was able to transfer to the Hawaiian language to great advantage; and the newness of the Mormon approach to baptism, modern revelation, the concept of God, and spiritual gifts and blessings, as well as the plainness of the message, which appealed to the Hawaiians.[17]

Success did not come so quickly to the elders on Oahu, who had more difficulty learning the language. Farrer, more advanced than Bigler, started teaching the Hawaiians in late April. His first missionary campaign took him on a circuit over the Pali to the windward side of the island, around the north shore, and back to Honolulu. He walked through Koolau, Kahana, Hauula, Laie, Kahuku, Waialua, and into the Ewa district. He spent his time with the Hawaiian people, attempting to teach the gospel with his limited but growing ability in the language. He ate their food and slept in their huts and homes. Finally, he returned to Honolulu in early June.

Bigler and Farrer remained in Honolulu until 16 June when they decided their language skills would probably improve if they left the city atmosphere. In Kaneohe, on the windward side, they worked hard at the language and at trying to interest people in their work but had little success at either. Farrer's journal reflects his day-to-day struggle with the language. Then on 4 July he decided to get out and push his cause. Once again he proceeded in the direction of Laie and at Hauula met a friend from Honolulu, Mr. J. W. H. Kauwahi. Kauwahi invited the elder to his home at Laie where he stayed for several weeks, studying the language, talking with the people, and even locking horns with the local minister, the Reverend Mr. John Emerson.

During the second week in August Farrer's references to his language difficulty decrease, and at about the same time he performed his first baptism. His convert was his host, Mr. Kauwahi. The following day, 18 August, Farrer baptized a man from Hauula named Kealoha.[18] Elder Farrer had finally conquered the language barrier, and work on Oahu was under way.

NEW ARRIVALS

The day of his first baptism Farrer received a letter from Elder Bigler in Honolulu telling him of the arrival of new missionaries and urging him to hurry to Honolulu for a meeting. The next day, on a borrowed horse, Farrer went to Honolulu where he met Elders Philip B. Lewis and Francis A. Hammond. Together they boarded a schooner for Lahaina. The two missionaries had arrived at Lahaina with their wives and Elder John S. Woodbury on 10 August.[19] Finding no missionaries, they asked around and discovered that Cannon and Keeler were in Kula or Keanae. After sending them a letter suggesting a Lahaina conference, Lewis and Hammond then embarked for Oahu, where they found Bigler and Farrer.

Lewis, age forty-seven, and Hammond, age twenty-nine, were seasoned veterans in the service of the Church. Lewis was born in 1804 in Massachusetts. After converting to Mormonism he served as a branch president in Massachusetts, where he contributed liberally of his financial resources to send Addison Pratt and his three companions on the mission that opened the South Pacific to the preaching of the restored gospel in 1844. Lewis gathered with the Saints in Nauvoo before the Prophet was martyred in 1844. With his wife he was driven from Nauvoo, and she died soon after. Before leaving Winter Quarters, Nebraska, for Utah, he married Jane Amanda Stevens, who later accompanied him on his mission to Hawaii.

Francis Asbury Hammond, born in 1822, was the only early Sandwich Islands LDS missionary who had previously been to the islands. Reared on Long Island, Hammond went to sea at fourteen, becoming an able seaman who was employed full-time by age eighteen. When he was twenty-two he was seriously injured while at sea and put ashore at Lahaina. From 1844 until 1847 he worked there as a shoemaker and bootmaker, an occupation learned from his father. During this time Hammond learned to speak Hawaiian and developed a love for the islands and the Hawaiian people. In 1847 he decided to go home and find a wife, but stopped to work in San Francisco where he met some Latter-day Saints. He was converted to the gospel by members of the Mormon Battalion and other Saints who had come to San Francisco on the ship *Brooklynn*. Hammond was baptized on 31 December.

After digging gold for a while to get money for traveling gear and a horse, Hammond journeyed to Salt Lake Valley, arriving there in September 1848. Two months later he married the valley's first schoolteacher, youthful Mary Jane Dilworth. In 1851 the Hammonds were called to the Sandwich Islands as missionaries. They brought with them their six-month-old child.

All the missionaries, except James Hawkins on Hawaii island, met together on 20 August 1851.[20] At that first meeting Philip B. Lewis, who had been called by Apostle Parley P. Pratt (president of all Pacific area missions) to be president of the Sandwich Islands Mission, was sustained by all present. The following day it was decided that President Lewis should remain at Lahaina. Hammond, who had lived at Lahaina during his years as a sailor, decided to stay there too and set up a shoe repair shop to sustain himself and his wife and child.[21] Woodbury was assigned to Hawaii to work with Hawkins. The other missionaries would continue as before.

Because of his wife's presence Lewis was not free from financial burden. He decided to teach English for a while until he learned the Hawaiian language. It was obvious to the new elders that the course taken by Cannon and his companions was the best way to succeed. The new elders were surprised that so much had been accomplished. Cannon and Farrer, as well as Bigler and Keeler, felt a certain relief that they did not have families to "fetter" them.[22] Within a few days they returned to their areas of labor, and in early September Woodbury joined Hawkins on Hawaii.

Hardly a month had passed before President Lewis decided that Honolulu was the logical place for the mission headquarters. He ordained a haole named Kipp, whom Cannon had befriended and Hammond had baptized, and suggested that he work with Hammond. Lewis then sailed with his wife for Oahu.[23] Honolulu remained the headquarters of the mission president for some time.

DIFFICULTIES IN THE FIELD

A number of factors complicated the efforts of the missionaries, among them the language, their virtually destitute state "without purse or scrip" (the married elders excepted), their lack of permanent homes in some instances, the instability of their new converts because of local customs and—not least—the persecutions and harassments caused by the Protestant and Catholic clergy.

A constant battle waged between the LDS missionaries and other ministers, a struggle that has never fully abated. Ministers occasionally used threats and other means of "persuading" new Mormon converts to return to their former religious affiliations. The first serious confrontation of this kind occurred in the Kula and Keanae districts of Maui. When Cannon returned there in September 1851 he found that the local minister of the Koolau area had stopped all LDS meetings and even threatened the Hawaiians, telling them that if they continued in their new-found beliefs they would be bound and sent out of the area. The local representative of the king, or *konohiki,* a man who had control over the royal lands, backed these threats. Enemies of the Church claimed that even higher officials were involved. Due to the critical nature of these threats, Cannon made a visit to Honolulu to clear up the difficulties.

He arrived in Honolulu early in October. With President Lewis he visited the appropriate government ministers, both American and Hawaiian. Although Cannon failed to gain written assurance that the Latter-day Saints had permission to preach and establish their Church, a portion of a letter from the Reverend Mr. Richard Armstrong, minister of public instruction, was used to justify the legality of the Mormon cause. Armstrong wrote, "The King's Government has given no sanction to the proceedings complained of; and so long as Messrs. Lewis and Cannon continue to respect the laws of the King they will be entitled to protection sought through the proper channels." Cannon later talked to Princes Alexander and Lot, who assured him that the Latter-day Saints would be protected.[24] Armstrong's letter was copied and sent to the other missionaries, who used it as a letter of permission to preach. It turned out to be a much-used document.

Elder Farrer experienced harassment similar to what had occurred on Maui. He used Cannon's experience to fight for his position and was able to put down the opposition without too much trouble. One argument used against him was that the Mormons were "rebelling against the Kingdom."[25] Two years later President Lewis reported that Protestant missionaries had "told the natives we are a gang of 'Filibusters' come here to overthrow the government and make slaves of them and then they will be pilikia (in trouble)."[26] The Hawaiian government was worried about such rumors at the same time but did not connect them with the Mormons.

By the end of the first year missionary work was moving along at a rapid pace. Cannon and Keeler had firmly established the Church in Kula and Keanae and had recently moved back to Wailuku, where their success continued. Farrer and Bigler were doing well on the windward side of Oahu. Farrer had progressed rapidly in the language after August and founded a branch at Hakipuu. Progress was slow at Honolulu but would improve within the next two years. By the first anniversary of the establishment of the mission, Hawkins had spent most of a year on Hawaii; he was joined briefly there by Woodbury, who soon decided to go to the dryer side of the island. On 10 November Hawkins joined the Maui elders and labored there for many months. Woodbury, who was joined by Elder and Sister Perkins, worked on Hawaii for a time, and the three were later sent to work on Molokai.

After the arrival of Elvira Woodbury and William and Patsy Perkins on 30 November 1851, no more missionaries came until 17 February 1853.

THE SECOND YEAR

The second year of the mission brought uneven progress. The missionaries settled into a routine of traveling from place to place, living on poi (either taro poi or potato poi), fruits, fish, chicken, and pig (the latter two on special occasions), and sleeping in the homes of friends or under trees if no friends were found. They did most of their own sewing and often even repaired their own shoes.

The elders struggled to keep their new converts interested and active. They were frequently frustrated because they could not get the Hawaiians to understand "reason." They considered Hawaiians naturally kind and hospitable, but found them hard to convince on the basis of logic. Farrer, discouraged with his unsuccessful attempts to develop testimonies (deep convictions) in the minds of the people based on logic and scriptural reasoning, said that they thought with their emotions.

During November and December 1851 a number of Farrer's converts fell away. He found their reasons for doing so capricious and without reason. On 13 December he wrote: "It appears to me—that it will be a hard job to do much with this people and get them to understand principle of which they are very ignorant but perhaps when we get a thorough knowlege of the language we may be enabled to get them to understand principle better." Though disgusted with the behavior of such apostates, he decided to "let these remain a little while and not cut them from the church at present as they may perhaps come back again."[27] In most cases his hopes proved vain.

From the beginning the elders taught the gospel in its fullness. They stressed so-called first principles—faith, repentance, baptism, and the gift of the Holy Ghost—and basic ideas, but did not hesitate to teach every aspect of the Mormon belief as it was taught elsewhere. They treated the Hawaiian members as complete equals from the beginning. Missionary journals reveal the following topics of discussion in Church meetings during late 1851 and early 1852: revelation, baptism, faith, priesthood authority, the second coming of the Savior, moral transgressions, visitations from heavenly messengers, the Church in the wilderness, Church organization, spiritual gifts and blessings, the coming forth of the Book of Mormon, diligence, the gift of the Holy Ghost, repentance, and the meaning of the sacrament.

By the end of the second year the elders had seen the Church grow, but apostasy had entered the flock. The gospel was being preached with all the knowledge available to the missionaries but the work was not easy. For the present progress seemed slow.

– 3 –

MISSION GROWTH

TRANSLATING THE BOOK OF MORMON

FROM the beginning the elders had recognized the necessity of having written materials available in Hawaiian for their new converts. At first no one had the ability to produce such information, but in late January 1852 Cannon began working on a translation of the Book of Mormon.[1] A few months later, in June, Farrer started work on a translation of Orson Pratt's pamphlet on the origin of the Book of Mormon. By August this small work was completed and ready for publication.[2] Cannon's work, being much larger and much more demanding of accuracy and correct interpretation, took longer.

Cannon lived with J. H. Napela at Wailuku, Maui, during this period. It was difficult to find time for his translating because all other aspects of mission work still had to be cared for. Brother Napela, a very intelligent man who knew the Hawaiian language exceptionally well, was of great help in selecting words and in criticizing every line written. He could give "the exact meaning of words." Use of the proper idiom was vital to the correct translation of the book. Cannon wrote of his task: "It was important, therefore, in translating, to know that the words used conveyed the correct idea. Unless the language used carried to the Hawaiian mind the same meaning precisely which the words in our translation gave to us, it would not be correct."[3] Other Hawaiian men of experience and education listened and gave advice for the necessary revisions. In this way Cannon and his Hawaiian associates adjusted the language of the translation to fit local cultural requirements and meanings. It was fortunate that there was but one native language in the Sandwich Islands. One translation of the Book of Mormon was enough.

Cannon's companions were aware of his efforts, as was the First Presidency in Salt Lake City. There was some discussion of alternate approaches, such as dividing up the book and having each elder assigned to a part, with Cannon revising the finished product so that the style would be consistent throughout. However, since Cannon had started the project and obviously had the spirit to finish the work, it was decided that he should be set apart to complete it by himself.[4]

The first draft was completed by July 1853, but it was necessary to check and revise the work carefully. To do this Cannon later went to Kauai to work with Farrer and some Hawaiian Saints there, particularly Elder Kauwahi. By the October conference it was apparent that the translation was nearly finished and some action should be taken regarding its publication. On the last day of January 1854, almost exactly two years since the project had begun, the book was complete and ready for publication.[5]

Much took place at the October conference in 1853. The Saints had grown in number and were over three thousand strong, this despite the unfortunate deaths of almost 180 who had succumbed to smallpox. There were fifty-three organized branches represented at the meetings. The first matter of business was the necessity of printing the Book of Mormon.[6] The missionaries decided that the best course of action would be for them to buy a press and publish the book themselves. They wanted to print a number of other items such as a synopsis of the scriptures, the portions of the Doctrine and Covenants relating to Church government, a selection of hymns, and various tracts and pamphlets. Having their own press seemed the least expensive course as well as the most convenient means of achieving their ends. It was decided that a committee of three men—George Q. Cannon, Philip B. Lewis, and Benjamin F. Johnson—would be appointed to raise the funds required to purchase the press. Cannon was released from his calling as president of the Maui conference and charged to travel throughout the islands to collect the money.[7]

In his appointed travels Cannon first encouraged the Saints on Maui to subscribe to the book by paying for their copies in advance. He later used this measure on Oahu and Kauai. Most of the Hawaiian members were poverty stricken and could give very little. The missionaries were touched by the "mites" they gave. The ordeal of gathering funds might have lasted a long time had collections and subscriptions been the only means of getting the money. Fortunately friends came forth and helped the cause. A Hawaiian high chief named Levi Haalelea had become interested in the gospel and was attending meetings regularly. He was a man of considerable influence and wealth, as well as a member of the king's privy council. Less than a month after the conference, he suggested his willingness to help finance the press. In January 1854 he loaned the mission five hundred dollars for one year to be paid back with interest.[8] On 2 December 1853 Elder Dennis, a convert to the Church in Hawaii and a man of considerable means and great generosity, promised to loan the mission one thousand dollars, to be paid back when possible. Brother Dennis and his Hawaiian wife were in the process of selling their tin and sheet metal business in preparation for emigration to San Bernardino, California, or Utah.[9] The money became available when their home was sold in January.

One of the elders, William McBride, was not well. Because President Lewis thought the climate of California would be better for McBride's health, it was decided that he should take the funds to San Francisco and there, with the help of a prominent member, John M. Horner, buy a printing press. McBride sailed from Hawaii on 21 January. When he arrived in California, he discovered that no presses were available, and so a press was ordered from Boston. It was finally sent from New York and arrived in Honolulu 6 October 1854. Once the press arrived, the brethren were at a loss to know what to do with it because Cannon had been released from service and no one in the mission knew how to operate it. The press was stored for six months. In the interim a letter arrived from Elder Parley P. Pratt, who was still presiding in California. He asked that the press be forwarded to California, where paper and experienced printers were more readily available. On 14 March 1855 the press was sent to California.

President Lewis and the Saints in Hawaii had hoped that Cannon would be sent back to Hawaii to assist in the actual printing of the Book of Mormon. This did not occur, but Cannon was sent to California only five months after he arrived home in Utah. In California he set up the press and supervised the printing of the book. This was accomplished late in 1855, but the assembling and binding of the book took some additional time. The record does not reveal exactly when the Hawaiian Book of Mormon was finally distributed to the *kanaka* (Hawaiian) Saints.[10]

Apparently Cannon had problems, perhaps financial, for he did not quickly finish the binding and shipping of the volume. Henry Bigler recorded receiving twelve cases of unbound copies on 24 November 1857. He was angry with the customs officer who said that "they could hardly be considered religious books" and would not allow them to be entered duty free. Bigler had a copy of the translation before this time, but he may have acquired it on his way through California on his second mission. It is really not known whether many copies were bound and distributed to the local Saints. It is unlikely that many members had the opportunity to use it until years later, when it was distributed widely. It was only about six months after the books arrived that the missionaries were called home on account of the Utah War (see p. 47), and the books were stored to await the eventual return of the elders.[11]

Chapel Building and Local Leadership

The missionaries were not content, even during the early years, to allow their converts to remain without basic facilities. Meetinghouses were constructed in many parts of the islands, the earliest in August 1852. During that month two chapels were dedicated on Maui; the next month another chapel was completed at Keanae, Maui. Farrer described it as "a frame building 56 feet long by 21 wide, built after the native fashion and covered with lauhala."[12] The roof was of *pili* grass, used for thatch. This description seems to fit most of the early meetinghouses. In some instances frame homes were rented and fitted out with rude benches. Finding property on which to build such structures was not always an easy job. Protestant ministers and others opposed to the Mormon cause fought the intrusion of such physical evidence of success. On the other hand, some help did come from influential Hawaiians such as Levi Haalelea. He helped locate suitable land for meetinghouses and homes for the elders. Some of these sites were on his own property.

Local Saints were immediately involved in ecclesiastical duties when they joined the Church. They built the chapels with their own hands and their own funds. When branches were organized, at least two and usually more local brethren were ordained to the priesthood and placed in authority over the people. Not many months passed after the first branches were organized before Hawaiian men were ordained elders in the higher or Melchizedek Priesthood and sent on six-month missions to their own people. Native elders were called in fairly large numbers, beginning with the October conference in 1852. A year later twenty-two native elders and priests were called, and the following April ten more joined the ranks as missionaries. Their efforts yielded good results during the first year or two, until about 1854 when the work slowed on all fronts. Thus Hawaiian members of the Church were not left as passive onlookers but were involved in responsible ways from the beginning.

On 31 December 1854 there were thirty-one foreign missionaries in Hawaii. The number of Hawaiian missionaries is not known. Foreign elders held all the mission and conference (district) offices. But the majority of the branches were presided over by local Saints. By this time there were seventy-five branches. Obviously, haole missionaries could not lead each flock.

The journals of the missionaries are replete with references to the degraded state of the Hawaiian people, and they frequently include derogatory statements about some of the members as well. These statements reflect a generally accepted attitude on the part of the haoles that by Christian standards the Hawaiians were morally loose, poverty stricken, slothful, and unreliable. All this notwithstanding, the foreign elders still gave their Hawaiian charges responsibilities in the Church in the hopeful expectation that service in the kingdom would raise them to a higher quality of life. To a degree, at least, their hopes were fulfilled.

Several Hawaiian Saints stand out as examples of integrity and devotion to the work. Elders Napela and Kauwahi were spiritually strong, and there were many others who almost matched their stature. Napela was a member of the Maui conference presidency. An example of the kind of work local members could do was Napela's founding of the first language training school for LDS missionaries in the Pacific area. On 9 April 1853, Napela suggested that all newly arrived missionaries should come to his house to live for a time so that he could teach them the language.[13] On the sixteenth he began his school by teaching from the Bible. Apparently the sounds emerging from the newly arrived elders were less than encouraging. In the evening Napela made them recite again. Two days later Elder Ephraim Green wrote: "I have all ways bin a hard working man all the days of my life but this is the hardist work I ever dun to set and study all day our teacher is very atentive sum of the Brethring have got so thay can read quite well but cant tell the mening of what thay read."[14] The sessions did not last many weeks; there was too much work to be done. But Napela did give his pupils a boost in learning the language.

EARLY EDUCATIONAL EFFORTS

The economic and sanitary conditions of the Hawaiian Saints troubled the missionaries, and they sincerely wanted to help them improve their living conditions. Much was written in the missionaries' journals concerning the poor influence the Protestants had had upon the Hawaiians. Several elders rhetorically asked themselves why something had not been done by the Protestants to teach the Hawaiians the arts of husbandry and other civilized skills. Such criticisms were unfair. The first Protestant missionaries to arrive in 1820 had brought farmers along to teach such skills. Again in 1837 a sincere attempt had been made to teach the Hawaiians how to farm and thus gain more from the soil. But these efforts did not prove fruitful because the Hawaiian people were used to a different pattern of life—one in which there was less structure and fewer demands. The LDS missionaries learned that they were not any more skillful at teaching the arts of Western civilization than were their predecessors. Nevertheless they tried.

Different kinds of "civilizing" efforts were attempted. LDS schools were started as early as April 1852. Farrer started schools at Hakipuu and "Kaawe" (probably Kaaawa). He hoped, as did President Lewis, who had suggested such a move, that he could influence his scholars in the ways of Mormonism as much as in the skills of the English language and the benefits that would bring.[15] Few students were attracted, and this first effort was soon given up.

About a year later during August 1853 the elders concluded that there were sufficient Church members to create LDS schools separate from the government institutions. They based this claim, which was made to Richard Armstrong, minister of public instruction, on the somewhat mistaken idea that there was already a double system of Protestant and Catholic schools supported by the state. In effect this was almost true because the local people of each area had the right to elect the board of directors for their school, and it was only natural that they would choose people of their own sect. Thus Protestant areas elected Protestants to their boards, and Catholic-dominated areas did the same thing. These boards in turn hired teachers of their own faith, thus giving the appearance of two sectarian school systems. It was unfortunate and somewhat ironic for the Latter-day Saints that they grew in numbers at a time when the population of the islands was sharply diminished by disease. The population had steadily declined over the years since the arrival of white men, and during the months from September 1853 to January 1854 approximately six thousand more natives died of smallpox. Thus the Mormons wanted to expand the school system at the very time when it was most practical to eliminate schools already in existence. It was also unfortunate that serious problems existed at this time between Protestants and Catholics. Armstrong wanted to change the status quo but was restrained from doing so by a French naval officer who had two warships under his command.[16]

President Lewis and others held meetings with Armstrong in an attempt to gain support for LDS schools, but he explained that he did not have the authority to give money to the Mormon cause.[17] The elders were not convinced of this and continued to discuss their grievances and possible courses of action during the following year.

It is not known how many schools were finally founded by the LDS missionaries during these early years, but schools were operated on Oahu, Kauai, Maui, Molokai, and Lanai. What difficulties were encountered are also unknown, but some problems did occur on Molokai when Elder Woodbury and the Saints organized their school. The problems were quickly resolved when the local Protestant missionary told the Hawaiians they could attend any school they wanted.[18]

The LDS missionaries also attempted to teach the Hawaiians how to farm using typical American methods. The best-known effort of this kind, which took place on Lanai, will be discussed later (see chapter 4). But an earlier attempt was made to teach the Saints of Maui how to grow wheat. The project was carried out by nonmissionary haole members of the Church. President Lewis was not warm to the idea but allowed it to continue. It soon proved a failure.[19] But failure or not, it was an effort in what the participants thought was the right direction.

The Doctrine of Polygamy

Joseph Smith was persecuted and reviled from the time he publicly made known his vision of the Father and the Son. Persecution grew when he published the Book of Mormon. As the Church expanded degrading stories preceded the missionaries wherever they went. But belief in modern visions and revelations and a book translated from golden plates caused minor abuse in comparison with the problems raised when the doctrine of plural marriage or "polygamy" was made known.

This concept is believed to have first been revealed to the Prophet in 1831.[20] Because of its controversial nature only a few trusted associates of the Prophet were taught the principle. Joseph Smith's first publicly recognized plural marriage came in 1841 at Nauvoo, Illinois. James B. Allen and Glen M. Leonard explain the development of the doctrine this way:

> Perhaps the most controversial doctrines taught at Nauvoo were those relating to sealing and plural marriage. . . .
>
> The same revelation that clarified the sealing power also explained the doctrine of plural marriage. Under priesthood authority, it declared, ancient prophets had been given more than one wife, and if the Lord for

> any reason should command it again, the practice was right and valid when entered into under the direction of the priesthood. . . .[21]

But even though several prominent men in Nauvoo were asked to take plural wives and did, the practice remained confidential until the Church moved to Utah. Then, on 29 August 1852 the practice was publicly announced. After this only a small part of the Church membership participated. Most of the men who took additional wives did so because they were asked to by priesthood leaders above them. Approximately 85 to 90 percent of the Mormon community continued to live monogamously and were happy to do so.[22]

The polygamy issue had preceded the first Mormon missionaries to the islands but was not a serious issue during the first two and a half years of the mission. But from August 1853 on the tensions between the Church and the government of Hawaii increased. The missionaries did not preach about the doctrine of plural marriage at all until April of that year, and then only because they thought it would be wiser to teach the doctrine themselves than to allow their converts to learn about it from their enemies. A copy of the revelation, section 132 of the Book of Doctrine and Covenants, was brought to the islands with the third group of missionaries, who arrived 17 February 1853. Elder Cannon translated it and preached on the subject for over two hours at the April conference in Wailuku. He explained the concept of plurality of wives but "impressed very forcibly upon them the necessity of not medling [*sic*] with those things that at present were not for them."[23] From there the elders carried the new doctrine (i.e., new to the Hawaiians) to other islands. A few weeks after the conference Elder Woodbury preached a sermon on polygamy to some Saints on Molokai. He was careful to make sure the Hawaiian Saints did not think they were licensed to enter the practice. The system was "for those who were commanded of the Lord," he said, and further explained "that we had nothing to do with it here" in Hawaii.[24] There is no evidence that the Hawaiian Saints were ever counseled to enter the practice of plural marriage or that any did. But the fact that the concept of polygamy had been introduced to the Hawaiian Saints came to the attention, naturally enough, of government officials and contributed to further friction.

What the elders taught their converts and what the press had to say about the matter were two different things. The same stories about the purported lascivious, lustful, vain, and vulgar behavior of the Saints in Utah, especially the stories about Brigham Young, were circulated in Hawaii that were spread all over America and the Western world. There is no question that the doctrine of polygamy greatly harmed the LDS cause in Hawaii. All manner of abuse was heaped upon the elders and Saints there just as in other parts of the world. Many newly converted members fell away because they could not stand the harassment to which they were subjected by their former associates and friends.

The most direct result of the discussions of the doctrine of plural marriage was refusal by the government to grant the right to perform marriages to LDS Church officials. This was a serious problem that continued until 1877. The missionaries fought this issue with every means available. They wrote letters to government officials and arranged personal interviews with people of influence, but all to no avail. The public justification used by the government was that the Mormons allegedly did not abide by the law of the land. However, there was nothing that proved this to be so and no attempt was made by officials even to suggest names of people who were actually practicing polygamy in Hawaii. Nevertheless the ruling stood. The Saints deeply disliked having to go to Protestant ministers to be married, but this had to be endured.[25]

The government newspaper, the *Polynesian,* ran articles about polygamy on a number of occasions. Every time this happened the elders penned responses to the editor in the hope that they could counteract the misinformation being spread. But not a word they wrote appeared in print. President Lewis wrote Brigham Young in August 1854 to report on the issue. A fact that troubled him was that the Latter-day Saints, thousands of them, were being taxed to support a newspaper that was so "slanderous and cowardly." On a few occasions the *Argus,* another newspaper, did print some of the letters from the elders. Elder Benjamin F. Johnson wrote a tract defending the cause, but it did not sway most antagonists.[26] The polygamy issue remained a problem in Hawaii until the concept was abandoned by the Church in 1890.

A number of other confrontations arose that brought the mission president into contact with government officials. One Hawaiian, Elder Kauwahi, a lawyer, was arrested for breaking the marriage laws. In truth he had been divorced for several years before he remarried and entered the Church. At the time he was seeking election as marshal of Kauai and was favored to win. Nevertheless he was arrested, placed in prison for a time, tried, fined, imprisoned again, and finally allowed to appeal to the supreme court. The missionaries were convinced that this was all done to discredit one of the most intelligent and influential Hawaiians in the islands because he had become a Mormon.[27]

Another problem was the destruction of two small meetinghouses on Hawaii by some overzealous Catholics. Again the elders went to the government for help. Enough difficulties had occurred by the end of 1853 that Brother Dennis bought Benjamin F. Johnson a complete copy of the legal code of the kingdom for reference. Johnson acted as legal counselor to the mission on this and many other occasions.[28]

THE "GREAT" SMALLPOX EPIDEMIC

Some of the saddest incidents in the mission's history took place during a terrible smallpox epidemic in late 1853. The elders, probably immune to the disease because of vaccinations used in Europe and America since 1798, spent their time administering to the sick with holy oil and blessing them, using more than two quarts of oil a day.[29] But many good members of the Church died on Oahu. Fewer suffered from the disease on the outer islands, but the effects were sorely felt there as well. Several of the elders were perplexed that the Lord had taken the best and strongest members from their midst.[30] In an effort to try to find meaning in these difficult losses, Elder Johnson wrote about his feelings at the time. He was heartsick to see the pain and agony as whole families suffered from the dreaded disease.

> So went most of our dearest and most zealous brethren and friends—our most active help in the ministry—and my heart wept, and my whole soul cried out to the Lord for that poor people. I was in great affliction, and marveled that the Lord would permit all his most faithful servants to die, so dear to us, and whose help we so much needed. I pondered the subject prayerfully until the light of the Lord shone upon my understanding, and I saw multitudes of their race in the spirit world who had lived before them, and there was not one there with the priesthood to teach them the gospel. The voice of the Spirit said to me, "Sorrow not, for they are now doing that greater work for which they were ordained, and it is all of the Lord."[31]

In this way, convinced that the gospel was now being preached to the Hawaiian people who had died prior to the introduction of the gospel in that land, one elder received solace for his grief.

–4–

THE LANAI COLONY

THE LDS missionaries to Hawaii came armed with the same spiritual beliefs that had motivated and guided their colleagues in other parts of the world. Since the 1840s Church doctrine had required Saints to flee from the sinful world and come to "Zion," a place where the pure in heart could dwell in peace. The missionaries who left the Utah gathering place to teach the gospel in Hawaii carried this concept of a separate gathering place with them.[1]

With the Hawaiian membership of the Mormon Church having reached a fairly large number, 3,008, and the antagonism of the government, Protestant and Catholic missionaries, and others becoming stronger, the missionaries made the decision to find a temporary gathering place in Hawaii. This action had actually been suggested by President Brigham Young before it was officially acted on at the October conference of 1853. A committee of elders was appointed to search for suitable locations. They hoped to find a place somewhat removed from the larger centers, a place where they could develop strong Saints without outside harassment. At the same meeting there was discussion concerning the advisability of buying a ship for the use of the Saints. Nathan Tanner suggested that a ship be bought to transport Hawaiian converts to and from California, so they could gather with the Church there, and also to carry missionaries from island to island. The proposal was tabled, but Tanner persisted in his idea.[2]

About two weeks after the conference, on 19 October, the committee visited the little island of Lanai. The visit was the suggestion of Elder Hammond, who had previously been there, and all hoped it would make a suitable gathering place for the Hawaiian Saints. Benjamin F. Johnson described the excursion:

> The following morning . . . we started to explore this island, which is nearly circular in shape, and about 20 miles in diameter, and had been

> upheaved, a melted, dripping mass of rock. . . . In ascending this island mountain about one mile was rugged and rocky, but another mile of smooth and beautiful grasslands brought us to a summit or rim of a basin or valley, which as a concave occupied its whole top; and as we gazed down upon it we were charmed with its beauty. Never had we seen a valley of such symmetry and beauty, and as we proceeded, we found the soil very rich, the only question of importance being the needed supply of water to sustain the population through the dry season. . . .
>
> We were told of springs over a high ridge. . . . At the bottom we found a number of small basins dry in the clay banks, filled by the seeping waters. . . .
>
> Exploring the interior portion of the valley we found beautiful fields of sweet potatoes, with melon vines and beans that had grown year after year. . . .
>
> We could not see how to procure water for a settlement, as to construct tanks would be expensive and take time, and one member of the committee [Tanner] was opposed to any move that interfered with his plan of procuring a ship and emigrating the native saints to the coast. . . .[3]

After the committee returned to Lahaina, they met to consider their findings and their impressions concerning Lanai. Most of the group felt good about the site, but Tanner created a spirit of dissension in the ranks, and a decision was put off for the time being.[4]

During the next nine months several locations on Molokai and Kauai were seriously considered as settlement sites. Nearly every tract of land proposed belonged to Chief Haalelea. He had offered to lease or sell land in late October 1853 and spent a great deal of time with the elders trying to help them find the right site. The missionaries in Honolulu studied his plans carefully. In January 1854 the elders on Kauai were convinced that they had found the best place, but after talking over the financial arrangements with Haalelea, they concluded that the rent would be impossibly high. Again they turned their attention to Lanai.

In February 1854 the missionaries and Chief Haalelea made a tentative agreement. Elder Hammond met with Haalelea in Honolulu, and the chief offered to "give us the privilege of going onto his land there [on Lanai] for the space of four years and try what we could do, without any charge, and after that if we wanted it longer we should then pay something for it."[5] Other locations were still considered, but the elders were moving more and more in the direction of Lanai.

In late May or early June President Lewis received a letter from Brigham Young in which he discussed the concept of "temporary or subsidiary gathering places" and asked the Saints in Hawaii to find a suitable location and proceed with the gathering.[6] Until this letter arrived the elders had been hesitant to make their move, possibly because Elder Tanner was still lobbying for a vessel. But when they came together for their annual July conference, the missionaries decided to use the valley of Palawai, Lanai, as their local Zion. When Lewis wrote to Brigham Young a few days after the meeting, he sounded a bit unsure about the decision, yet he did his best to make the place sound attractive. "This valley is supposed to be of sufficient altitude to admit the growth of wheat, corn, sweet potatoes; with many of the tropical fruits, and we hope that it will prove sufficiently moist to admit of the cultivation of the coffee and grape." Lewis mentioned that there was serious concern about the availability of water, but that they were planning to construct large reservoirs to sustain the settlement through the dry season. He felt that this valley had been preserved for their special use as a place where the "oppressed and dispised [*sic*]" could be exiled to a haven of peace.[7]

Ephraim Green, a man of experience, patience, and good humor, was appointed to supervise the farming and lay out the village. Francis Hammond and Benjamin F. Johnson were to help select the best site, with Hammond, who lived at Lahaina, to assist in carrying out whatever measures were necessary to make the new community a success.[8] According to the final agreement with Chief Haalelea, Lanai could be used on an experimental basis for four or five years, after which a small rent that amounted to $175 a year would be charged.[9]

SETTLEMENT

When Green, Hammond, and Johnson arrived on Lanai on 28 August 1854, they were greeted by twenty-one Hawaiian pioneers who had moved there to take part in the gathering, and by fifty Saints who lived there permanently. Both the missionaries and the local Saints regularly referred to the new settlers as pioneers. Although Lanai was already inhabited (total population of the island was around six hundred), the area surrounding the new settlement was essentially barren and required the same kind of effort as had been needed in Utah. After exploring the valley of Palawai for two days, Green and Johnson found a satisfactory place for the settlement. When they took the other brethren there, "all with one voice said, 'This is the place,' and joy seemed to fill all." Johnson then suggested that it be called the Valley of Ephraim (a name President Lewis had suggested to Brigham Young a few weeks before), and that the city be called Joseph. All agreed. They knelt together, and Johnson, who was first counselor in the mission presidency (see appendix B), dedicated the land and people to the Lord.[10]

The Lanai pioneers came primarily from Kula and Wailuku. They had been called on missions by Elder Hammond to settle this new and "barren" land. Their calls came to them in words similar to those used by President Young when he sent groups to open new communities in the valleys of the Mountain West. Hammond told the Saints at Kula that a few should get ready to go to Lanai. They should "commence farming there as pioneers for the Church—building houses, digging wells, making roads, &c." They were "to get ready in the course of a few days, with all the different seeds they can obtain suited for planting."[11]

At Kula Hammond had recruited eleven men, one plow, two yoke of oxen, and one cart for the "Lanai experiment," and he did just about as well at Wailuku. It was not easy to convince the Saints there or elsewhere in established Church centers to move to Lanai and leave their friends, relatives, and familiar surroundings. But these two areas, as later years were to make even more evident, were the strongest in the mission.

Conditions on Lanai were difficult because little food was available, and water had to be obtained from a spring located more than a mile from the new settlement. Family and friends had to provide food for the pioneers by transporting it by canoe or boat from Maui. For the first eight months or so it was an almost all-male community. Families would come later, after a good crop had been raised to sustain them.

One of the first things Elder Green did was to divide the pioneers into groups of ten, with captains at the head of each group. Because nine or ten Lanai residents wanted to be considered pioneers, they were also grouped together, making a total of three groups. When this was done, Hammond offered a prayer dedicating the pioneers and their works to the Lord. They then began clearing land to plant their first crops: corn, melons, and a few Irish potatoes. The next day, 6 September, Green started digging a well. The work of creating a settlement had begun.

Over the next year an amazing variety of seeds, slips, and starts were planted, including wheat, oats, barley, grapes, sweet potatoes and Irish potatoes, beans of several kinds, peas, squash, pumpkins, bananas, corn, melons, peaches, plums, quinces, pears, tomatoes, cabbage, and "many kinds of garden seed."[12] The process of planting was fairly well thought out. Seeds and starts were ordered from California, Oregon, Maine, Long Island, and Boston. New varieties were tested, and experimental planting was done at different times of the year to find the best growing seasons for various crops. Some of the seeds died in the ground and other plants were totally destroyed by worms. The dry weather almost killed some acreage, and heavy rains from January to April 1855 caused problems and ruined some crops. But during the first year there were some successes, and the experiment was deemed worth the effort. The wheat had produced well, as had the corn. Over fifty acres were planted during the first year.

The work was hard and the ground did not yield its fruits without a struggle. The first planting was done in unplowed ground. Later, four head of oxen, brought from Maui in a scow, pulled the plows. The ground was so dry and hard that the plow beams broke several times, along with at least one plowshare. But such slowdowns were a regular occurrence, and Elder Green took them in stride.

Green was less patient with his native charges. His journal registers repeated complaints about how their "laziness" disgusted him, and he said that he would have given up on them if they were not descendants of Abraham, Joseph, and Lehi and therefore full of promise and favored with blessings of the Lord. Green was not the first, nor the last, to give in to impatience. Most Hawaiians had difficulty following the aggressive haole life-style. Their ancient work patterns were far more casual, and a strict regimen held little appeal for them, either historically or emotionally. The missionaries were neither historians nor anthropologists who were interested in the problems of the people they were leading. To the elders, there was but one way to complete the job they were doing and that was through work. The Hawaiians knew they would have to work, but they wondered why it all had to be done so soon.

Green's poor command of the Hawaiian language exacerbated the problem because he did not recognize the difficulties arising among them. Even before the pioneering work officially commenced, trouble was brewing, for Hawaiians were already clearing private areas without thought of their obligation to provide for the later settlers. Hammond, who spoke the language fluently, observed their actions. He taught them how to behave in the new Zion, telling them they should not allow themselves "to be covetous and get greedy and want to go and plant great fields for your own selves and families. . . ." He asked them to set good examples for all who would come after them. If they worked hard, the Lord would prosper them.[13]

The matter of how much time should be spent working for the Church and how much for themselves was a serious problem. In the beginning Hammond and Green asked the pioneers to work for the Church full-time. But because some of the Saints requested time for themselves, it was decided that after they had worked all day, they could plant private fields in the evening and at night. This plan did not work because they toiled harder at night than in the day and were too tired to work industriously on the Church lands. By January 1855 Green had modified his demands, allowing the natives to work on their own fields two days a week. "They are very busy on them days. I think they plant more them two days than they do in the other four." He said he did not care how or when they did it, but he hoped they would get all the potatoes planted.[14]

All the missionaries gathered at Lanai for the July conference, where it was resolved that the native pioneers should devote two days a week to the Church and have the remaining time to do as they wished.

Settling this community was not very different from doing the same thing in Utah or Idaho. In Utah each village and town had started from barren wilderness where almost every comfort had to be created. Land had to be cleared, water obtained, homes built, and streets laid out. The same kinds of work needed to be done on Lanai. First a decision had to be made concerning how large the city should be and where the roads should run. Since Green was in charge, he made the decision:

> This morning Br. Hammon left for Maui. I tuck my cumpas and commenst to lay out a town at the fut of the mountain and laid out one stret runing south to the sea three mildes to a fine litle harbour whare we land our boats hear we intendt to build a store hou[se] to leave our produse. I then laid out three more streats thruing the town in to blocks fore acres each with the streats fore rods wide this is a butiful location for a town.[15]

The next task was to assign lots to the pioneers for their houses. Timber had to be acquired either in the mountains above the town or from other islands. Since water was in short supply, cisterns were dug, faced with rock, and cemented. A corral was built for the oxen, mules, and donkeys, and the pigs were provided with a pen, but the chickens and turkeys were allowed to forage for themselves. Also, the original meetinghouse, built by local Saints before the arrival of the pioneers in August, was replaced by a larger one. After several months of hard work, the new building was finished and dedicated on 30 December 1854.

Homes for the pioneers, like the meetinghouse, were built in the native style. George Q. Cannon described the homes, called *hale*s:

> These native houses are built by putting posts in the ground on which a board is laid as a plate for the rafters to rest upon. When the frame of posts and rafters is built, poles . . . are lashed horizontally, about six inches apart, on to the posts and rafters. The house is then thatched by fastening a

> durable grass, which they have in that country, on to the poles. When finished, a house looks, in shape and size, like a well built hay stack. . . .
>
> Inside the house they have no board floors. The ground is covered with grass, on which mats are laid. The making of these mats constitutes one of the chief employments of the women, and a good housewife in that country is known by the quality and fineness of the mats in her home. Such a woman is very particular to have no dirt brought into her house; for the mats answer the purpose of beds, tables and chairs. They sit upon them; when they eat, their food is placed upon them, and they form their bed, though in many houses they have the place of sleeping raised above the ordinary floor; but even then, they have mats spread out, upon which to sleep.[16]

Elders Green and Hammond were the prime movers of the Lanai project, but other men also helped. The Hawaiian Saints were the most important, for without them the project could never have been put into operation. Two haole converts, Brothers Baker and Rice, helped with the building and planting, spending considerable time on Lanai during the first year. Elders Thomas Karren and Silas Smith also spent time working with the Hawaiian Saints.

Karren's involvement in the Lanai experiment was rather awkward for all concerned. Around the first week in October 1854, Hammond received a letter from President Lewis stating that Karren was coming from Oahu and would, from the time of his arrival on Lanai, be in charge of farming and business affairs. Though Green had handled this part of the project, Hammond had overseen all activities and was deeply hurt by this new order from Lewis. He believed that Karren had been sent because of a disagreement he, Hammond, had had with Benjamin F. Johnson concerning the possible planting of tobacco on Lanai. Even at this time use of tobacco was discouraged by the LDS health code, called the Word of Wisdom. Johnson, an intelligent, strong-willed man, thought it would be a quick way to earn money and take care of the mission debts. But Hammond thought it was wrong to plant a product that the Church was teaching the Hawaiians not to use. He also mentioned that the "weed" destroys the soil faster than any other crop he knew. Hammond was convinced that Johnson had influenced Lewis to send Karren because he thought Karren would plant tobacco.

Before this problem was solved, strong words had passed between the elders involved. Green, who was also being displaced, was terribly disappointed that his authority and ability had been questioned, and Karren felt bad that he had ended up in the middle of an issue he had not created. Through it all Hammond sought the Lord for strength to endure what he felt to be an affront to his character. The men did resolve their differences and worked together for several months until Karren left the island to prepare to return home.[17] The record does not reveal the planting of any tobacco on Lanai.

Although creating a settlement on Lanai was difficult, the pioneers had time for some lighter moments too. They enjoyed hunting wild goats for meat in the mountains, and on a number of occasions during the first year were successful. Fishing was also a routine but enjoyable part of every Hawaiian's life. The pioneers held several feasts that were a delight to all who participated.

Green frequently mentioned that he wished the rain would come—or that the rain would stop—but he loved his little colony. On several occasions he wrote about the beauty of his island home. "This morning the sun has risen clear and spreads its golden rays over the Sandwich Isles and all nature seems to rejoice at its appearance."[18] In June 1855, when corn had been harvested and dried, he wrote, paraphrasing the style of the Book of Mormon:

> This day we have spent in preparing and fiting up for Conference the boat arived from Maui loded with goats for Conference This evening Bro Silas Smith and Silas S. Smith made a grater and grated a fine panful of indian meal. and it came to pass that I Ephraim being born of Yanky parence and som what lurnd in all the arts of that people proceded to make a cake which was choice above all uther cakes that I had ever seen even in my own land and thus ended the thurtieth day of June 1855.[19]

THE *LANAI*

The dreams of the elders for the success and prosperity of Lanai were large indeed. In November 1854 Elder Hammond had purchased a whaleboat to make transportation to and from Lanai more convenient. But by spring he was convinced that this boat would not suffice for all the traveling that needed to be done. New settlers would have to be transported from all the islands, and the abundant crops later to be harvested would need to be taken to appropriate marketplaces. A bigger vessel, he argued to President Lewis and the other missionaries, would have to be acquired.[20]

Apparently Hammond convinced his colleagues, for they began looking in earnest for a suitable vessel during March and April 1855. Funds were very limited, but fortunately (they thought) a German convert named Baumann was building a sloop. Although not a sailor, nor an experienced shipbuilder, he did have a boat and offered the mission half interest in it for eight hundred dollars. The offer was accepted. Half the money was to be paid before the boat was launched, with the remainder to come from the earnings of the boat. When the idea was suggested to the native Saints, they were eager to be part of the excitement and subscribed four hundred dollars very quickly. Collecting this money proved to be the problem. About three hundred dollars was paid to Brother Baumann by the July conference in 1855, but one hundred dollars of that had to be borrowed elsewhere. The other hundred never was collected.[21]

Hammond was released from his mission in July 1855 and was thus free to be the first captain of the little sloop. He described the 21.5-ton vessel this way: "The *Lanai* sails well, but is cranky and needs a good deal of ballast. She is a vessel of about 21 tons and as ugly looking as anything I ever saw afloat."[22] Launched 8 August 1855 on the island of Oahu,[23] the sloop *Lanai* turned out to be nothing but a nightmare. The idea was good, but the choice of vessels was poor.

TROUBLED TIMES

The July conference of 1855 on Lanai was a very important meeting. The decisions to buy the sloop *Lanai* and to release President Lewis and Elders Green, Hammond, A. Allred, Woodbury, and Linn were made. Such releases were standard after men and women had served several years as missionaries. Silas Smith was chosen as the new president of the mission. The elders also decided to start a school on Lanai, where Elder Ward E. Pack would teach the Hawaiians English. It was further decided that the mission would assume all debts that had been incurred by Hammond and others to establish the Lanai settlement.

When the old group of elders departed, they left the mission in the hands of men who had very little language expertise. Most of these new missionaries acquired proficiency within a few months, but work was nonetheless slowed down for a time.

The following year, from July 1855 to July 1856, was not as successful as the elders had hoped. The crops on Lanai turned out poorly. Saints throughout the islands generally refused to move to the new colony. Strong sermons on the necessity of gathering out of Babylon or out of Egypt were given regularly in all parts of the mission, but to little avail. Perhaps their message seemed harsh and difficult to follow. Success was attained only among the very strongest converts. Elder Joseph F. Smith said: "The gathering at the island of Lanai has gleaned out most of the faithful and diligent brethren, and that, perhaps, is one cause why the Saints feel so discouraged on the other islands."[24]

Joseph F. Smith (1838–1918), who later served as an apostle, as counselor to Presidents Taylor, Woodruff, and Snow, and as president of the Church from 1901 to 1918, was called to the Hawaiian mission at the age of fifteen. His first mission to Hawaii lasted from 27 September 1854 until 6 October 1857. Like George Q. Cannon, he learned the Hawaiian language quickly. During his first mission he served primarily on Maui, Molokai, and Hawaii, his experiences there shaping his love not only for the Hawaiian people, but also for the gospel and the Lord. While he was serving on Molokai Smith became extremely ill. For three months he was cared for and nursed by a young Hawaiian woman named Ma Manuhii and her husband. The story of his meeting with this good woman is familiar throughout the Church, and his warm reunion with his aged Hawaiian "mama" when she welcomed him again to Hawaii after so many years is recounted in *The Life of Joseph F. Smith* by Joseph Fielding Smith, Jr.

Even as a young man Smith was blessed with wisdom. He perceived the mission's most serious problem—that the Lanai colony benefited those who gathered there, but weakened branches elsewhere.

At the July 1855 conference it was apparent that growth had slowed to a near standstill. There were 4,650 members in the islands at that time.[25] By the time of the April conference in 1856, after a careful census of Saints had been taken, there was actually a drop in the total. This was due to previously unrecorded deaths, some apostasy, and the loss of some members who simply could not be located. The loss notwithstanding, mission leaders felt that progress was being made.[26]

Among the missionaries laboring in Hawaii at this time were strong men, but opposition to their work grew and hindered them. Discouragement set in and began to cause problems. After June 1856 the momentum of the mission changed. Efforts that before had yielded converts now seemed useless. President Silas Smith tried to be positive but could not hold back his discouragement: "We are forced to acknowledge that despite all our exertions to strengthen, build up and increase the Church on these Islands, there is a very manifest falling away, both in numbers, and in the faith and good works of those who pretend to hold on to the work."[27]

During the next year matters became even worse. A number of previously active and successful branches suffered from mass apostasy. Reports of apostasy came from Elder William Naylor on Oahu in December 1856, from Elder Smith B. Thurston six months later, and from Elder John R. Young at Keanae, Maui, in September 1857. In April 1857 Joseph F. Smith reported that many of the Saints on Molokai had lost their faith and were indifferent.[28] Apparently the only area that remained strong was Lanai, and even there, problems arose.

From July 1856 on, letters from President Silas Smith to President Young carried many such negative reports: The newness of the Church had worn off, and people were no longer attracted to the novel ideas and doctrines of the Mormon Church. Within the Church some members were critical of the failure of the *Lanai* venture, which had resulted in great debt to the Church and had served virtually no useful purpose. Some Saints were also critical of the Church because other debts, such as those incurred to buy seeds and tools for Lanai, had not been paid off. Others complained about the failure of the crops on Lanai. This criticism is ironic in that at this very time people were starving in all parts of the islands due to an extended drought lasting from 1856 into late 1857.

In addition to the internal difficulties, there were serious problems from outside the Church. Smith reported that two apostates had come to Hawaii. The first, unidentified, spread vicious stories about the behavior of Saints in the Mormon colony of San Bernardino, California, and elsewhere. Some local Protestant ministers welcomed such stories, using them in sermons and in the local press. A second apostate was John Hyde, Jr., a man who had presided over a group of missionaries to Hawaii. When he arrived he left the Church and proceeded to hurt the Mormon cause more than any other individual. He was escorted from place to place by Protestant ministers who willingly volunteered to translate his message. Hyde later became one of the most famous apostate writers of the early Utah period. In May 1857 President Smith reported: "the past six months has been for us a season of unprecedented opposition from Apostates, Editors, and hireling Priests who have spared no pain to belie and misrepresent the Church, and do all in their power to impede its progress."[29]

During the summer of 1857 another group of elders was called to Hawaii. At its head was Henry W. Bigler, now forty-two years old. Two other veterans of the Hawaiian mission were also called—John S. Woodbury and James Keeler. Bigler sailed from San Francisco on 22 August, having been advised by George Q. Cannon, now president of the California mission, that he should prepare the way for the other elders.

When he arrived on 4 September, Bigler could hardly believe how much things had changed since 1854. Attending church in Honolulu, he felt like "everything [was] dead or dieing." To his dismay he found that elders were working as hired labor simply to sustain themselves. Previously, they had relied upon the local people for support. His companions told him their belief that there were not more than one or two Hawaiians in the whole mission "but had more faith in their old religion than they had in the Truth." Bigler's journal records that this did not include the two or three hundred Saints on Lanai, who were still faithful and obedient.[30]

A conference was held on 4 October at which twelve missionaries were released to return home to Utah or California. Both Silas Smith and Joseph F. Smith were released, and Bigler was sustained as president of the mission. President Bigler chose James Keeler (expected to arrive soon) and John Woodbury as his counselors. A number of matters of business were discussed, most important being the mission debt (which was relatively low at this point, although the conference report does not give a dollar amount), the fact that George Q. Cannon had decided to send the printing press to Hawaii from San Francisco, and the proper disposition of the Lanai settlement. It was resolved that a more suitable gathering place than Lanai should be sought.[31]

The next Sunday attendance was poor, with hardly a dozen Saints showing up. It was "like preaching to the walls," said Bigler, contrasting it with the apparent faith of the Saints three years before. "The faith of the native Saints is gone."[32] He blamed two factors: the failure of the *Lanai* project and the removal of the press. Both ventures had been real disappointments to the Hawaiians.

With so few Saints to help support them, it was obvious to the recently returned elders that they would have to work to maintain themselves. Woodbury started a school to teach Hawaiians and Chinese the English language. Bigler went to work for a Mr. Duncan (who also hired several other elders from time to time) a mile or two outside Honolulu. He was paid room and board plus twenty dollars per month. On their hours off the elders worked to reform the Church, but their efforts were of no avail.

THE CLOSING OF THE MISSION

For the next month work moved along at a slow pace and with little promise of improvement. Then on 20 November 1857 the mail arrived from San Francisco, bringing several letters of vital importance. One, a letter from President Brigham Young dated 4 September, read in part:

> The reports from the Sandwich Islands have for a number of years agreed in one thing, that is, that the majority of the Saints on these Islands have either been dead or dieing Spiritually—it would appear that they occasionally spasmodically resuscitate for a few moments, only to sink lower than they were before . . . I think it best for all of the Elders (with one or two exceptions) to come home. . . . You had better wind up the whole of your business and return with most of the Elders as soon as possible.[33]

Although Young did not mention problems at home in this letter, a letter written the same day to his nephew, John R. Young, detailed difficulties between the Saints and the U.S. government and the possibility of war. This did not come as a surprise to the elders. Honolulu and San Francisco newspapers had kept them well abreast of the issues in Utah.

President Young explained his actions, saying that he knew there were some faithful Saints there, men who were "experienced enough in the work to enable them to stand firm in the faith." On the other hand, those who were "filled with the lusts of the flesh will float off with the current and if at any time it should be thought wisdom to renew the work there, the Church will flourish more rapidly through the testimony of those who are faithful to their God."[34]

The letters that day also informed the elders that the new missionaries who had supposedly left for Hawaii had been recalled home before leaving San Francisco. Furthermore, President Young had told Elder Cannon not to send the printing press to Hawaii.[35]

The impending closing of the mission was announced to the Saints the following Sunday. It was a cause of much grief among the faithful few who loved the Church and believed strongly. On 9 December 1857 the remaining elders who had been released in October left the islands. Since their release, they had been working at various occupations to earn the money for their passage. Only eleven Zion missionaries were left, and they were doing their best to earn funds to pay their passage home.

The situation in Utah grew more serious with each passing week. Perhaps for this reason President Young was moved to write to the Hawaii-based elders again in October. His letter, which arrived in Honolulu on 22 December, showed his alarm about the growing threat to the Mormon cause. He included information on the size of the army coming against them and its location. He reiterated his advice to them to come home, but added that they should "return home as speedily as they may be able to procure outfits." He further stated that George Q. Cannon had been instructed to help the missionaries pay their way home with any funds obtained from the sale of the Book of Mormon in California. Young was concerned about leaving the Hawaiian Saints without proper leadership, but he rationalized the situation and said that he "presumed that the Books of Mormon [in Hawaiian], the native Elders and one or two now from here will answer on that mission for the present."[36] This call to return home was not peculiar to Hawaii. All missionaries in the United States and Europe were also called home. Young was concerned for the welfare of the political entity called Utah, but he was also concerned that the men of the Church should be home to take care of their wives and children. The majority of the missionaries were married men; thus it is not surprising that they became anxious about returning as quickly as possible to Zion.

In his first two letters Young had told the mission leaders to leave one or two men to watch over the Saints. In his third letter, however, dated 4 February 1858, President Young said: "You are all, without regard as to when you were sent, counseled to start for home as speedily as you can wind up your affairs and obtain passage money, not even leaving in that mission one Elder who has been sent there, unless you should deem it wisdom so to do."[37] The six remaining missionaries (four had left in mid-March) met together on 25 April and decided that they should all leave. On 1 May all but Elder Clayton, who sailed soon after, left Hawaii.

President Young has been criticized for pulling the missionaries out of Hawaii. Significantly, though, he did not change his original order without first receiving the suggestion from the missionaries. On 3 December 1857 President Bigler and Elder Woodbury wrote Young that they did not think it necessary for anyone to stay.[38] President Young heeded their counsel and changed his mind. Thus responsibility for leaving the Hawaiian Saints without supervision rests on the local mission president and his counselor at least as much if not more than on Young. As will be seen later, the closing of the mission led to serious difficulties within several years.

When the mission closed, the Saints on Lanai had one year left in their experimental period. A better gathering place had not yet been found. Haalelea had assured the missionaries that the Saints were free to stay until the fifth year was up and then he would make arrangements to collect rent on the land or sell it to the Church. Thus stood this matter when the Utah elders left.[39]

The annual Lanai rent, set at $175, was large considering the relatively poor crops that had been produced. Not long after the Utah elders departed, Haalelea offered the Lanai Saints all his holdings, around ten thousand acres, for the small sum of three hundred dollars. It seems likely that he had been willing to lease the land to the Saints in the first place not only because he was friendly to the Church but because he considered the land useless. He may have felt that it would be to his advantage to unload the property at any cost. But the Hawaiian Saints ran into financial problems and did not purchase the land. Some kind of arrangement may have been made with Haalelea, for the Saints were not forced to leave Lanai. It may be surmised that he either received rent or simply remained patient with the Lanai Saints. The latter course would be in keeping with his previous actions and with the kindly temperament of the Hawaiian people.[40]

Unfortunately almost no records exist to tell the story of the Hawaiian Saints from 1 May 1858 until July 1861, when Walter Murray Gibson arrived in the islands. There is no question that the total number of members declined during those years and the years that followed. Fifteen native elders were appointed to positions of authority, such as conference presidencies. At the last mission conference with the Utah elders on 25 April 1858, there were still 3,067 members of record. But at the next conference in October only 632 members were reported, although this probably indicates more about the quality of record keeping than the actual number of Saints. It can be said, though, that the next three years were dark indeed.[41]

–5–

THE ERA OF WALTER MURRAY GIBSON

The Hawaiian Saints Alone

AFTER the Utah missionaries returned home, records of only one semi-annual conference were submitted to the Salt Lake City headquarters of the Church. The records reveal that efforts were being made to continue on without outside leadership. However, because the last mission president, Henry W. Bigler, had not appointed a leader or presiding elder for the islands, there was some contention as to who was the leading Church authority. (Why Bigler did not is unclear. Perhaps he did not want to give one man that much power.) Elder Kailehune of Lanai claimed to hold this position. He did not claim to be president of the mission but believed that because he was president of the Lanai conference, he was superior to all other presidents. Apparently he was sustained in his claims by the other conference representatives.

At that time local missionaries were still being called and baptisms performed. Local Saints were also being encouraged to come to Lanai as pioneers. Priesthood leaders were trying to maintain a standard of righteousness among members, but there were some serious problems. For example, the Saints on Molokai had been so inactive and inattentive to duty that they were all cut off from the Church at the October 1858 conference. Obviously, this was an unorthodox action.[1] Better leadership could have avoided such a reversal.

After reports of these actions were sent to Salt Lake City, the record of events in Hawaii becomes silent. Many years later, in 1895, Assistant Church Historian Andrew Jenson visited the Hawaiian Islands and through interviews found that the organization of the Church had gradually become less and less orderly. Contentions had arisen among the Hawaiian elders that were difficult to settle. An unfortunate incident relating to the purchase of Palawai occurred during these years. Money that had been collected throughout the islands for the purpose of purchasing the Palawai lands was used by President Kailehune for his own purposes. Although he was excommunicated, the money, over three hundred dollars, was not recovered.

WALTER MURRAY GIBSON AND HIS ASSOCIATION WITH THE CHURCH

Three years passed after the Utah elders left Hawaii before an authorized representative from the center of the Church visited the islands. It was the adventurer Walter Murray Gibson who stepped into this divided and disoriented setting to take charge. The story of Captain Gibson is probably the most frequently written-about incident in LDS Church history in the Pacific and Asia.[2] Gibson was a complex man. He was very bright and capable; however, with only one exception, authors who have studied his Mormon years have concluded that he was a dishonest man who defrauded Church members in Hawaii of their money and holdings in a selfish effort to establish a kingdom or empire in the Pacific.[3] Gibson was unsuccessful in his plans for an island kingdom, but he was able to accumulate a considerable amount of wealth and land at the expense of his trusting Hawaiian subordinates. The most unfortunate result of his fraudulent actions was not the loss of land and personal property by the Hawaiian Saints, however, but the destruction of morals and morale among them.

The story of Gibson's life reads like a novel. Reared in North Carolina, he went to sea at an early age and married while still under twenty. His life was filled with adventures, the most important being his expedition to the East Indies. This voyage ended in disaster because the Dutch in Indonesia considered Gibson hostile to their interests in the territory. He spent some time in prison, escaped, and returned to the United States, where he unsuccessfully sought redress for his grievance against the Dutch government. It appears from Gibson's own writings that he was interested in establishing some kind of personal kingdom in Southeast Asia, a desire that almost completely consumed his every thought and action for many years. It was this grandiose scheme that brought him into contact with the Latter-day Saints.

In 1856, before he joined the Latter-day Saints, Gibson conceived the idea of relocating the Utah Mormons to New Guinea. He thought the U.S. government would like this plan because the Latter-day Saints were a thorn in its side, as is attested by the later Utah War. Gibson discussed his proposal with Utah's congressional representative, John M. Bernhisel, and the plan was also presented to President James Buchanan. Buchanan deemed the project impractical and too expensive. But Gibson was not easily defeated. He next decided to visit Utah and convert Church leaders to his scheme. In the fall of 1859 Gibson traveled to Salt Lake City, where he was hospitably received. He was completely frank about his intentions. The *Deseret News* reported that he had come to "influence" President Young to move the Saints to New Guinea. During the days following his arrival in Salt Lake he lectured on the East Indies. This was his principal means of financial support in Utah and elsewhere.

Brigham Young was not convinced that the Saints should move. In fact he told Gibson that if he really wanted to help the people of the East Indies, he should investigate the gospel and be baptized; he would ordain Gibson an elder and send him there on a mission. Gibson appeared to take Young's advice seriously, remaining in Salt Lake City during the winter to be baptized a member of the Church during January 1860. His daughter Talulah also joined the Church at that time.

Later that year Gibson was sent on a mission to the eastern states, but he returned to Salt Lake City only six months later on 4 November. He had not been able to get the East Indies out of his mind. Only three weeks passed before he talked President Young into giving him a commission to teach the restored gospel in Japan and Malaysia. The authority he received from Young was very broad: he was "fully authorized to negotiate with all the nations of this world who would obey the gospel of Christ. . . ."[4]

Gibson's route to his mission field took him to San Francisco and on to Hawaii. While in San Francisco he lectured frequently on the geography of the East Indies. He seems to have carefully avoided preaching the gospel, even though he was now a high priest in the Melchizedek Priesthood of the Church and had participated in the Church's highest ordinances. Gibson wrote several letters to President Young at this time. Each reported on the good works he had performed, but other observers did not report any open representation on his part that he was a Latter-day Saint. Gibson's motive for avoiding identification as a Mormon missionary in San Francisco and later during his first weeks in Honolulu can only be inferred from his later actions. Once he did reveal his affiliation with the Church, he was eager to be identified as the highest LDS official in the islands. To conclude that he had no plan for personal aggrandizement in mind even before he arrived in Hawaii takes some tricky mental gymnastics.

The question might be raised why Gibson went to Hawaii. President

Brigham Young had suggested to Gibson that if it was not inconvenient, he might visit the Saints there and in Tahiti and look after their welfare. Gibson took this suggestion seriously and began gathering information about the Hawaiian Saints while he was still in San Francisco. He was aware of their poverty-stricken state before he sailed for Honolulu and thus was not surprised by conditions when he arrived on 4 July 1861.

Upon his arrival, Gibson immediately identified himself as a world traveler and expert on Malaysia and the East Indies. Newspapers were interested in him because he announced that he intended to offer lectures on his experiences in the East Indies. Two months passed before he publicly affiliated himself with the Hawaiian Saints. Although he did meet the members at the Oahu conference, he told these people to keep his membership in the Church a secret. In October 1861 newspaper reporters from the *Pacific Commercial Advertiser* asked Gibson whether he was a member of the Church. He replied that "he himself believed in no creed or sect whatever."[5] He later wrote the same thing in his diary. This being true there must have been some other reason for his affiliating himself with the Latter-day Saints. As months passed, his real intentions with regard to the Church became evident.

Because there was no president of the Hawaiian mission when he arrived, Gibson assumed this title for himself. He was not satisfied, however, with the limited nature of the office and so enlarged the scope of the title, becoming "Chief President of the Islands of the Sea and of the Hawaiian Islands, for the Church of the Latter Day Saints." Gibson was never appointed to this position by Church leaders in Salt Lake City, although he did write to President Young to report his activities—at least some of them. In effect Brigham Young did give Gibson tacit authority to lead the Church in Hawaii, but he did not have a full picture of Gibson's activities.

Captain Gibson assumed control of the Church in Hawaii during September 1861. When the regular October conference of the Hawaiian Saints was held, Gibson was there and in charge. The Saints obeyed him in almost everything he asked them to do. This seems strange in retrospect, but Gibson had a powerful, charismatic personality. He accomplished more than his predecessors. Perhaps he was not as patient with the Hawaiian Saints as they had been. One of his first official acts was to issue certificates of membership and of office in the Church. These were sold to all members who desired to remain active in the Church. Membership certificates were only fifty cents, but higher offices carried a higher price. Gibson continued this practice throughout the three years of his presidency.

Selling offices in the Church was just the beginning of the changes Gibson made in its organization. He also ordained seventies (a position reserved for stakes), bishops, an archbishop (the Church had none elsewhere), a quorum of twelve apostles, and a first presidency. All these officers paid well for their positions, although it was abnormal for a mission to have any of these offices, and apostles and a first presidency were positions reserved for the top leadership of the Church as a whole. These offenses alone would have in all likelihood brought Gibson's disfellowshipment or excommunication from the Church; however, he was guilty of still other infractions of Church rules. The best-known incidents relating to Gibson's misuse of his Church authority revolve around his scheme to acquire a portion of the island of Lanai.

When Gibson arrived in Honolulu in July 1861, he soon learned about the settlement of Hawaiian Saints on Lanai. Haalelea, who owned the land, was still willing to sell the portion of the island that he owned, the valley of Palawai. At this time he was asking five hundred dollars for three thousand acres. Immediately Gibson determined that the Church should have this property. He told Brigham Young that if a good water supply could be developed, the land could be worth fifty thousand dollars. During September 1861 he visited Lanai and observed that it was very desolate and hardly worth owning, but he was determined to turn it into a valuable piece of property. He reported to Young that the Saints needed Lanai as a place to call their own. By the end of September Gibson had men searching for water, planting new crops, repairing huts, and rebuilding the "City of Joseph," as it had been named in 1854. Before long he settled on Lanai and took direct control of all affairs there.

Gibson was a demanding administrator. He insisted on work from his Hawaiian charges, and he received it. Visitors to Lanai were much impressed with the orderliness of the village and the apparent enthusiasm of the Hawaiians for work. New seeds and plants were ordered from various parts of the United States, and the island produced fairly well for a time. Unfortunately, Gibson's intentions were not altruistic. Everything he did was for his own benefit and aggrandizement, and Lanai was merely a means to a selfish end. Consider the following quotations from his diary:

> I could make a glorious little kingdom out of this, or any such chance, with such people; so loving and obedient. . . . I would fill this lovely crater with corn and wine and oil and babies and love and health and brotherly rejoicing and sisters kisses and the memory of me for evermore.[6]

Late in January he wrote,

> I view him [the Hawaiian] and treat him as an interesting yet feeble younger brother, a subject of an oceanic empire. . . . Who or what shall I fear where I am King—and I shall keep within my Kingdom. . . . I am King; not of oceanica, not of Malaysia, not of Hawaii nei, not of Lanai, but of Palawai on this day of grace. But this is but the baby of my Kingdom. Oh smiling Palawai, thou infant hope of my glorious kingdom.[7]

Gibson worked consistently toward his goal of controlling and owning the Church lands in Lanai. He demanded that members of the Church contribute to a fund for the purchase of the land. Under his direction numerous properties were sold—chapels, Church lands on other islands, homes of members, lands owned by members, and other private properties—sometimes at ridiculously low prices and all in order to raise enough money to buy the lands owned by Haalelea. Friction developed between Gibson and Haalelea, but Gibson did finally acquire the land.

But for whom did he buy it? Throughout his campaign to raise money, Gibson told the Hawaiian brethren that they were giving their means so that a gathering place could be acquired for all of them. But in truth, he had had the titles of the property placed in his own name. It has been argued that he had the land put in his name because he was the trustee for the Church in Hawaii. Such a procedure does have precedents; however, in other such instances the trustee was willing to relinquish control of the property when the time came to turn it over to another administrator. Gibson proved his bad faith by refusing to sign the Lanai property over to the Church when he was asked to do so. He did not actually steal the property; but he defrauded the members of the Church by telling them that he would serve their interests and then doing otherwise. Gibson was also responsible for acquiring a vast amount of Hawaiian government land on a lease arrangement. This too was done in his own name. The Church never laid claim to this land, but it was supposed to be used by Church members. This lease land and Haalelea's Palawai property together made up the major portion of the island, making it easy to understand why many Hawaiian members of the Church since Gibson's time have said that he stole the island of Lanai from the Church.

Gibson almost completely controlled the Church in Hawaii for three years. But a number of Hawaiian elders who could remember how the earlier missionaries behaved toward them became discontented. These people left Lanai and jointly wrote to some of their former missionary friends—to Alma L. Smith in particular—questioning Gibson's actions and his strange use of authority. These questions were brought to the attention of the First Presidency, which immediately dispatched a select committee made up of Apostles Ezra T. Benson and Lorenzo Snow and former missionaries Joseph F. Smith, Alma L. Smith, and William W. Cluff to go to Hawaii to investigate Gibson's activities.

When these brethren visited Gibson on Lanai, they found his practices conflicted with the accepted patterns of Church government. Gibson did lack Church government experience and may have felt that many of his changes in administrative procedure were justified by local circumstance. Nevertheless, the offenses mentioned above, such as simony, the selling of Church offices, and appointing men to offices that were reserved for the top leadership, were discovered. In addition, Gibson had consecrated a large stone and set it apart as the cornerstone of a great temple to be built on Lanai. Priestesses of the temple had been appointed, and ritualistic ceremonies, presumably dances, were carried out by these women.

A number of firsthand reports concerning the proceedings against Gibson are available. Two provide especially useful information on the activities of the visiting apostles and their relations with Gibson. On 12 April 1864, four days after Gibson was excommunicated, Elder Benson wrote:

> We reached his house on Sunday morning and found him and his daughter in possession of good health, but apparently more surprised than rejoiced at seeing us. We found that in the district of Palawai 6,000 acres of land had been bought by the Church, and that besides this Captain Gibson had got possession of all the government land on the island of Lanai. The Saints had been constrained to turn over all their substance, horses, sheep, goats, poultry, houses and lands to the Church to gather up to Lanai giving their time for the cultivation of the soil and this many had done receiving their food once a day from the hands of the head bishop. . . .[8]

Several weeks later on 4 May 1864 Joseph F. Smith wrote a letter to George Q. Cannon adding the following details:

> On arriving at Palawai, we found Captain Gibson snugly settled in a small village of some fifty grass houses. . . .
>
> We found that he had ordained twelve apostles. High priests, seventys, elders, bishops, and "priestesses of temples," all of whom had to pay a certain sum corresponding to the various degrees of honor bestowed upon them. What the "priestesses of the temple" signified we were at a loss to

> know, but we soon found it was only to gull the poor natives and obtain their money. Gibson had bought the district of Palawai (6,000 acres) by the donation of the Saints, assuring them he was doing it all for them for the Church. He persuaded them to give all they had to the Church and made it a test of fellowship. Many could not bear it and were excommunicated, while the faithful remained and became wholly dependent on him for both food and clothing.
>
> Brothers Benson and Snow required him to sign the land over to the Church as it was deeded to him and his heirs. This he flatly refused to do informing them he should take his own course, that he was not sent here by the Church, had received no counsel from Brigham Young, had acted upon his own responsibility in what he had done, and he was not beholden to the Church.
>
> He also told them he should ask no counsel of them, but would pursue his own course for the future. . . . He declared he should use his influence to keep the natives in his power, and persuade more to come there if he could, that they should receive no benefit from the land they had bought only as they would become subject to him. It is useless to say more. He was cut off from the Church. . . .[9]

When it became apparent to the visiting Church authorities that the charges against Gibson were true, a meeting of the priesthood was held on 7 April 1864 at which it was proposed by the apostles that he be excommunicated. Only one Hawaiian elder voted for this proposition; evidently those Church members who had remained on Lanai were still under Gibson's influence. But the official excommunication took place a day later at Lahaina.

After Gibson's excommunication from the Church, Elders Benson and Snow departed almost immediately for home. Elder Joseph F. Smith was left to preside over the Hawaiian Saints, along with Elders Alma L. Smith and William W. Cluff. These three elders were a capable trio. Joseph F. Smith later became an apostle and Church president. Cluff, at the time thirty-two years old, had already served missions in Hawaii from 1854 to 1858 and in Scandinavia from 1860 to 1863. He later served as a territorial legislator in Utah and as stake president of Summit Stake in central Utah from 1877 to 1901. Although little biographical information is available concerning Alma L. Smith, he was a diligent missionary. His first mission was from 1856 to 1858. His second mission lasted from 1864 to 1868, and he later returned as mission president from 1874 to 1875. These were good men, qualified to set the Church back in order.

Gibson, meanwhile, was left on Lanai with those Saints who would remain with him. Although his influence had been strong among them, when it was learned that he had been officially cut off from the Church, the people of Lanai left him very quickly. In October 1864, only six months later, only fourteen members of the Church were reported still living under Gibson on Lanai. These people requested to be cut off from the Church in October 1864, and their request was granted.

Gibson was a complex character. Some men, offended by the Church's action, would have used all their influence to fight back, yet Gibson gave no outward indication of any sort of malice toward the Latter-day Saints in years to come. On 7 April 1864 he wrote a letter to President Young in which he expressed regret that they were no longer working in the same channels. He said he did not feel that he would ever be hostile to President Young or the Church.[10] He remained true to this statement. In fact, he later spoke warmly of his respect for the LDS cause and donated fifty dollars to the Laie chapel building fund in 1882.

Although the native Saints made a brief but feeble attempt to recover the lands purchased on Lanai, no legal effort was ever made by the missionaries to win back the land. The reason for this was twofold. First, Joseph F. Smith, who was in Hawaii in 1857 when the decision had been made to look for a new gathering place, would have had to institute such litigation, but he did not believe that Lanai was worth fighting for. His feelings about the matter had apparently not changed since 1857. Second, Elder Smith was convinced that the cost of a court battle would be greater than the value of the land. Thus Gibson was left alone to do as he desired with the Palawai plantation. He had difficulty accomplishing much there after the Saints left because he could not duplicate his subservient labor force from another source.[11]

–PART II–

1864–1892

BEGINNING AGAIN AND YEARS OF STRUGGLE

–6–

LAIE: THE NEW GATHERING PLACE

Reconsolidation and Reformation

When Elders Benson and Snow left the islands in 1864 the Church was in almost total disarray. Many chapels had been sold. Lands had been turned over to Gibson, as had crops and livestock. Bitterness filled the minds and hearts of many Hawaiian Saints. The task before the remaining elders was to rebuild, as far as possible, the Church structure that had existed before the Utah elders departed in 1858.

It soon became apparent to the missionaries that it would not be possible to "reactivate," as Latter-day Saints say, all or even most of the former Saints. Much apostasy had taken place in the islands during the Gibson years; unwholesome practices had entered the lives of many members who had formerly been faithful.

The first task before the elders was to organize branches and regulate the affairs of the Church. New leaders had to be appointed and many former leaders had to be reprimanded for improper activities and immoral behavior. John R. Young, twenty-seven, who had recently arrived, and Alma L. Smith went to Hawaii island in June 1864, while Benjamin Cluff, thirty-four, another new arrival, stayed on the windward side of Oahu. William W. Cluff and Joseph F. Smith worked on Maui and Kauai. This division of labor was necessary to extend the missionaries' influence on the scattered Saints and preserve good feelings and friendships among the people.

Twenty-four-year-old Joseph F. Smith, the president of the mission, could not see any evidence that the gospel had "benefited the Hawaiians one iota." He stated that it looked like not one "of them has lived it." Nevertheless, even though discouraged, he still loved the Hawaiian people and hoped for their success as Latter-day Saints. Out of this hope he developed the idea of establishing a new gathering place somewhere in the islands where the Saints could be taught manual skills and how to live according to gospel principles. This suggestion was passed on to Brigham Young.[1]

President Young's attitude toward the Hawaiian Saints is important. He felt that little should be done in Hawaii. His letters to Joseph F. Smith reveal that he was disturbed by the unfaithfulness of the natives and wanted to see some indication of repentance before he committed more Church resources, either missionary time or money. He repeatedly stated that he felt the Church was under no obligation to the Hawaiian people until they repented and showed they were worth the trouble. In 1864 he told not only Smith but Francis A. Hammond (who returned to the islands in late 1864) that if they felt moved by the Spirit to close the whole operation and come home, they were at liberty to do so.[2] Young was very pragmatic about the Hawaiian mission. He placed almost total authority in the hands of the mission presidents, who he correctly judged to have the best insight into the problems and possibilities of Hawaii.

Brigham Young's confidence in his assigned leaders is borne out by the way he accepted their advice, even when it went against his own feelings. An example of this is his full support of Joseph F. Smith's suggestion that land be bought for a gathering place. Although land was not actually acquired at this time, the attempt to find a suitable piece of land led to further efforts to establish a new gathering place, culminating in the purchase of the plantation called Laie.

A mission conference was held during the first three days of October 1864. Although only two hundred Saints were present, they manifested a strong spirit of determination. The sermons were direct and pointed and the counsel given by President Smith was particularly strong: the Saints were gathered together "to inaugurate a reformation. . . ." He mentioned the disappointment he had felt when he and his companions returned the previous March, and he told the local Saints that they needed to recommit themselves totally to the gospel. He then read the names of fifty men and women whom he deemed worthy to be rebaptized if they were willing to make their commitments again. The practice of rebaptizing members, which ceased in the nineteenth century, was a symbolic renewal of the first baptismal covenant. The fifty members were rebaptized that same night after the meeting. The following day sixty-three more names were read and these Saints were also rebaptized. In this manner a "reformation" was begun.[3]

That the missionaries had not lost confidence in the local Saints is evidenced by the responsibilities they gave them. They called native elders to preside over the Maui, Hawaii, Molokai, and Kauai conferences. They called other men to serve as traveling elders and to spend their time in missionary work.

At the close of the conference it was announced that Joseph F. Smith, William W. Cluff, and John R. Young were released to return home, and that Alma L. Smith and Benjamin Cluff would temporarily preside over the mission.

THE FOUNDING OF LAIE

The suggestion to find a new gathering place came from Joseph F. Smith, but the follow-through for the project came from Brigham Young. In October 1864 he called Francis A. Hammond and George Nebeker as co-presidents of the mission. President Young asked them to find a suitable place or places for the gathering of the Hawaiian Saints. George Nebeker, who was thirty-eight years old at that time, brought a great deal of previous church experience to his call. He had already served a mission among the Indians of Nevada, helped colonize an area near Carson City, Nevada, and been a member of the high council of Salt Lake Stake from 1859 to 1864.

Hammond and Nebeker left Salt Lake City on 10 November 1864. They met Elders Smith, Young, and Cluff in San Francisco and learned of conditions in the islands. It pleased the returning elders to learn that land was to be purchased by the Church for the specific purpose of gathering the Saints. Brigham Young had told Hammond and Nebeker that they were to teach the Saints how to labor and how to live the principles of the gospel. Over the next several years this point was reiterated by Young many times. The clearest statement of purpose for the new settlement was made in a letter from Young to King Kamehameha V in March 1865. He wrote that the missionaries were going to Hawaii as

> religious teachers, but . . . they will not confine their labors to spiritual matters only. According to the precepts of our religion, the spiritual and temporal are so intimately blended that we view no salvation or system of salvation as being complete, which does not provide means for the welfare and preservation of the body as well as the salvation of the Spirit. . . . Mr. Hammond, and my other friends . . . will therefore endeavor to teach your Majesty's subjects . . . practical salvation.[4]

The disappointments suffered by the Hawaiian Saints during the Gibson experience led President Young to establish the new gathering place on a different basis than the Lanai experiment. It would not be purchased with their own contributions but would be obtained and owned by the Church's leaders in the islands and held for the benefit of the native Saints.

The matter of land ownership was a problem. The Morrill "Anti-Bigamy Law" of 1862 not only forbade plural marriages but also made it illegal for churches in the territories of the United States to own property valued in excess of fifty thousand dollars. Thus it was impossible for the Utah-based Church to purchase any further property in its name. This was a technicality outside U.S. territory, such as in the independent kingdom of Hawaii, but because of the Church's tenuous status at home it was wise for the leaders to follow the course they took. Because Brigham Young was considered the trustee of the Church, he could not buy the property in his own name. Therefore, when Hammond and Nebeker were sent to Hawaii to buy land, they were told by Young that the Church would support them and loan them money to buy it, but the land would have to be in their names. The financial arrangements for the purchase were supposed to be reasonable enough that the new gathering place could pay for itself and return the original loan payments to the Church.

When Brothers Hammond and Nebeker arrived in the islands, they found the financial situation there to be in a serious state of flux. The American Civil War and the introduction of inexpensive kerosene had rung the death knell for the whaling industry, but it had helped to create the Hawaiian sugar industry. The war years had given rise to much land speculation throughout the islands and had also raised the value of sugar. But the end of the war brought a depression in the sugar market; although not ruined, it was unstable. Many speculators lost everything, and others were eager to sell their properties even at a loss.[5] The time was right for the purchase of good property.

Hammond and Nebeker arrived in Honolulu on 23 December 1864 and were warmly greeted by many of Hammond's old friends. He was asked to speak in a sacrament meeting the same day. To his relief he still had command of the Hawaiian language. The next day he and Nebeker began a careful search for land. They contacted past friends and acquaintances, questioned businessmen, and visited the king's personal attorney, finding out all they could about land values and possible pieces for purchase. Their quest led them to Kauai for two weeks during early January and then back to Honolulu.

By 16 January they were satisfied that they could buy all the land they wanted; it was only a question of time. That day they decided that Nebe-

View of Honolulu from the harbor, 1853, showing the town and Nuuanu Valley. (Paul Emmert lithograph, courtesy Hawaiian Historical Society)

William Henry Bigler, one of the first ten LDS missionaries to Hawaii, was at Sutter's Mill when gold was discovered in California. (Courtesy LDS Church Archives)

George Q. Cannon had much success as a missionary to Hawaii from 1851 to 1854, and devoted most of his adult life to serving the Church. (Courtesy LDS Church Archives)

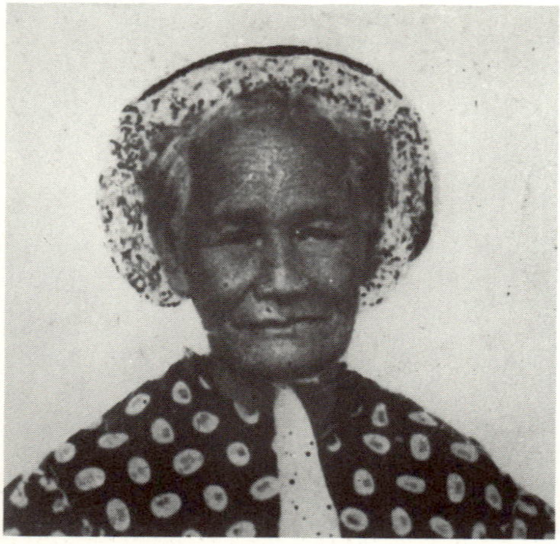

Nalimanui, whose name means "big hands." From her hands came food and shelter for the first LDS missionaries to Lahaina, Maui. (Courtesy LDS Church Archives.)

Jonatana H. Napela, among the first converts to Mormonism in Hawaii, helped George Q. Cannon translate the Book of Mormon into the Hawaiian language. (Courtesy LDS Church Archives)

Traditional thatched *hale*s were commonly used as chapels during the early years of the mission and could be found in remote communities even after the turn of the century, such as this meetinghouse at Hanalei-Uka, Kauai, where Elder Castle H. Murphy posed with Relief Society sisters in 1909. (Courtesy Mr. and Mrs. Kay Young)

Ma Manuhii was Joseph F. Smith's Hawaiian "mother." Some sources refer to her as Ma Naoheakamalu or Ma Huihui. (Courtesy LDS Church Archives)

Joseph F. Smith, here shown as a young adult, served his first mission in Hawaii at age fifteen. (Courtesy BYU–Hawaii Archives)

Walter Murray Gibson took over the Mormon colony on Lanai and proclaimed himself "President of the Church for the isles of the sea." (Courtesy LDS Church Archives)

George Nebeker presided over the Laie plantation and the Sandwich Islands Mission from 1865 to 1873. (Courtesy LDS Church Archives)

President Matthew and Libbie Noall presided over construction of Lanihuli House. He also placed Laie plantation on a firm financial footing. (*Improvement Era* photo)

Laie Sugar Mill, 1888. This is the second mill to operate on the plantation, larger than the first and powered by steam. (Courtesy LDS Church Archives)

In the 1860s and 1870s, Laie was frequently described as dry, desolate, and windy. Here, four Hawaiian boys pose on the hillside overlooking the plantation's main buildings. (Courtesy LDS Church Archives)

A typical early Laie home. LDS women often wore white for church services, a custom borrowed from Protestantism. (Courtesy LDS Church Archives)

Laie Chapel, dedicated in 1882, stood where the Hawaii Temple now stands. (Courtesy BYU–Hawaii Archives)

View of Laie looking toward the ocean from the old cemetery behind the present temple, taken by Castle H. Murphy about 1912. Note the trees and other foliage, showing the effects of the water wells put into use beginning in the 1880s. (Courtesy Mr. and Mrs. Kay Young)

Laie Relief Society sewing class in the Octagon Room, Lanihuli House, around 1910. (Courtesy Mr. and Mrs. Kay Young)

Lanihuli House, completed 1894, served for many years as mission headquarters. In the 1950s it became the first women's dorm for the Church College of Hawaii. (Courtesy Mr. and Mrs. Kay Young)

Laie rice flats looking south from *makai* (the sea), with *kalo loi* (taro ponds) in the foreground, 1899. (Courtesy LDS Church Archives)

Abraham Fernandez, friend of Queen Liliuokalani, baptized her a Latter-day Saint in 1906. (Courtesy LDS Church Archives)

Auwaiolimu Chapel was the first substantial LDS structure in Honolulu. (Courtesy LDS Church Archives)

ker should sail for home immediately and bring their families back. Hammond was to buy property as soon as it was feasible and get crops started.

On 20 January Hammond talked to Thomas T. Dougherty, who owned six thousand acres of land on the north side of Oahu. His plantation was called "Laie." In earlier times it had been a "city" of refuge. From description the plantation seemed to be what Hammond was looking for. During five days he traveled to Laie, rode over the crop land, investigated the mountain part of the property, looked over the buildings, and then rode back to Honolulu.

On 26 January 1865 Hammond met with Dougherty and negotiated an agreement to purchase the plantation.

> Called on Mr. T. T. Dougherty and offered him 12,000 dollars for "Laie" with all the stock, horses and improvements thereon—he would not take less than 14,000 dollars. I finally after a little consideration consented to give it. I agreed to send him a draft for 3000 dollars in ten weeks from date and pay 5000 dollars more by the 1st of July/65—6000 dollars in two years from date bearing at 12 per cent per annum—giving a mortgage on the place for security. I take possession immediately.[6]

Hammond believed he had made a good bargain—and he had. Dollar costs are of course relative to time and subject to the constant effects of inflation and deflation. Yet from any point of view the cost of the Laie plantation was nominal. Perhaps $2.33 an acre seemed high to Brigham Young, who objected to the cost, but he was accustomed to settling land that was virtually free. However, by Hawaii standards since the Great Mahele, the great land division of 1848, the price was fair.

Not only was the price relatively low, but the land was fertile and productive. The tract was wedge-shaped, having three miles of coast and running to the top of the Koolau mountain range behind. There was sufficient water available to handle needs at that time. There was also livestock—600 cattle, 500 sheep, 250 goats, and 20 horses—that added to the value of the purchase. A large frame house and five native houses, all furnished, stood on the land. Finally, five acres planted with cotton promised to bear a crop.[7]

Laie had two other advantages. It was close to the capital city—only thirty-seven miles from Honolulu—but not too close. Also, it was already the location of an active branch of seventy Latter-day Saints. These members were to form the nucleus of the new gathering.

After settling affairs in Honolulu, President Hammond sailed for home on 30 January 1865, leaving Elders Alma L. Smith and Benjamin Cluff in charge. They were to move to Laie and begin planting cotton. Hammond hoped that by March they would have one hundred acres planted. He was eager to report his progress to President Young.

Much has been written concerning Laie and its role as a gathering place for the Hawaiian people and other Polynesian Saints. A common impression is that the enterprise followed almost the same pattern as the Lanai settlement. Indeed, some aspects of the Lanai venture were duplicated, but in many ways the Laie effort was quite different.

The Lanai settlement had been created to provide a temporary gathering place for the growing number of Hawaiian Saints in order to bring them out of Babylon. At the time much was said by the missionaries concerning the nature of the new Zion in the Pacific. It was their expectation that they would effect a spiritual revolution among the Hawaiians. The Lanai colony was founded at a time when the Church was strong and the attitudes of missionaries and members positive. The Lanai gathering, however, ended in failure and disappointment.

The Laie settlement was created under vastly different circumstances. By 1865 President Young did not expect to save many Hawaiians. He hoped at best for the salvation of a few, for he was aware of the down-graded conditions under which most Hawaiians suffered. The Hawaiian population was decreasing yearly because of various diseases, particularly venereal diseases. Many Hawaiians were having a difficult time adjusting to the ever encroaching Western style of life. Some had given up in despair. Although he had almost lost hope, with encouragement from the missionaries, Joseph F. Smith in particular, Brigham Young went ahead because he believed that the Hawaiian people were literally of the house of Israel. He felt that he and the missionaries were obligated to try to save a remnant of those people.

President Young's master plan for the new gathering place seems never to have been clearly transmitted to the missionaries involved. When Francis A. Hammond arrived back in Salt Lake City, he and Elder Nebeker were charged with the responsibility of selecting a skilled group of missionaries—such as mechanics and farmers—who could then pass on their skills to the Hawaiians. Previous missionaries were also to be included. Although it was hoped that some of these settlers would be men of means who could buy large plots of land in Hawaii as gathering places, this did not develop.

In nearly all instances the missionaries were called with their wives. Those called included four former missionaries and their wives: Ephraim and Mary Green, James and Harriet Lawson, Eli and Louisa Jane Bell, and William and Emma Wright. All four men had served in Hawaii during the 1850s. Other missionaries new to Hawaii were Charles and Mary Boyden, Alfred and Mildred Randall, Caleb and Anna World (and six children), Philip Pugsley, Maria Louisa Nebeker, Mary Ellen Cluff, and Talitha Smith—the latter three being wives of missionaries already assigned and/or in the field. A number of children accompanied the group, which numbered forty when settled in Hawaii.

The families were part of President Young's plan to show the Hawaiians how proper Saints lived and conducted their lives. He expected the Utah Saints to take sufficient funds with them to be able to live at a standard well above that of the Hawaiians, for he didn't want his missionaries living like Hawaiians or depending on them for sustenance.

Laie was not to be a gathering place in the normal Mormon sense of the term. It is clear that it was to be a refuge from the world. But it was also to be a school in proper behavior, in hard work, in virtue, and in morality. It was to be not only a place where the Saints could gather to strengthen each other in their determination to live Christian lives, but also a center for learning. The haoles were to be the teachers, the Hawaiians the students. It was paternalism, although altruistic in intention. Brigham Young had basically one purpose—to elevate the Hawaiian Saints. Also part of Young's plan was the hope that both cotton and sugar could be produced in Hawaii and shipped to Utah to take care of the Saints' needs. Cotton and sugar were grown with only marginal success in the St. George area of southern Utah; the Hawaii plantation seemed to provide a logical solution to these basic needs.[8]

SETTLING IN

Time was required for the new missionaries to prepare for the trip to Hawaii. Hammond returned to the islands before their arrival to make sure all was well with the legal and financial arrangements for the plantation.

On 1 May 1865, four days after his arrival, Hammond and Benjamin Cluff saddled their horses and rode through the Laie fields. Much had been accomplished since Hammond left in January. He wrote, "the late planting of corn and cotton look well—but all of the first planting has been destroyed by the wind and worms."[9] Unfortunately, this kind of observation would become much too common in the journals and letters of the missionaries. The elements and pests were constant adversaries of crops at Laie plantation.

Hammond's task was not easy. He had to make decisions concerning land-use policy: where to build roads and fences, and where to plant crops. Livestock had to be either sold or given proper care, and decisions had to be made whether to plant corn, rice, Irish potatoes, or sugarcane. A dedicated man, Hammond worked long hours with only one goal in mind—that of serving the Lord. He frequently wrote of his poor health, occasionally of loneliness, but most frequently of his desire to fulfill his mission in the Lord's way. On Sunday, 7 May 1865, he preached about his mission: "I then addressed them for a short time on the necessity of connecting temporal matters with spiritual matters, taught them the doctrine of obedience being the foundation of all happiness—and told them our object of our coming unto them again, that it was to improve their temporal condition."[10]

During this time, a serious matter was under consideration in the king's court. Brigham Young had sent a rather lengthy letter to King Kamehameha V (quoted in part above), in which he detailed the LDS beliefs concerning the Hawaiian people, that they were descendants of Lehi, the Book of Mormon prophet. The letter also elaborated on the intentions and purposes of the mission to Laie. Although he emphasized the temporal nature of the mission, Young also expressed the intention of the Church to proselyte the Hawaiian people, if possible, to the restored gospel.

Even though the laws of the kingdom protected religious freedom for all, the king and his advisors did not feel that these laws applied to the Latter-day Saints because many of their teachings were foreign to the typical doctrines of Christianity. The temporal aspects of the new LDS mission were acceptable; the spiritual ones were not. "As long as your friends limit themselves to carrying on their agricultural and mechanical operations," wrote John O. Dominis, the king's private secretary and husband of later Queen Liliuokalani, "they will be protected in their industry, but they can never be recognized here on a footing with Christian missionaries as teachers, as those words are ordinarily understood."[11] This problem, fortunately, was resolved without serious difficulty. Within a year the king passed away, and the matter was not raised again. But as a result of this governmental position the Church was not given the right to perform marriages for a number of years.

Hammond sailed for San Francisco on 18 May to escort the new missionaries to Hawaii. The company sailed for Honolulu on 22 June, arriving in Hawaii on 5 July. Without stopping to see Honolulu, they chartered a schooner to take them to Laie.

The Laie missionaries and their families sacrificed a great deal, worked diligently, and suffered many hardships to establish a community. Homes had to be built for both the Utah missionaries and the Hawaiian Saints. Food had to be provided for all and jobs created for the male members of the village.

Some serious problems confronted the entire group. A cash crop had to be found to help support the community. Both cotton and sugarcane were considered. Cotton was the primary crop during the first couple of years, but by then it was evident that the chance of consistently losing the crop to worms was very high. Sugarcane then replaced cotton. A good crop of cane required a lot of water, but fortunately there was sufficient rain to provide a fair yield most years. As the plantation grew in acreage, however, the water supply became a problem.

Unity among the missionaries was another difficulty. All went well until President Hammond was released in the fall of 1865; when President Nebeker assumed control, tensions and conflicts began to surface. The goals and objectives of the mission were not clear in the minds of some missionaries, and Nebeker's view of his responsibilities was different from that of the men working with him.

The most serious problem related to the basic subsistence of several of the families. Though this problem should not be blown out of proportion, it helps provide an understanding of how the mission operated. When the plantation was purchased, Hammond and Nebeker were told that it would be their responsibility to pay off the debt. This seems like an almost unreasonable obligation until one remembers that if the plantation wasn't able to support itself and pay for itself it should never have been purchased in the first place. Nebeker felt keenly the burden of this debt. He believed that the whole operation should be run on a businesslike basis and that the missionaries should pay for everything with either cash or labor. But other missionaries felt the enterprise should be operated more like a present-day bishops' storehouse, with the worthy poor having the right to draw upon the resources of the Church community. Ironically, although Nebeker had not paid for the property that was in his name, and was holding it for the Church, he operated it as though he owned it himself. The missionaries felt like "hired men," and even the Hawaiians wondered about the true status of the elders. By March 1867 the total debt owed to Nebeker by Elders Smith, Cluff, Green, Bell, and World (the others had already been released to return home) was $2,423.60. Most of this debt was worked off on the plantation, but it troubled the elders to be in debt to one of their fellow missionaries. President Young ultimately intervened in the matter and loaned the indebted elders enough to throw off their financial yoke.[12]

Another problem arose between President Nebeker and Elders Boyden, Lawson, Randall, and Wright. These men perceived the goal of their missions to be one thing: the purchase of real estate. Even though two of them had filled previous missions in Hawaii, they did not think they had been called to preach or to work on the plantation. In an effort to bring the missionaries into accord, Brigham Young wrote:

> It was the intention in sending the brethren who went from here last spring to have them, and those who were already there, labor together for the good of the mission, either in preaching or in working on a place or places where the people could be gathered and instructed in the practical as well as the theoretical principles of their religion. They were not sent there to work here and there, where they could make the most money, and to have that alone in view, neither was it expected that they would scatter [some had moved to Honolulu], but it was hoped that by concentrating places of effort, places might be secured and cultivated profitably, where the natives might gather and be taught the arts of industry and those correct habits which are necessary for them to acquire to be the respected fellow-laborers of the white race in building up Zion.[13]

But even this encouragement from the president of the Church did not alter the views of these disaffected elders. They gave Nebeker much worry and ultimately were released, having accomplished little.

One of Nebeker's regrets was that he had difficulty providing work for all of the men who wanted to make their living on the plantation. As early as January 1866 there were over twenty Hawaiians who depended on the plantation for the support of their families. The number continued to grow over the years. This was of course the purpose of the plantation, but the problem of providing work for the growing numbers also caused much anxiety for Nebeker and the mission presidents who followed him.

PROGRESS

Education was traditionally important to LDS missionaries. In late October 1865 Sister Mildred E. Randall opened two schools: one for haole children and the other for young Hawaiians. English was the language of instruction in both schools, but some Hawaiian was used with the native children when necessary. The difference in English-language ability was the reason given by the mission president for the separate schools. Sister Randall continued the schools until November 1866 when she returned home to Utah.[14]

Many months passed before the schools opened again. In August 1867 the missionaries decided to share the responsibility of teaching the children. By that time the veteran elders who could speak Hawaiian were traveling regularly to the other islands to preach, but it was decided that whoever was left at home in Laie would supervise the schools. This approach was not wholly satisfactory to anyone but was considered better than having no school at all.

The LDS schools at Laie seem not to have conformed well to the government system, at least at this early date. Elsewhere in the kingdom there were both common (public) and select (private) schools. Generally, students in the common schools were taught in Hawaiian. But the medium of instruction had already been a hotly debated issue at the national school-board level for more than a decade, and it remained an issue in years to follow. The Mormon schools at Laie did not fit the mold of other more prestigious private residential or day schools, but showed the good intentions of the missionaries.[15]

The settlers divided the land and built homes. Some Hawaiians were able to construct frame homes, but most lived in traditional grass houses. President Nebeker lived in the so-called mansion, a larger home already on the property when purchased. Each Polynesian family was given—that is, loaned—enough land for a home and garden. The land was owned by the Church and rented on a share basis. In an effort to make the land-holding system clear to the local Saints, President Nebeker announced at the April conference of 1866 that "it [Laie plantation] was purchased by the servants of God and it [is] entirely under their control and direction. It is expected of the native brethren that come here to go to work [to] improve their condition by laboring under the direction of the servants of God and receive a just remuneration for all their labors."[16]

Almost as soon as building of the homes was under way, a chapel was begun. It was not a large building (24 by 36 feet), but it was of frame construction and was a great improvement over the temporary shelter made of boughs or the crowded situation in the mansion. Church meetings were held in the traditional manner, however, separate meetings were held for the Hawaiians and the haoles. Again the separation was justified on grounds of language.

It is difficult to say how many people lived in Laie at any given time. An October 1866 reference says about two hundred Hawaiians were living on the land, "mostly members."[17] Throughout the entire mission the number of members was not impressive, especially when one remembers the four thousand Saints of 1855. In October 1865 President Nebeker could account for only five hundred rebaptized or newly baptized

Church members. Six months later the number had grown by fifty. Apparently he discovered some active members in other parts of the islands soon after, for in October 1866 he reported one thousand Saints in Hawaii. This was still two thousand under the 1858 figure.

In a letter to Brigham Young written 14 October 1866, Nebeker reported on the spiritual health of the mission. Oahu was doing quite well and the same could be said of Kauai. But the Saints on Maui, Molokai, and Lanai were apathetic, and the Church was reportedly dead on the Big Island. In some ways the beginning of the Laie period was like the beginning of a new mission, except that the tasks were even greater than they would have been in a completely new mission.

The original plan called for the elders with language ability to travel among the Saints and teach the gospel. New converts were also to be taught and baptized. Because much had to be done to establish a settlement at Laie, it took a long time to institute this plan. Twice President Young wrote to Nebeker and asked him to send the missionaries out to visit other groups of Saints. Finally, beginning in mid-April 1867 Elders Smith, Cluff, and Bell began taking tours of the various islands. They visited the branches and encouraged the local leaders to conduct their activities according to approved procedures. As they traveled they sought out potential converts but were disappointed in their quest. About the same time some native elders were called to do similar work as missionaries, and they added considerable strength to the work. This pattern became the regular procedure in the coming years.

During the fall of 1866 economic matters reached a low ebb in the islands. The high-flown land speculations of the Civil War years were now coming to roost. When sugar prices dropped, many investors found themselves in financial trouble. One large financial house, Walker, Allen and Company, went bankrupt in January 1867.[18] With it went six or seven of the largest sugar plantations in the islands. Nebeker, aware of these events, was greatly concerned. The final payment on the Laie land came due in late January 1867, and the money was loaned to Nebeker by Brigham Young. Two months before Walker, Allen and Company went under, Nebeker had warned President Young not to send the final payment on the plantation through that banking firm. This advice was followed, and thus a large amount of money, six thousand dollars, was saved from the legal entanglement of bankruptcy. By April 1867 all papers of ownership were properly completed, and the Laie plantation belonged to the Church.

A month later Elder James Lawson and his family were released from their missions. When Lawson reported to President Young, he painted a dark picture of affairs in Laie. He was concerned about the subsistence of the missionaries and their families. As a result Brigham Young suggested to Nebeker that if he could sell the plantation without a loss he should do so.[19] This suggestion was gently worded, but it still placed the existence of the Laie project on unsure footing. Many months passed before a decision was finally made to go ahead with the community as originally planned. Nebeker believed that he could not sell the land without taking a serious loss. The price of Hawaiian sugar in San Francisco, the principal market, was controlled by San Francisco & Pacific Refineries. The previous year it had glutted the market with Manila sugar and driven the price down, causing Hawaiian planters, agents, and refiners to suffer. Author Gavan Daws viewed the situation in Hawaii as a crisis.[20] Considering the depressed economic condition of the islands at that time, Nebeker's assessment was probably correct. But he had still another concern. He and the other missionaries were afraid that if they put the land up for sale it would discourage the Hawaiian Saints and others living on the land, whether a sale was made or not. The risk was too high. Brigham Young ultimately agreed, and it was decided to move ahead with the sugarcane planting and milling in a vigorous way.[21] After the spring of 1868, the continued existence of Laie as a gathering place for the Hawaiian Saints was never in serious question. It would become the center of Zion in the Pacific.

–7–

THE PLANTATION YEARS

THE YEAR 1868 was an especially good one for the Sandwich Islands Mission. Most of the missionaries and Saints were in agreement with the objectives of the mission, and the work moved forward. The decision to raise sugarcane was well accepted by the native Saints. The Hawaiians now saw themselves as a more equal part of a cooperative financial venture rather than as lowly serfs, as they had generally been regarded on other plantations. Through the leadership of Jonatana H. Napela, who years earlier had worked with George Q. Cannon to translate the Book of Mormon into Hawaiian, the Hawaiian men of Laie were organized into work teams. For many months during 1868 and into 1869 the work progressed at a rapid and exhilarating pace. Everyone seemed to be caught up in the new project.

President Nebeker soon had to make some difficult decisions. The cane was growing, and before long he would have to have it ground and processed. He considered various arrangements, but then he found a mill, almost new, and for around two thousand dollars the Church went into the sugar milling business. A large amount of labor and some additional money were necessary to get the mill into operating order. A stone building (30 by 90 feet) was constructed to house the operation. Between March and October of 1868, Nebeker's letters to Brigham Young give a step by step, almost stone by stone account of the progress of the new building.

Finally, on 12 November, after seven months of preparation, milling began. Power for the grinder was provided by twelve mules. Twenty men, most Hawaiians, were required to operate the mill. The first cane crop was exceptionally large. Milling operations went on from November until the next May. The average output was fifteen hundred pounds of sugar and five hundred pounds of molasses daily. That first harvest produced approximately one hundred tons of sugar.

If every year had been as wet as 1868, the plantation would have been a magnificent success. Unfortunately, the following year was dry. The crop was smaller and of inferior quality. In fact, sugar production over the years was disappointing almost as often as it was satisfactory.[1] Several problems plagued the plantation over time. First was the insufficient water supply. This problem was overcome in the early 1880s by the construction of a flume over two miles long to bring a consistent water supply from the mountains, and the drilling of an artesian well. A number of large wells were drilled in later years.

A second problem for the plantation was to find a consistent sales outlet for the sugar produced each year. Nebeker, acting on the suggestion of Brigham Young, tried to establish marketing relationships with Salt Lake City merchants. A number of tons of Laie sugar were taken to Salt Lake City in 1869. Unfortunately, the color of the sugar was not as light as that of other sugar available, and the Salt Lake City buyers were willing to pay a higher price for what they wanted. Over the years most of the sugar produced on the Laie plantation was sold to Waterhouse and Company in Honolulu, who in turn shipped it to San Francisco. John Thomas Waterhouse and his son Henry became the principal financial backers of the Laie operation. They were the eighth largest agents for sugar plantations in the islands. At one time Waterhouse held a substantial mortgage on the plantation, and in fact the Laie plantation was almost always deeply in debt to this company until the 1890s. However, relations between Waterhouse and the Church were generally satisfactory to both parties.

Another problem was the constant struggle to keep the mill going. The original mill was small and inexpensive, and as the years passed the equipment became rusty, broken, and dilapidated. Lack of working capital for upkeep was the most persistent problem. When Nebeker was relieved of his post in 1873, the once-new mill was in poor condition; during the next year or two it almost fell apart. The sugar produced was of low quality and the amount of waste was high. Many months of "downtime" passed before new copper boiling pans and other equipment could be installed.

When Harvey H. Cluff took over as mission president and plantation manager in 1879, he soon recognized that it would be necessary either to ship the cane to another mill or to build a new one. He decided on the latter course because it would keep the local Saints employed. The new facility was much larger and more modern than the old one. Steam was used to power the grinders instead of mules, and other new equipment was installed. An entirely new building was constructed a few hundred feet from the old mill. This facility served the plantation for many years.

In addition to these problems, which were fundamental to the sugar industry, there were others peculiar to the LDS operation. The nature of the Laie plantation was different from other similar operations in Hawaii. One of the principal differences related to ownership and management.

Different mission president-managers had different styles of leadership. George Nebeker seems to have been difficult to get along with. He was without question a good manager, but he also kept some of his fellow Utah missionaries at odds with him most of the time. Even though Brigham Young had loaned Nebeker the entire purchase amount for Church use, Nebeker behaved as though he himself owned Laie. He was charged with the responsibility of paying off the mortgage, but with profits from the plantation. In an effort to do this he tried many approaches. The one that made his fellow missionaries most unhappy was his near demand that they buy half of the farm from him, to be paid for from their regular wages as laborers on the plantation or in the mill. They were upset that Nebeker wanted to sell them their shares at the current market value of the plantation (around $50,000), and not at the original amount for which he had purchased it ($14,000). The elders went along with Nebeker's plan, but not without feeling they were being mistreated.

Another problem with the operation was the plantation "company" store. Nebeker was the sole owner and manager of this small retail outlet, and he occasionally raised costs of goods by as much as 30 percent. These inflationary price hikes seemed unjustified to most people who used the store. The social and economic implications of this small retail operation can only be conjectured. The store was started to serve the needs of the members of the growing Laie community. Laie was somewhat isolated from other market areas such as Honolulu, which caused prices to be higher than in the city because of transportation and handling costs. Laie residents were not required to buy their goods at this store (except during President Mitchell's tenure), but the difficulty of traveling to Honolulu or other smaller towns closer to Laie made the company store more convenient. As the decades passed the store grew according to the needs of Laie residents and to meet competition from merchants who moved into the area.

The company store issue became a major problem during the presidency of Fred A. Mitchell, from June 1873 to September 1874. The thirty-eight-year-old Englishman forbade the Laie Saints to purchase goods from any other store. Many Hawaiian Saints complained that he also gave them bills in English that they could not understand. The company store was only part of a larger issue for Mitchell, that is, the use and sale of *awa* (pronounced ah-va). Awa is a mild narcotic made from the root of a kind of pepper plant. Called *kava* elsewhere, it is used in ceremonies in island countries throughout the Pacific area, and can damage the nervous system of a regular user. Today it is used in formal ceremonies and as a means of honoring special guests such as General Authorities of the Church in Samoa, Tonga, French Polynesia, and Fiji. Its use has virtually ceased in Hawaii.

On New Year's Day 1874 a great feast was held at the Laie chapel. At its conclusion President Mitchell stood at the door in the traditional fashion of the old lords of the land (*konohikis*) and declared that there would be no more drinking of awa; selling it to persons outside of the plantation was also prohibited. This ultimatum shocked the assembled group because they had used plantation land to cultivate the awa plant with the intention of selling most of the crop for profit. But Mitchell said it had to be destroyed. This pronouncement almost caused a riot in the chapel.

President Mitchell's decision was motivated by the fact that the Word of Wisdom, the Church health code, was receiving much emphasis in Utah. His objective was to be completely in tune with the Church leaders in Salt Lake City. From 1833, when Joseph Smith disclosed the revelation concerning health,[2] until 1867 the suggestions made concerning the non-use of tobacco, tea, coffee, and alcoholic drink were not considered binding commandments. But in 1867 Brigham Young strongly suggested that the men who were participants in the newly created School of the Prophets should stop using these habit-forming substances and donate the money saved to bring "the poor" (i.e., immigrants) home to Zion. Women of the Relief Society, a Church organization, also joined in the movement to abstain from tea and coffee. As Leonard Arrington points out, "So effective was the Word of Wisdom campaign in 1867 and following years that in less than two decades abstinence from tea, coffee, tobacco, and intoxicating beverages was almost as strong a test of faith as carrying out a colonizing or missionary assignment."[3]

But the elders from Utah were not united on Mitchell's ban of awa, possibly because some Church leaders in Salt Lake City had encouraged the cultivation of coffee trees on the Laie plantation, and some elders felt there was very little difference between awa and coffee. Why Mitchell was so adamant about awa but not coffee is unclear. Nevertheless, his refusal to allow the Laie Saints even to sell their existing crop of awa made feelings run high.

The issue would probably have died a natural death were it not for the offer of a Chinese landholder to sell his land to the Laie Saints. The land, called Kahana, which was located eight miles from Laie and consisted of 3,600 fertile acres, seemed to the Hawaiians the answer to their problems; by purchasing this land they could remove themselves from the iron hand of Mitchell. The land was priced at six thousand dollars.

Mitchell wanted to take Church court action against the dissidents as early as April 1874 but did not. However, when the Hawaiians went through with their plan to buy Kahana, he called a meeting of the priesthood in late June to consider the matter. Elder Harvey H. Cluff recorded the event:

> The meeting was filled to overflowing. . . . President Mitchell . . . asked those who had combined together if they still were determined to go ahead with the organization and draw off from Laie, to which they answered in the affirmative. Whereupon President Mitchell "moved that they be disfellowshipped from the Church of Jesus Christ of Latter-day Saints" and when put to vote there were only about thirty voted for the motion including the foreigners [missionaries]. At this Brother Mitchell asked to sing at which the congregation went into demonic yells and the greater part of the audience rushed out before the benediction was offered.[4]

The next day Mitchell sent a letter to all the Saints in the mission telling them not to support the Kahana project in spirit or with contributions.

Not many days after the meeting of the Church court, a number of angry Hawaiian Saints wrote to President Brigham Young to express their feelings and complaints. The company store problem, high rents for land use, and even Mitchell's stringent enforcement of the law of tithing were all mentioned. But the chief complaint centered on President Mitchell's "giving away to passion so easily, with his indisposition to listen to more than one side." The feeling among the Hawaiians was that the plantation belonged to Mitchell and they had "no lot in Laie." The Saints also said they did not realize that buying new land for themselves was an offense that could bring disfellowshipment to twelve of their number.[5]

The immediate result of these events was Mitchell's release as mission president and the calling of Alma L. Smith to replace him; the long-term result was the founding of Kahana village. This settlement was eight miles east of Laie, toward Honolulu; the present village is close to the shore. Within a year of its purchase, Kahana had become an established village with a chapel, branch presidency, and full status in the eyes of the mission presidency. By the early 1880s Kahana was the second largest Mormon settlement in the islands. Almost half of the Laie Saints moved to this new "native" gathering place in the months following the confrontation with Mitchell. There cultivation of the awa plant continued; in the early 1880s part of the Laie plantation land was being used for the cultivation of awa. The missionaries reported that they discouraged its use by the Saints, but it brought a fine price in the market.[6]

CHURCH GROWTH IN HAWAII

Despite these problems, the mission made steady progress. Laie, however, did not grow very rapidly. Most Hawaiian Saints preferred to live in or near their ancestral villages, and the facilities at Laie could not easily support a larger population. The missionaries never stopped preaching about the importance of gathering at Laie, but their words generally went unheeded. The actual size of Laie village through the years is very difficult to establish as official records do not disclose this information. Several approximations were recorded, however. According to Harvey H. Cluff, there were around three hundred natives living in Laie in 1870. Four years later Alma L. Smith reported a membership of 377. In 1877 Ward E. Pack numbered the Hawaiian population of Laie at 275.[7] One in every fifteen Latter-day Saints in Hawaii lived in Laie at this time. The significant drop in numbers between 1874 and 1877 can be attributed to the establishment of Kahana. Descriptions of the Laie settlement in the 1890s lead to the conclusion that there had been little population gain since the late 1870s.

Church growth throughout the mission was more impressive (see table 1), although its erratic growth over the years was a source of constant anxiety to the foreign missionaries. It was not unusual to have from two hundred to four hundred convert baptisms in as little as a six-month period, but the converts seemed to be seed cast upon shallow soil. One missionary commented that the native missionaries in particular seemed to want to make converts regardless of who or what the converts were. "They seem to make converts by persuasion and by getting the best of their opponents in argument than by convincing the sinner of the error of his ways and teaching him the true plan of salvation. . . ."[8]

The rapid growth in the Church between 1872 and 1874 is in direct correlation with the number of missionaries working in the field. The size of the Utah missionary contingent did not increase, but the number of Hawaiian missionaries did grow. The practice of using local elders for missionary work had been started in the 1850s. It was used by Walter Murray Gibson and later reinstituted in 1867, but only on a small scale. Eleven Hawaiian elders were called to serve six-month missions during

TABLE 1 **Mission Growth Patterns, 1865–1906**

Year	Members	Missionaries*
1865	500	19
1866	1,000	16
1867	1,277	14
1870	1,611	10
1872	2,627	77
1875	4,092	10
1877	3,806	99
1879	4,408	11
1890	4,119	17
1894	4,899	23
1900	6,978	22
1905	6,842	27
1906	7,212	37

Sources: MHHM, October 1866; Cluff, Autobiography, 125; Bock, "Church in the Hawaiian Islands," 75; MHHM, April 1872; A. L. Smith to Brigham Young, 9 November, 1874; Ward E. Pack to Brigham Young, 19 April 1877, Letters to Brigham Young; MHHM, 1894–1906, passim.

*Excludes native Hawaiian missionaries.

1869; in 1871, 10 were called; in 1872, 25; 1873, 22; and 1874, 20.[9] Although they were very successful in performing baptisms, they apparently lacked the experience and background in church government and doctrine to be allowed to continue on their own.

In April 1875 it was discovered that the Hawaiian elders were teaching a number of incorrect doctrines and procedures. Alma L. Smith wrote, "During the last six months the foreign Elders have had a big job on their hands in discovering, ferreting out, correcting and undoing many false and erroneous doctrines and principles introduced by the native elders who have been sent out as missionaries during the last number of years. . . ." Among the erroneous practices discovered were several incorrect modes of baptism and styles of administering to the sick, and the empowering of a number of Polynesian officers with the authority to forgive sins. This last problem included the widespread practice of having the guilty person appear before any of the appointed officers, confess sins of any kind, and receive a certificate stating his "sins were all forgiven" and he "was clean and spotless from the crown of his head to the soles of his feet." Besides these practices, Smith wrote that there were many "other false, heathenish, idolatrous, and superstitious ideas and notions" that had crept in.[10]

No native elders were called to serve missions for the next year. The use of the local brethren as missionaries was gradually resumed, but never on the same large scale as between 1872 and 1875,[11] which resulted in a significant drop in the number of baptisms during the next two decades. Apparently Hawaiian elders were not called into the mission field for a year (until October 1876), and then they were assigned to travel with a haole companion. It was hoped that the association of the native elders with the haoles would "train them [the native elders] so they will be free from false traditions. . . ."[12] In October 1878 the mission president decided to increase the native force of elders, and called and set apart ten Hawaiian elders—four to go to Hawaii island, four to Maui, and two to Kauai. Later, in 1890, twenty local elders were called into the mission field. At that point, although the rate of baptisms did not increase too rapidly, the total membership grew from 4,119 in 1890 to 4,899 in 1894.

HAWAII'S CHANGING LIFE-STYLE

The Hawaiian Islands made much material progress between 1865 and 1895. Much happened within the Church in Hawaii, but many developments in Hawaii in general also helped change the complexion of the Church and the mission.

As late as the 1850s Hawaii was still a wide-open whaling center whose foreign residents were generally ex-sailors or adventurers hostile to missionaries of any kind and drawn toward a liberated style of life. The plantation men who arrived after 1860, however, were generally respectable capitalists who were at least outwardly God-fearing men. But Honolulu, although a large city, still lacked the refinements of San Francisco and other similar coastal centers.

Descriptions of the Hawaiian way of life, even in the 1860s and 1870s, include their "haystack" type of house with its "crude" *lauhala* mats for furniture. But by the 1880s grass houses were becoming unusual as frame houses took their place. By then Honolulu boasted most of the refinements of San Francisco, although on a much smaller scale. In 1888 electric lamps were installed to light Honolulu's principal streets. Work commenced that year on a mule-drawn streetcar line; another project was a short-line railroad from Honolulu to Ewa. The first Royal Hawaiian

Hotel was sixteen years old that year, and tourists were beginning to frequent the islands in greater numbers. One missionary reported to Salt Lake City that more than a hundred tourists were visiting the islands every month. Interisland steamship service made a rude beginning in the 1850s but by 1890 was a well-organized operation with fourteen regular ships in service. LDS Relief Society sisters reported that these ships were clean and comfortable. Around 1890 telephone service began to expand in Honolulu.

Laie was founded by pioneers. By the 1890s, however, the missionaries were typical Americans accustomed to modern conveniences. Whereas the early missionaries came by wagon to San Francisco and by sailing ship to Hawaii, later groups traveled by railroad to the West Coast and by steamship to Honolulu. The letters of Mormon missionaries reflect different life-styles and attitudes. The emphasis of the early missionaries was generally on toil and sacrifice; that of the later missionaries (i.e., those of the late 1880s and the 1890s) was on adventure and dedication. All desired to teach the gospel, but their perceptions of the world were different.

The population of the islands also changed significantly during these years. As the sugar industry developed, it was early recognized that three things were necessary for success: a market, capital, and labor. The United States became the principal sugar market, although some was sold in New Zealand and Australia during the 1870s. Capital seemed to be no problem, but labor was a serious matter. Most planters concluded that Hawaiians simply could not or would not work on the plantations. Hawaiians seemed to like the life of the cowboy and sailor, but the tedious nature of sugar cultivation did not appeal to them. In an effort to develop a steady labor supply, government officials took two approaches. First, they legalized contracts of up to five years for the Hawaiians. The result of this arrangement was that Hawaiians felt more like slaves than employees. It was not unusual for them to become indebted to the company store, which further tied them to the plantations. According to the mission presidents, the Laie plantation received a considerable amount of public attention during its first several years in the sugar business because the Hawaiians who worked the fields were not bound by contract as on the other plantations. They were paid by the month and could leave if they wanted to. But this arrangement sometimes resulted in labor shortages on the plantation.

A second means of obtaining labor was through immigration. Three hundred Chinese laborers were brought to the islands in 1851–1852. Several of these men joined the Church in Hilo in 1854, probably the first Chinese anywhere to become Mormons. But the Chinese laborers did not bring the desired economic results, and Chinese immigration was halted for over a decade.

But because the native population was decreasing steadily and often would not work on the plantations, immigrant laborers were again sought. In 1864 the Hawaiian government organized the Bureau of Immigration. Foreign labor was recruited, and immigration in general was encouraged. By the end of 1865, 1,306 Chinese coolies had come to Hawaii under contract. Three years later around 150 Japanese laborers were brought in.

The influx of foreign labor was steady for the next two decades. By 1890, when the total population had reached 90,000, over 55,000 laborers had been imported into Hawaii, including 15,000 Chinese, 12,000 Japanese, and 9,000 Portuguese.[13] The polyglot, polyracial nature of Hawaii had been established. The Caucasian population also grew rapidly during these years. The Hawaiian population seems to have started an uphill climb in the middle or late 1870s, although, unfortunately, by that time Hawaiians had descended to the lowest rung of the islands' social ladder.

THE CHURCH AND THE HAWAIIAN GOVERNMENT

When the Laie colony was established in 1865, King Kamehameha V allowed the Latter-day Saints to establish a temporal mission, but he told them that they could never be recognized as Christians "as those words are ordinarily understood."[14] Despite this unfriendly attitude toward the Mormon cause, Kamehameha V was not hostile toward the Saints themselves. Mission work was carried on without hindrance or problems.

Kamehameha V died on his forty-second birthday, 11 December 1872. His successor, Lunalilo, served but a short time before his early death on 3 February 1874. David Kalakaua was elected king by the Hawaiian legislature on 12 February 1874 and reigned until 1891. During Kalakaua's time relations between government and the Church were friendly. The Latter-day Saints had no reason to fear or resent him. Many of his goals and desires, such as the growth of the Hawaiian population and the concept of Hawaii for the Hawaiians, were also espoused by the Latter-day Saints. It is somewhat ironic that Kalakaua chose Walter Murray Gibson as his prime minister. But Gibson, who served from 1884 until he was forced from office in 1887, treated representatives of the Church with respect and kindness.

The long and friendly relationship between the Saints of Laie and the king began only ten weeks after his election. On 30 April 1874 the missionaries received notice that Kalakaua, who was touring the island of Oahu with a large retinue, would be in Laie the following day. Elaborate preparations were frantically made, and the Laie Saints were ready when the king arrived. He seemed to like what he saw for he complimented the citizens of Laie for their industry and for the beauty of the community. But the number of children impressed him most. He told the assembled crowd that there were more children there than at any other village of similar size he had visited.[15]

Kalakaua and his wife, Kapiolani, visited Laie on many occasions. They made most of their visits as private citizens. Kapiolani attended Relief Society occasionally and was apparently pleased with what she saw and heard. In fact, a government-sponsored "Female Relief Society" was founded by the king and queen in an effort to assist the kingdom's poor.

During these years the LDS Church was involved with the government over two minor matters. The first concerned the right of LDS elders to perform marriages. They had had difficulty obtaining such permission during the early years of the mission, and since 1865 they had still not received permission to perform this ordinance. In 1876 the problem was brought to the attention of the proper government authorities. Because some rapport had been established with the king, President Ward E. Pack broached the matter with him. Soon, the minister of the interior received a letter informing him of the king's desire that the Latter-day Saints should have the right to perform marriages. Several months later, in late 1877, this permission was finally granted to the fourteen missionaries of the Church.

The other problem concerned taxes. Even though LDS elders had for many years been exempt from personal taxes, and Church lands had been exempt from property taxes, the tax assessor in the Laie area suddenly decided to tax several of the missionaries and the Church property.[16] Elder Henry P. Richards made a test case of the issue in 1879, which was decided in his favor. But even after this, many local assessors continued to levy the five dollar poll tax on the elders. Finally, in 1882, the issue was brought before the minister of foreign affairs, who resolved it in favor of the Church.[17]

Kalakaua's reign, at least in the early years, was stronger and more satisfactory than those of his predecessors the decade before. Various kinds of corruption were uncovered during the later years, much of which was blamed on Gibson. But in 1887 the king was forced to give up a significant amount of his power. From then until his death in 1891 he accomplished very little. Strong pressure was applied by whites in Honolulu during these years to have Hawaii made part of the United States.

At his death, Kalakaua was succeeded by Queen Liliuokalani. Her reign was brief, hardly more than two years, because of a revolution that brought an end to the Hawaiian kingdom during its ninety-ninth year. The Hawaiian republic was formed in 1893, but in 1898 an act was passed in Washington, D.C., calling for annexation of the islands as a territory of the United States. Hawaii officially became a territory on 14 June 1900. Although the LDS missionaries stayed out of politics, they found that they were sometimes treated coolly by Hawaiian members and nonmembers alike. The missionaries were white and thus considered guilty of anti-native attitudes. As late as 1896 some of the elders complained that the Saints were treating them with indifference. After that the native animosity toward the government and toward whites diminished and the missionaries were once again treated with hospitality.

Liliuokalani was well educated, a devoted Christian, and a strong leader; however, history was not on her side. She gained the throne at the wrong time. Like her predecessor, she was a friend to the Latter-day Saints. On many occasions she visited Relief Society meetings in Honolulu and at Laie. According to Jenson's "History of the Hawaiian Mission," Queen Liliuokalani requested that LDS services be held at the palace on 13 March 1892. After this, LDS services were regularly held there until she was deposed. Liliuokalani was a close friend of Libbie Noall, wife of mission president Matthew Noall, and sought her advice on a number of occasions. Unfortunately, she did not follow Mrs. Noall's advice opposing the opening of a gambling lottery,[18] instead pushing it through to become law. This was a major contributing factor in the fall of her regime. Along with other actions, it gave the annexationists the excuse they had been looking for to overthrow the queen. Her downfall came within the year.

Liliuokalani joined the Church in 1906. Her old friend, Abraham Fernandez, performed the ceremony. She did not become an active member, however, and Mormonism never became her exclusive religion.[19] Liliuokalani appreciated and affiliated with several different churches. It is likely that she included Mormonism in her religious life not only because of its affinity with old Hawaiian ways and because of her friendship with Mormons such as Libby Noall and Abraham Fernandez, but also because she, like many Hawaiians, deeply resented the role played by the sons of Protestant missionaries, the so-called "mission boys," in the revolutions of 1887 and 1893. It is possible that she sought company with people and a church that were not so closely associated with her downfall.[20]

–8–

ORGANIZATIONAL DEVELOPMENTS AND JOSEPH F. SMITH'S EXILE IN HAWAII

ONE OF the strengths of the LDS missionary system is the regular turnover of the men and women involved in the missions. Although some problems arise because the missionaries do not remain long in the field (e.g., language and cultural problems), there are also advantages from the regular changes. Probably the most important benefit is the constant contact with the Church center and new developments that arise there. In the nineteenth century it was usually only a matter of months before innovations developed in Salt Lake City were disseminated throughout the world. Hawaii benefited from this circumstance considerably.

ESTABLISHMENT OF CHURCH AUXILIARIES IN HAWAII

During the years 1865 to 1895 the Church in Hawaii came abreast of the Church in Salt Lake City. All the Church auxiliaries were organized in Hawaii: Sunday School, Relief Society, Mutual Improvement Association, and Primary. Choirs and other musical organizations were founded. Chapels and a school were built and printed material was prepared in the Hawaiian language. A brief resume of the organization of each of these institutions follows.

Sunday Schools

First organized in Hawaii during the 1850s, Sunday schools were not widespread nor was their curriculum fully developed. They were simply morning worship meetings that differed little from sacrament meetings.

In Laie, the first organized Sunday school began 31 December 1871. Three years later, Sister Mildred E. Randall reported that about fifty pupils, aged five to fifty, were attending regularly.[1] In 1879 Joseph H.

Dean was given responsibility for this work. With his companion, Elder Kaihe, he organized six Sunday schools during June, five on Oahu and one on Maui. By the mid-1880s twelve Sunday schools were organized with a membership of 453. After that time a mission superintendent was called from among the missionaries, and the organization received constant attention.[2]

The Women's Relief Society

The Women's Relief Society, also called the Hui Manawalea, began at Laie branch on 6 July 1875. President Fred A. Mitchell called a woman named Kapo and two other Hawaiian sisters to preside. Within a year fifty-six members were enrolled. Progress was rapid. As mentioned, Queen Kapiolani took an interest in the relief work of the society and created an organization in its image. Kapiolani visited various relief societies over the years. Her first visit was to the Third Annual Festival Meeting in 1878, a gathering of over two hundred people.

By the summer of 1880 there were enough relief organizations that President Harvey H. Cluff decided to call his wife as superintendent of all relief societies in the mission.[3] Two years later there were fourteen societies functioning in Hawaii with a total membership of around 250. A year later another hundred women had been added to the ranks. Under the leadership of the missionary sisters and with the strong support of the local Saints, the number of societies grew to thirty-one in 1889 and to thirty-six by 1895. Most of the 619 members lived in small, scattered branches, but strong, well-organized groups had been developed at Laie, Kahana, Kaneohe, Honolulu, and Waikiki. The Wailuku, Maui, Relief Society also carried on a full program.

Hawaii's Relief Society followed the same program that had been created in Utah. Emphasis was placed on compassionate service and charitable acts. Handicrafts, sewing, and other home industries were taught. Funds were raised to help the poor, and the sick were ministered to. The sisters also regularly sent money to Salt Lake City to assist in the construction of the temple. Visiting teaching of a sort was carried on by the sisters, as were frequent supervisory visits from the mission superintendency.

The sister missionaries were not to be outdone by their husbands. In 1892 eight sisters formed "a school of missionary sisters" and held regular weekly meetings in which they studied the gospel. On 6 July they selected part of their number to visit the adjacent islands to teach and direct the societies there. Each haole sister was assisted by a Hawaiian sister as a companion. Sister Elizabeth (Libbie) Noall, wife of the mission president, was assigned to Hawaii island. With a companion she traveled on foot, and by horse, cart, and train around the north end of the island from Hilo to Kona, holding frequent meetings. During the entire venture, completed with considerable discomfort, she carried a new-born infant.[4] She seemed to expect such labor. In addition to her travels she also translated some lesson material into Hawaiian and wrote a short manual of instructions regarding Relief Society work in the Hawaiian language.[5]

Mutual Improvement Associations (MIAs)

First called "Retrenchment Societies" of the Church, these associations were organized in November 1869 by Brigham Young. He gathered his daughters together and asked them to create a style of their own, a manner of dress and deportment different from that of other people. This organization soon became part of the Church in Zion. In the mid-1870s the name was changed to the Young Ladies' Mutual Improvement Association (YLMIA). A similar association for young men was organized in October 1872. One of the founders was Richard G. C. Lambert. He was called to Hawaii on a mission in 1873 and was instrumental in establishing both organizations in Laie in 1876.[6] After one year thirty-one ladies and thirty-three young men belonged. By that time a fife and drum corps had been organized as part of the MIA. The missionaries were much impressed by the musical ability of the native Saints. A few years later a brass band was organized.

The progress of MIAs was not as rapid as that of the Relief Society. There were five groups with 142 members in 1883, ten groups by 1885, and only 27 MIAs in 1895. However, they did meet a need for recreation and self-improvement.[7]

Primary

Relatively little information is available concerning early Hawaii activities of this organization, devoted to teaching gospel principles to children under twelve in a weekday setting. The first Primary, the Hui Kamalii, was organized by Sarah L. Partridge on 19 August 1883. This auxiliary, like the Relief Society and the MIA, had its Hawaii beginning at Laie. There were about forty children in the first group. Apparently Primary did not receive much emphasis during these early years, for as late as 1895 only two groups had been organized. However, the number of members had grown to 162.

The Primary curriculum was rather demanding. At the conference on 5 April 1895, the various skills of the Primary children were demonstrated. These skills included recitations, readings, testimonies, Bible verses, memorized questions and answers, songs, essays, dialogues, stories, manuscript papers, and correspondence.[8]

Publishing

The first important publication in Hawaiian was the Book of Mormon, which was translated by Elder George Q. Cannon and published in California in the mid-1850s. Unfortunately it was not readily available after 1865. President Noall saw a need for the book and in May 1892 initiated a request to have a new edition published. It was finally republished in 1903.

In addition to the Book of Mormon, only a few other items had been printed by 1895. These included several tracts, some lesson manuals, a book of hymns, the Articles of Faith, and some instructions for Relief Society leaders. After 1895 the use of English became more and more common both in the secular world and in the Church.

Chapel Building

From the early days the Saints of Hawaii engaged in the work and sacrifice necessary to build chapels. The early chapels have previously been described. Apparently the post-1865 chapels were generally not much more substantial than those of the 1850s. The Laie chapel, constructed of rock, was the first to be built for long-term use. But in 1881 it became obvious that, with the growth of the Church in the islands and the increasing size of the semiannual conferences, it would be necessary to build a new meeting hall.

The chapel was to stand on a small knoll, the choicest spot in all of Laie, the same site where the temple now stands.[9] Much planning and fund-raising was done before construction commenced. When the foundation was completed and the work moved upward, a celebration was held to mark the laying of the cornerstones. King Kalakaua attended and added his support to the work, donating one hundred dollars. Six months later, on 6 October 1882, the meeting hall was dedicated. The king once again graced Laie with his presence. Like the rest of the assembled throng, he was impressed with the large structure. It was 35 feet wide by 65 feet long, with a ceiling that was 19 feet high inside. It had a raised stand and pulpit for those who presided. A choir loft spanned one end, and the high building was graced with a belfry with a 250-pound bell. The total cost was nearly eight thousand dollars.

President Edward Partridge, Jr., dedicated the building, after which the king was invited to speak. He did not speak long but told the Saints that they were his best subjects in "fulfilling the laws and keeping the peace of the Kingdom."[10] Three choirs, from Kahana, Honolulu, and Laie, participated in the ceremonies. Between five hundred and six hundred Saints jammed the new meetinghouse, and over one thousand participated in the feast that followed. It was a landmark occasion.

In 1885 there were twenty-five chapels in the mission, but only the Laie chapel could be considered a permanent structure. Others were flimsy frame buildings or makeshift grass pavilions. At about that time one of these buildings caught fire and burned to the ground, causing considerable inconvenience to the members of the district who had assembled for a conference meeting.

The second permanent building constructed was the Honolulu chapel, which was completed in 1889 with Elder Matthew Noall as the head builder. It was not as large as the Laie building (the Honolulu chapel seated two hundred), but it was a credit to the Church. The Honolulu branch, with its 891 members, was probably the largest branch of the Church west of the Rockies at that time.

One other permanent building was a mission home built on the same property as the new Honolulu chapel. It was constructed in 1879–1880 under the direction of Joseph H. Dean and William D. Alexander, carpenters and missionaries. The home was a stopping place for the many elders and sisters constantly arriving at and embarking from Honolulu. The elders assigned to the Honolulu-Waikiki area also lived there.[11]

The Laie School

One of the most important and creditable efforts of the Hawaiian mission during these early years was the establishment and maintenance of a school for the children in and around Laie. The efforts of Sister Mildred E. Randall during the first several years of the Laie colony were admirable. After her departure, the elders struggled to keep the school open by shifting teaching responsibilities among those not assigned to the outside areas. This proved unsatisfactory.

Word of the educational problems was sent to Salt Lake City, and in the spring of 1873 Sister Randall was called to fill a second mission. She arrived in Hawaii on 3 June 1873 and within two weeks had started a school. It was held in the Laie chapel, the small rock building. Only four students were enrolled in the school when it opened, all Hawaiians. By January 1874 the number had increased to around twenty pupils and it leveled off there. Sister Randall was a demanding teacher and the courses were taught in English. Subjects studied were spelling, reading, writing, mental and written arithmetic, and geography, as well as recitations, dialogues, and singing. Financially the school was not a success. Sister Randall was to support herself from the tuition paid by her pupils. She wrote: "I charge them 20¢ per week per scholar, which is 5¢ cheaper than other schools of the same grade that have assistance from the government. But I am here on a mission to benefit the people all I can and not to oppress them by charging exorbitant prices for what I can do for them. I only want a living, and that in the most economical style."[12] If all her pupils had paid their tuition, her pay would have been sixteen dollars per month.

Because Sister Randall was eager to improve the school's financial situation, she applied to the Board of Education for government assistance. Although the answer she received was not hostile, she was told that the government had no extra funds to allocate for the next budget year. Before she could follow through on the matter the following year, she was released to return home.[13] Her release from this second mission came 20 June 1876. Whether the school closed for a time after Sister Randall's release is not clear from the record. The next teacher of the Laie English school was Sister Jane E. Molen. It is evident that after Sister Molen's release the school closed. In April 1883 Marvin E. Pack was appointed teacher of a school "about to be established at Laie."[14]

After 1883 the school grew rapidly and required the full attention of one missionary, usually an elder. By 1885 there were fifty students enrolled, aged six to eighteen. Several elders taught the school between 1883 and 1887. In 1887 Elder Fred Beesley petitioned the government school board in Honolulu for financial aid. To the joy of the missionaries, the board agreed to pay a teacher fifty dollars per month and provide maps, charts, and other materials if the Church would provide a building.[15] After that time the school continued to grow and make steady progress.

JOSEPH F. SMITH'S TWO-YEAR EXILE IN HAWAII

For two years, from 9 February 1885 until 25 June 1887, the Hawaiian mission was blessed with the presence of Joseph F. Smith, who since October 1880 had been second counselor in the First Presidency of the

Church. Smith had previously filled two missions to Hawaii. He was called and ordained an apostle in 1866.

Smith went to Hawaii to escape the persecutions growing out of the polygamy problem. After the passage of the Edmunds Act in 1882, federal agents constantly assaulted and harassed the Saints. Members of the First Presidency were considered especially important violators of the law and were zealously sought. The leaders of the Church held that plural marriage was a religious matter that should be protected by the First Amendment to the U.S. Constitution. Because they were sure their religious rights would be upheld before the Supreme Court of the United States, they deliberately broke the anti-polygamy laws in an effort that would now be called civil disobedience. Many Mormon polygamists went to prison rather than give up their wives and families. The first wife was considered a legal wife; others were outside the law.

Joseph F. Smith was particularly wanted by the U.S. marshals because he was an officiator and recorder in the Endowment House and had detailed information and records regarding plural marriage. When the pressure became too great, the Church president, John Taylor, told Smith to leave four of his five wives and go to Hawaii. With Julina, his legal wife, he departed. Although the two years he spent in Hawaii were a great blessing to the missionaries and Saints of the islands, they were years of suffering, tears, grief, and trouble for the Smiths. His families left at home had to move about and endure much hardship. Young Joseph Fielding was left without a father during most of his early teen years. Another child died during the exile. During this time President Smith regularly wrote about the importance of learning from difficulty and trials. "Adversity is often the cradle of courage and heroism," he wrote to Elder Jacob F. Gates. To another missionary he said, "Trials are necessary to the perfection of mankind."

But there were also positive aspects of President Smith's stay in the islands. One unexpected result was the discovery of the original Spaulding manuscript—a source of much trouble for the Latter-day Saints—in the hands of a man named L. L. Rice who was living with his daughter in Honolulu. Smith obtained permission from Rice to print the manuscript and thus make clear through the contents of the work that Joseph Smith had not stolen the basic ideas for the Book of Mormon from this purportedly similar document.[16]

The major benefit of Joseph F. Smith's residence was his great spiritual leadership and administrative experience. He regularly taught the missionaries and their president concerning the organization of the Church and correct procedures. He encouraged better record keeping and stricter attention to statistical matters. His ability to use the Hawaiian language had diminished little since his last mission in 1864. He frequently spoke in Sunday meetings and also in every conference session while in the islands.

One result of Smith's leadership during this period was an inspiring prophecy, which has become an important tradition among the Hawaiian Saints. Though it was recorded many years afterward, the best evidence indicates that the ideas expressed in the written document were indeed those of Joseph F. Smith.[17] The prophecy grew out of problems of the times. The Saints of Laie were discouraged about the plantation in 1885 or 1886, and brought their complaints to President Smith. After listening to the people for a while, he arose and said:

> My brothers and sisters, do not leave this land, for this place has been chosen by the Lord as a gathering place for the Saints of the Church of Jesus Christ of Latter-day Saints in Hawaii nei. Do not complain because of the many trials which come to you, because of the barrenness of the land, the lack of water, the scarcity of foods to which you are accustomed, and the poverty as well. Be patient, for the day is coming when this land will become a most beautiful land. Water shall spring forth in abundance, and upon the barren land you now see, the Saints will build homes, taro will be planted, and there will be plenty to eat and drink. Many trees will be planted and this place will become verdant, the fragrance of flowers will fill the air, and trees which are now seen growing on the mountains will be moved by the Saints and will grow in this place near the sea, and because of the great beauty of the land, inland birds will come here and sing their songs.
>
> And upon this place the glory of the Lord will rest, to bless the Saints who believe in Him and His commandments. And there are some in this house who will live to see all these things fulfilled, which I have spoken from the Lord.
>
> Therefore, do not waver, work with patience, continue on, stand firm, keep the commandments and also the laws of the gathering, and you will receive greater blessings, both spiritual and temporal, than you now enjoy or have enjoyed in the past. May the Lord be with us all.[18]

The words given here may not be precisely accurate, but the important thing is that years later the Laie plantation developed in almost precisely the manner predicted by Smith. His words gave the discouraged Saints the reassurance they needed to carry on.

During these years the haole portion of Laie grew to the greatest size it would attain during the nineteenth century. There were twenty-eight elders (they were not always at Laie), ten sisters, and ten children. After observing that most of the women had at least one baby and seeing how busy they were with the basic responsibilities of motherhood, Smith suggested to President Taylor that no more newly married couples be sent to Hawaii. He asked that two elders be sent every six months so that transitions could be effected smoothly and the language would not be a problem. His advice and counsel were followed. Few couples were called into the field after 1886.

In March 1887 Julina sailed from Hawaii. She took with her a one-year-old child, E. Wesley, who had been born at Laie. He would later serve as president of the Hawaiian mission. In late June Smith departed for home. He had been called back because of the ill health of President Taylor, who died on 25 July 1887.[19]

LAIE'S EARLY YEARS ASSESSED

Laie's first twenty-five years (1865–1890) brought growth and change to the mission and to Church members. But these were not easy years. The plantation was not an economic success. The missionaries were generally discouraged with the slow moral progress of their Hawaiian brothers and sisters, and often wondered and asked whether the entire operation had not been a failure from the beginning.

The economic outlook was seldom bright at Laie. Church leaders in Salt Lake City frequently sent loans to help redeem the plantation's credit rating. The operation was very small in comparison with other enormous plantations that had been developed in the islands by the 1890s. In fact, one of the mission presidents reported that the entire Laie sugar crop would hardly keep some of the large mills operating more than a day or two. The plantation mill required experienced supervision and constant upkeep by specialists that the mission seldom could provide. The point, however, is that the plantation had not been purchased to make men rich. From its inception it was a place where faithful Saints could gather away from the world and labor for a just remuneration. The Laie idea was to help the local Saints develop character while they developed skill, or at least while they earned an honest living. Over the years this goal was achieved for the relatively few Saints who heeded the call to gather at Laie.

Probably the greatest weakness in the Laie scheme was the uneven quality of supervision from the mission presidents. This is not personal criticism, for they were seldom in Hawaii for more than three years, and while they were there they not only had to learn the sugar business, but also to supervise the activities of many employees on the plantation. In addition, they oversaw the store, kept the books and records, made sure the community was kept clean and neat, hosted visiting dignitaries such as the king and queen, and took care of the numerous other tasks that devolved upon them. And of course, the other tasks of the presidency, involving the missionaries and all the branches and members, also required much time and energy. The mission presidents generally deserve nothing but admiration for their devoted and selfless service. Nevertheless, it was difficult for these busy men to handle the sugar plantation effectively.

Beyond the economic issue lies the question of social progress. Did Laie fulfill its purpose for the Saints? A reading of letters from the mission presidents to President Brigham Young gives the exaggerated impression that there was not a moral Hawaiian either in the Church or without. The mission presidents constantly lamented the moral looseness of the converts and members. Even the best Hawaiian Saints were sometimes brought before Church leaders on charges of adultery. But the Hawaiians were quick to repent and sorrowful for their lack of moral rectitude.

These reports notwithstanding, there is strong evidence that the Laie Saints did make progress. They lived cleaner lives, in a physical as well as a moral sense, than they had done when the community was founded. On two different visits, in 1874 and 1883, King Kalakaua complimented the Saints—first for their ability to have babies, which was directly related to their physical and moral health (missionaries reported few who suffered with social diseases), and second for their status as loyal, law-abiding subjects. In the late 1870s, when the islands were suffering a drought of many months, one report stated: "the natives who have gathered to Laie are in better condition than any of the native population on the Islands that I have seen, and I have traveled half around Hawaii, around Kauai and two-thirds around Oahu."[20]

Spiritual progress is difficult to evaluate. For the Latter-day Saints, it is very closely related to temporal welfare. This concept was recognized in Hawaii both when Brigham Young decided to found a gathering place and throughout the early years of the community. There was also some outward evidence of inner spirituality. The Relief Society sisters frequently reported that many kind and Christian acts were taking place. The sisters struggled to improve themselves. By the late 1890s Alice R. Woolley, wife of President Samuel E. Woolley, said she believed the Hawaiian relief societies could hold their own with most of those in Utah and that there were many good and faithful Saints in the islands.[21] Also it must be added that over the years the Hawaiian elders and other priesthood bearers had devoted many years to the service of the Lord as missionaries and in other priesthood capacities. Virtually all the branches were presided over by Hawaiian Saints, and many Hawaiians had filled missions with honor and success.

Although many aspects of the Church program in Hawaii could have been improved in the early 1890s, one thing is certain: the Church in Hawaii had made enormous strides since the time of Walter Murray Gibson.

–PART III–

1892–1919

A TIME OF SPIRITUAL AND TEMPORAL SUCCESS

–9–

A NEW ERA IN LEADERSHIP

THE ERA of Hawaiian Church history that began with President Matthew Noall in January 1892 and culminated in 1921 at the end of President Samuel E. Woolley's tenure was very different from the previous period. The 1890s and early 1900s were a time of transition. The Church situation in the 1890s was shaped by the Church's new position on polygamy. In 1890 President Wilford Woodruff announced to the Church and to the world that polygamy would no longer be practiced by the Saints. This proclamation did not immediately convince a skeptical world (and many devout Latter-day Saints) that polygamy had really ended. But by 1896 the politicians of America were sufficiently persuaded of the sincerity of the Church's position to grant statehood to Utah. This did not automatically bring acceptance to Utah's politicians in Washington, D.C., but the new state relatively quickly became part of mainstream American politics. Polygamy, however, continued to be a social and religious issue in the United States until World War I.

Presidents Woodruff and Lorenzo Snow were the last presidents of the Church to have known Joseph Smith well. Joseph F. Smith, who followed Snow, was six years old when the Prophet was martyred in 1844. With the beginning of his administration in 1901, the Church began a new era in some ways. Soon after Joseph F. Smith became president, several young apostles were called to the Quorum of the Twelve. In addition to Reed Smoot, thirty-eight, who was called in 1900, were George Albert Smith, thirty-three, called in 1903; David O. McKay, thirty-two, called in 1906; and Joseph Fielding Smith, thirty-three, called in 1910. These men and others brought not only devotion and spiritual strength to their assignments, but also youth and new ideas.

Three changes in emphasis and policy were important at this time: a significant change in economic outlook; a new emphasis on worldwide expansion of the faith; and a new attitude toward immigration, which encouraged converts to remain in their homelands and strengthen the Church there. In the late 1890s President Snow began selling some Church properties in order to pay the great debts that had accumulated as a result of the Morrill Act and the Edmunds–Tucker Act, which restricted the financial operations of the Church. But the Church also developed a different attitude toward business. Whereas the Church had been favorable toward communal and cooperative financial ventures, now emphasis was directed toward more typical capitalist American business practices.[1] This attitude can be seen to some degree in the administration of Laie plantation and village, and in the Iosepa colony, the Hawaiian gathering place founded at Skull Valley, Utah, in 1889 (see chapter 10).

The new emphasis on expanding the faith had little effect on the Hawaiian mission. However, efforts to make missionary work more efficient and productive did bring some changes to Hawaii. The construction of the Laie temple reflects the desire of Joseph F. Smith to take the full program of the Church to all peoples prepared to receive it.

Nor did the new decision to encourage converts to stay at home and build up their local churches change matters in Hawaii. The few Hawaiians who were determined to go to Utah went anyway, although the missionaries stopped encouraging them to leave Hawaii and gather in Utah.[2]

It was against this background that Presidents Matthew Noall and Samuel E. Woolley worked to bring the Hawaiian mission to a stage of religious, social, and economic maturity.

THE WORK OF MATTHEW NOALL

The work of Matthew Noall from 1892 to 1895 deserves more notice than it has received in the past. It was President Noall who started the mission on its way to better financial and statistical accounting and also toward better record keeping in general. It was Noall who finally placed the plantation on a profitable footing. He also did much to improve the general environment in and around Laie. His many contributions include the construction of a new mission house and a new company store and the establishment of better pay for the employees of the plantation.[3]

Noall and his wife Libbie had not been back in Utah from their first mission very long when they were asked to return to Hawaii to take charge of the mission. Only twenty-eight years old, he wondered how well he would be accepted by the missionaries and Saints. The Noalls arrived in Hawaii on 18 December 1891 and took control of the mission early in January 1892. Dissension had arisen between the native Saints and the missionaries, and problems even existed among the elders and sisters. President Ward E. Pack had been unable to solve these problems, and thus the responsibility of bringing peace to the mission rested on young President Noall. Through meetings, discussions, and constant supervision of the principal troublemakers, the matter was brought to a peaceful resolution within a month or so of Noall's arrival.

Perhaps the difficult circumstances surrounding Noall's beginning as mission president and plantation manager proved a positive factor in the long run. He was forced to study the whole situation carefully and take matters firmly in hand. Many areas of the plantation and mission concerned him. One of the first problems needing to be resolved was the mission-owned "company" store, which was part of the old mansion house. Chinese merchants had moved into the Laie area and were drawing off business from the mission store. In order to compete Noall built a new store, which was completed 29 February 1892.

Next Noall wrote to the First Presidency for permission to build a new mission home. The old building was deteriorating and he hoped that a new home would bring credit to the Church. While waiting for an answer, he tackled other problems. Hawaiians leased portions of the Laie land for *kalo* (taro) patches, and some less than honest individuals were able to avoid making full payment on their land. Also, there were arguments concerning boundary lines between home lots. Noall realized that the best solution would be to survey the land carefully and establish uniform rents due at a set time. Although some of the native Saints did not like this, it was not long before the matter was resolved.

The plantation's financial accounts also occupied Noall's early days as he tried to discover the true state of the operation. Few records existed for the period before 1890, and even those for 1890 and 1891 were far from accurate. Noall uncovered serious mistakes in the accounts (all of which were evidently unintentional) during the first two years of his mission. On two occasions he wrote to the First Presidency to make corrections in the mission accounts. By 1895 these matters had been corrected, and it was established that the plantation and all of the Laie property was worth $116,220. The gross value of the operation increased about $26,000 during Noall's administration. The plantation produced profits sufficient to allow Noall to send $30,000, over three years, to President Woodruff to help with financial problems at the Church headquarters in Salt Lake City.

These profits were made even though the price of sugar had fallen drastically between 1891 and 1895. Three factors contributed to the plantation's success. First and most important was a new agreement between Laie plantation and the newly formed Kahuku Plantation Company. Kahuku had built a large, modern sugar mill very close to Laie. An agreement was arranged in 1892 to have the Kahuku mill cut, haul, and process Laie's cane crop for half the end product. This was a great boon because the old mill built in 1882 was totally out of commission and the Laie plantation could not afford to construct a new one. Because the Kahuku mill was so efficient, the gross production per acre was higher than ever before. This arrangement with Kahuku plantation was modified almost yearly, but the broad terms of the agreement remained.

A second factor that increased profits was the cultivation of more acreage. This was made possible by a third factor, an improved water supply. A reservoir was built and more ditches and flumes added. President Woolley continued the expansion of land and the search for water during his tenure. Pumps were added in the late 1890s, making it possible to open higher land that had previously been inaccessible.

When permission came from the First Presidency to build a new mission home, President Noall was so busy with other matters that he almost wished he had never broached the matter. Nevertheless, there was a genuine need for the new home, and by April 1892 Noall had drawn up the plans—he had been a carpenter prior to his mission—and the new home was under construction. In late August the cornerstone was laid; the work continued for over two more years. Finally, on 6 October 1894, Lanihuli House was dedicated. The completed structure came to be the symbol of the mission and was pictured on the mission stationery during Woolley's administration. Until the completion of the temple it was the physical center of the Church in Hawaii, although being a home it served a totally different ecclesiastical function.

Lanihuli House, described at the time as a "building modern in all its designs," was an interesting combination of current continental U.S. styling with some Hawaiian modifications. It can best be classified as Hawaiian Victorian. In addition to the balcony gracing much of the second story, it had an octagonal turret that faced the sea. Inside it was spacious, with kitchen, dining room, hallways, and six "dwelling rooms." Probably the most used room, at least by missionaries and guests, was a special prayer room. It was also used as a council room and meeting hall, and many major decisions were made or announced there. This old home added to Laie's landscape until 1960, when it was razed to make way for the home that today houses the temple president.

Lanihuli House played an important role in every conference held in Laie. Long before it was constructed, when the old mission home was still in use, a tradition arose whereby Relief Society sisters would gather at the mission home and then walk in procession, two by two, to the meetinghouse. Each sister dressed in spotless white. It was described as a beautiful, striking sight.

The mission president was deeply concerned with both the missionaries and the members. Instructions from the mission president and his assistants were usually given orally at conference meetings. However, while Sister Noall was confined during her pregnancy in the first part of 1894, President Noall found it necessary to write an extensive letter of instructions to the missionaries.[4] It reveals the dedication of a mature young leader whose concern for the success of his missionaries was very deep. He counseled them on many topics and encouraged them to be prayerful, diligent, faithful, and strong, and to work in harmony and unity. He pointed out the pitfalls that could lead to failure and disgrace and pleaded with them to avoid doubt, uncertainty of purpose, and the wasting of time. He gave much counsel concerning the evils of fault finding and the blessings of overlooking disagreements. His letter ended with a restating of twenty-eight rules that had previously been accepted by the missionaries. Many of the rules pertained to principles of unity in the work, but most related to proper priesthood procedures. Rule 27 was to "make frequent reports to headquarters of your whereabouts, and the progress of your labors, that we may have a good understanding of the progress of the mission in all its parts." President Noall evidently made every effort to know what was happening in every part of his stewardship.[5]

THE WOOLLEYS IN HAWAII

One of the most important men to serve the Church in Hawaii was Samuel Edwin Woolley (1859–1925). He was called as mission president and plantation manager in 1895 and remained in Hawaii until 1921. An important influence in shaping the destiny of the mission and the Laie community, he made a significant contribution to the modernization and institutionalization of the mission and plantation.

Woolley was working for the Iosepa Agriculture and Stock Company, the Church's Hawaiian colony in Skull Valley, Utah, when he received a letter from the First Presidency asking him to take his wife and four children and go to Hawaii to serve as mission president. He accepted and was set apart on 9 August 1895. Both Joseph F. Smith and George Q. Cannon were involved in the ordinance.

The Woolleys arrived in Honolulu on 31 August. A phone call to Laie revealed that President Noall was sick and thus had been unable to meet them. Abraham Fernandez, one of the most faithful local Saints, loaded the Woolleys and their luggage into his cart and they started for Laie. When they arrived at the foot of the Pali they were met by missionaries from Laie with a team and wagon from the plantation. As they traveled night fell, and they watched the moon rise over the sea. According to President Woolley, it was a beautiful night, very bright. They arrived at Lanihuli at midnight and found their way to bed. Thus began a mission that would last almost twenty-five years; a mission that would oversee many changes in the Church and the plantation and would last long enough for the Woolleys to see their children grown. Woolley started his mission at age thirty-six and ended it in his early sixties, spending his most productive years in the service of the Lord.[6]

Noall and Woolley spent many days discussing the affairs of the mission. They carefully transferred all accounts in Honolulu and Kahuku to Woolley's name. Together they entered into several lease arrangements with Chinese farmers. They also spent many hours talking about the missionaries and local Church leaders. While together they started several projects on the plantation, an important one being the piping of water to Lanihuli House, a considerable effort. By the end of October 1895 the Noalls were ready to leave, and President Woolley had matters firmly in hand. The Noalls sailed from Honolulu on 4 November 1895.[7]

President Woolley was an energetic leader. His daily journal entries almost always begin with "up at daybreak" or "at work early." To him "early" meant anytime after 2:00 A.M. but before 6:00 A.M. He believed in the original idea and philosophy of the Laie community: the sole purpose of the settlement was to help the Hawaiians temporally and spiritually. For many years the population of Laie had remained static. The land would not provide a living for many more than the ninety to one hundred employees and their families. Woolley could see that if Laie was to grow as a gathering place, the plantation would have to be enlarged. He accomplished this by buying new land and by increasing the acreage under cultivation. This process of expansion continued throughout Woolley's administration.

One of the most important capital improvements made at Laie during Woolley's early years was the installation in 1898 of a steam-powered pump. The pump weighed over eleven tons and cost more than thirty thousand dollars to install. It raised 3.5 million gallons of water a day to land that was 110 feet above the well. Once it went into operation in June 1898 it was used twenty-four hours a day. In addition, many wells were drilled during Woolley's administration. The quest for water never ended because every time more water was procured, more land was cultivated. By 1930 there were five pumping units at Laie with a daily capacity of around eight million gallons.[8]

The expansion made it possible for the population of Laie to grow. By the early 1920s Laie was approaching the one thousand mark. From 1900 until the early 1920s the plantation paid its own way every year and supported the financial needs of the mission as well. By 1930 there were 432 people employed in various parts of the operation.[9]

One of Woolley's land acquisitions occurred in a rather unusual way. Around 1905–1906 a wealthy and influential sugar magnate, J. B. Castle, who controlled the Kahuku Plantation Company, developed a scheme that encompassed a major part of windward Oahu. In addition to his lands on the Kahuku side of Laie, he acquired the lands that adjoined the Laie plantation on the Honolulu side. A new company was formed called the Koolau Agricultural Company, Ltd. Not pleased with having his lands divided by the Laie plantation, Castle decided he wanted the upper part of the Church's property. This was a serious problem for President Woolley because he believed Laie was a sacred trust from the Lord. He was repeatedly pressured by Castle and his associates to sell the *mauka* (upper) lands, but Woolley did his best to put off the decision.

Finally, in 1906, Castle used the milling contract between the Kahuku company and the Laie plantation as a lever to achieve his purposes. In effect he told the Church that if it would not sell the lands, water, and rights he desired, its 1906 cane crop would be the last the Kahuku mill would process. This would have put Laie plantation out of business. All Woolley could do was to pray and wait. But somehow, year after year, arrangements with Kahuku plantation were made to mill the Laie cane. Years passed and Castle died. The Koolau Agriculture Company properties were put up for sale, and in 1918 Woolley acted as agent for the Laie plantation in buying the property. This new land, eight hundred acres, purportedly valued at a half million dollars, almost doubled the sugarcane acreage of Laie plantation.[10] Cane production was also increased by the denial of lease renewals to the Chinese farmers who had grown rice on Laie lands. By 1915 all of this land was back under the management of the plantation.

The production of Laie plantation increased steadily over the years. Under President Woolley's watchful eye and skillful leadership, the small-time farming enterprise of the nineteenth century grew into a major twentieth-century operation. The sugar crop of 1894–1895 was 339 tons. Woolley's best crop was 3,103 tons of sugar, an almost ten-fold increase, produced in 1917–1918 during World War I.[11] Woolley was encouraged to produce all the sugar possible to help with the war need: he met the challenge.

THE JUBILEE: FIFTIETH ANNIVERSARY OF THE HAWAIIAN MISSION

The fiftieth anniversary of the arrival of the first ten LDS missionaries in the Hawaiian Islands, 12 December 1900, began a four-day celebration. Preparations for the event began in early November, almost too late for plans to be carried out as the missionaries and Saints desired. But all the necessary preparations were made—arranging for a suitable hall, translating programs and brochures and printing them, preparing choirs and soloists, arranging for food and feasts, scheduling appropriate housing, planning programs and receptions, advertising the event, and finally inviting all past Hawaiian missionaries and certain special guests—and the exciting event came off without a major hitch.

The Jubilee committee hoped that President George Q. Cannon, first counselor in the First Presidency and the real leader of the first missionaries, would be able to attend. The first indication that President Cannon would come arrived on 5 December, only a week before the celebration was to begin. The fears of President Woolley and his associates were finally allayed when President Cannon, his family, William W. Cluff, and others arrived on the evening of 10 December 1900.

The next four days were a whirlwind of meetings and receptions. Six meetings were held at the Orpheum Theatre on Honolulu's Fort Street on 12 and 13 December. Cannon spoke at each session. To his own satisfaction he was able to speak a few words in Hawaiian, a language he had not used for forty-six years. Before he departed on 5 January 1901 he was using the language almost fluently, much to the delight of the Hawaiian Saints.

Two men stand out above all others during the first fifty years of the mission: Joseph F. Smith and George Q. Cannon. Joseph F. Smith had returned to Hawaii in 1864–1865, again in 1885–1887, and had visited as recently as 1899. In addition to visits in 1909, 1916, and 1917, he would return again to dedicate the site for the Laie temple in 1915. But President Cannon had not returned to Hawaii since the 1850s. A great tradition had grown concerning the works of Pukuniahi, as he was called in Hawaii, and local Saints almost worshiped his name. He wrote frequently during his visit of his sincere joy in being received so warmly after so many years.

The speeches, music, feasts, and receptions were important, but perhaps more important were the words of encouragement and strength, of wisdom and exhortation, that Cannon gave at various meetings held after the official celebration was over. He also gave many blessings to Saints who sought him out. Even ex-Queen Liliuokalani asked him to come to her home, where she knelt before him and asked for a special blessing. Cannon said in his journal, "I felt very free in blessing her and the Spirit rested upon us both."[12]

In addition to his time in Honolulu, Cannon spent eight days in Laie where he enjoyed himself immensely. He also took a trip to Maui where he had established the Church fifty years before.

Three significant revelatory experiences occurred while Cannon was in the islands. On Sunday, 23 December, he spoke to the Saints at Laie branch concerning the blessings the Lord still held in store for them. President Woolley wrote: "He told them of their forefathers and the many blessings that were in store for them if they would but obey the commandments of the Lord. He said if they would be faithful enough that the time would come when some would be given the power to seal husband and wife for time and eternity so that their children would be born under the New and Everlasting Covenant."[13] Cannon was moved to discuss the same subject a week later in Honolulu. In his journal he recorded that he had spoken on temple building and the necessity of the Hawaiian Saints' gathering information about their ancestors. In the afternoon meeting of the same day he spoke on the subject again. He wrote:

> I dwelt upon . . . the necessity of living lives of purity. I led them to believe that if they did so and exercised faith, the Lord might move upon His servant, the prophet, Lorenzo Snow, to authorize one of his servants to seal wives to husbands for time and eternity. I felt led to touch upon this point for I believe if that were done here in the cases of faithful saints it would be attended with excellent effects.[14]

Taken together, these expressions later gave rise to the tradition that Cannon had prophesied that a temple would be built in Hawaii. There is no evidence that he intended to give this impression. He did, however, hope for the time when the sealing powers would be given to the Hawaiian people in Hawaii.

The second revelatory clarification occurred at Lahaina, Maui. On the morning of 27 December, Cannon, in company with Woolley, Cluff, and some others, started out to find the place where Nalimanui had lived when she offered him food and shelter. Cannon journalized as follows:

> I wanted to find the site of this house and the garden where I sought the Lord in secret prayer and where He condescended to commune with me, for I heard His voice more than once as one man speaks with another, encouraging me and showing me the work which should be done among this people if I would follow the dictates of His Spirit, Glory to God in the highest that He has permitted me to live to behold the fulfillment of His words.[15]

The third experience took place at Waikapu, Maui. It concerned the LDS doctrine that the island peoples are descendants of Abraham through Lehi and are heirs to all the blessings of Abraham and his posterity. This doctrine had been accepted by Latter-day Saints ever since the time of Cannon's first mission, but the fact that it had its inception through him was not known until Cannon explained this to the Saints at Waikapu on 28 December 1900. President Woolley wrote that President Cannon "told them they were of the seed of Abraham, he knew it because the Lord told him so at Lahaina."[16]

The Jubilee was successful in bringing the Saints into closer harmony and unity of purpose. It also brought the Church to the attention of the peoples of Hawaii. Cannon met with many important people and left a good impression on those with whom he spoke. In 1854, at the end of Cannon's mission to Hawaii, there were over four thousand members of the Church. The Church had diminished greatly during the Gibson years, but by 1900 it was larger than ever before at between six and seven thousand members. Twenty-five of Cannon's own converts were still alive when he returned to Hawaii, and he conversed with eighteen or twenty of these old friends.

But the first fifty years do not belong to Cannon alone. American elders and sisters accepted 299 mission calls during those years. Some served two or even three missions. It is impossible to number the Hawaiian elders who served, except to say that their numbers may have been larger than those of the foreign missionaries. And beyond the missionaries were the many thousands of faithful Saints who had served in the numerous presidencies, choirs, and teaching and clerking positions that the Mormon Church requires of its members. One of the most remarkable features of the first fifty years of Church history in Hawaii, one that sets the Church apart from other faiths in all lands and at all times, is that the Church was a lay Church. The people, the native people, had worked to make it strong from the very beginning.

–10–

FROM PLANTATION TO TEMPLE

PROGRESS OF THE HAWAIIAN MISSION TO 1920

THE PROGRESS of the mission during the first two decades of this century was remarkable in many ways. Not only did the Saints move forward temporally, but they also entered a new era of spiritual strength.

Although Laie had been the pride of the Church in the islands prior to 1900, it was after this date that the little community developed aesthetically to become a showplace of the islands, a position it still holds. The beauty of the village was greatly enhanced when a large artesian well was drilled to supply water for all the homes, yards, and gardens of the residents. Trees hardy enough to withstand the brisk winds of the windward side of the island were found and planted, along with many varieties of shrubs and flowers. The roads were paved and kept clean, and the people of Laie developed an unusual pride in their little city. By 1913 there were not only eighty LDS families living there, but also many nonmember Chinese, Japanese, Korean, and Portuguese farmers as well.

Life in Laie was a modest proposition. Yearly rent was twenty-five cents per family, a charge levied only to remind residents that the land was owned by the Church. But there was another "cost" that contributed much to the environment of Laie. In a 1911 address President Woolley said, "History says this land was a place of refuge in ancient times, and I want it to continue so to be. . . . The price of a house and lot at Laie is *proper living*."[1] Proper living was constantly stressed by Woolley and his associates. However, the records reveal no expulsions for improper living.

The Laie school brought credit to the Church and the community. It was not large, but it did serve a growing number of children, both Church members and nonmembers. After the turn of the century the mission staff put more effort into the school to maintain well-trained teachers who could stay in Hawaii several years. Sisters were called from the Mountain West to teach in the school. The principal for many years was Ernest L. Miner. The school gradually developed a fine reputation because of the enlarged curriculum offered to students. In addition to courses in the three R's, training was also offered in music, gardening, domestic arts, and "manual training" as vocational or industrial arts were called. The school buildings were steadily improved over the years —even though the campus had been moved several times to make way for other developments, particularly the new temple—and by 1920 consisted of six separate cottages for the six grades. A Honolulu newspaper wrote concerning the Laie school in 1920, "This high-class establishment is for the use of 150 children of the settlement and represents, as in other sections of the islands, about every race on the face of the earth."[2]

President Woolley worked to improve the mission's chapels and amusement halls. Between April 1913 and April 1914, six meetinghouses, two amusement halls, and one additional building at the Laie school were added to the inventory of Church buildings at a cost of $16,600. A year later President Woolley reported that there were fifty-two meetinghouses in the mission, valued at $66,000. This was in addition to the Laie plantation and property and some mission homes.

Growth in financial and physical status was satisfactory, but growth in the number of lives touched by the gospel was more important. Membership growth was never spectacular, but it remained steady over the years (see table 2). Membership grew more rapidly when more missionaries were called into the field after 1919.

But more important than the total number of members was the moral strength and character among the Saints. Attendance is one indication of spiritual health in a mission, and about half the members were active in 1915. But this is only part of the picture.

What kind of people were the Hawaiian Latter-day Saints? Even though the returned missionaries from Hawaii had a deep love for the Hawaiian people, some of them were surprised when President Joseph F. Smith decided to build a temple in Hawaii. The older returned missionaries particularly questioned whether the Hawaiian people were strong enough to remain true to the demanding moral covenants of the temple. This had been a problem among Hawaiian Saints prior to 1900. Even after 1900 it was a standard practice for President Woolley to meet in council at least once each month to consider cases of alleged immorality.

But as the years passed, the number of moral infractions became fewer. The Hawaiians did not become perfect (nor did their haole teachers), but they did gain strength and character. Elder Moses Cowley, older brother of Elder Matthew Cowley, once wrote that he had talked with

TABLE 2 **Mission Growth Patterns, 1910–1925**

Year	Members	Missionaries
1910	8,170	37
1911	8,461	37
1912	8,689	35
1913	8,918	—
1914	9,146	38
1915	9,443	46
1916	9,771	42
1917	10,108	42
1918	10,434	40
1919	10,745	37
1920	11,078	51
1921	11,514	64
1922	12,157	72
1923	12,572	67
1924	13,083	61
1925	13,668	67

Source: Mission Financial and Statistical Reports, Hawaiian Mission, 1910–1925.

one of the most influential sugar men on Maui, who told him that the Mormon Hawaiians made up the "best class of Hawaiians." This kind of report of course encouraged the missionaries, even though it was only one man's opinion. Cowley also pointed out that there were many temptations among these people and that if a Hawaiian could remain true to his convictions, which many of them did, he could be considered among the best people on the earth.[3]

Cowley was convinced that the Hawaiians were a chosen people. In an all-mission conference address in April 1914 he said:

> I have taken notice of this mission, of the people here, and in comparing their numbers with the numbers of other missions, I believe that more people have believed the gospel here than have done in any other land in proportion to the number of its people. If we go to other places in these islands, from Hawaii to Kauai and visit the meetings, we will find that there are more Mormons going to meetings than other people.[4]

In 1913 the missionaries calculated the proportion of Latter-day Saints in the islands and concluded that Mormons made up 22 percent of the

Hawaiian population.[5] Unfortunately, by the second decade of the twentieth century the Hawaiian race had become only a small part of the total island population. The Church was considered a Hawaiian church. In 1914 the Doctrine and Covenants and the Pearl of Great Price were published in Hawaiian for the first time. This was a help to the older members; most younger people were now literate in English thanks to laws requiring that all education be in English.

The temple was the most important factor in motivating the Saints to keep the commandments of the Lord, and it stood as a positive motivation to all Church members. It is impossible to show a direct relationship between the behavior of the Saints and the promise of the temple, but it is interesting to observe that only one person was excommunicated from the Church in 1918. The cause for excommunication was usually immoral conduct, and earlier in the century as many as fifty had been cut off from the Church in one year.

President Woolley was also happy with the progress made in other areas. "The mission," he said in April 1916, "has made good progress during the last year. More are keeping the Word of Wisdom; more are paying their tithing; the number of baptisms and blessings is well up to the standard, and the work in general shows an increase in faith and good works among the people; yet there is need for repentance. None are perfect."[6]

The Hawaii Temple

President Joseph F. Smith kept a careful eye on Hawaii. He not only watched the growth of the Church there but also helped by sending a growing number of missionaries. Prior to 1900 there were seldom more than twenty-five missionaries in the islands, but the number serving after 1900 gradually edged up to about thirty-five in 1910. The number of Church members also grew to 8,170 in 1910 and 9,443 in 1915. Forty-six missionaries were laboring in the field at the end of that year.

Viewed today there were hardly enough Church members in Hawaii in 1915 to populate two or three stakes, to say nothing of justifying the operation of a temple. The number of members in the other Pacific missions was growing, but population was not the only issue involved in the decision to build a temple in Hawaii. As early as 1900 President Cannon had seen the need for the Hawaiians to have the blessings of being sealed as families for time and all eternity. After that time temple work was discussed frequently in mission conferences. President Woolley regularly encouraged his people to live lives of purity so they could enter the temple some day.

Perhaps Woolley had been told by Church leaders that they were seriously considering a temple for Hawaii. But this seems unlikely because President Smith, when telling his companions, Elder Reed Smoot and Bishop Charles W. Nibley, of his feeling that a temple should be built in Laie, also informed them that this idea had not been discussed with the Quorum of the Twelve and the First Presidency. Nevertheless, in April 1915 Woolley said: "Have we searched out our genealogies? Are we prepared for a temple to be built? . . . Who knows but what the Lord wants to build a temple in this land? I tell you that there are people here today who if they continue in the work of the Lord, shall enter into the temple or other temples; and the time will come, in my judgement, that a temple will be built here."[7] Woolley's admonition was prophetic, for two months later, while President Smith was visiting the islands, he selected a temple site and dedicated it to the Lord. Elder Reed Smoot, who was with the prophet, recounted this sacred occasion:

> President Smith came to me and said, "Reed, I want you to take a walk with me." And as we went out the door, he said to Bishop Nibley, "I wish you would accompany us." I never saw a more perfect night in all my life; the surroundings were perfect. You who have been to Laie know the surroundings; all nature smiles. We walked toward the meetinghouse. Nothing was said of what we were going for until we stood at the back of the meetinghouse, and President Smith then said: "Brethren, this is the birthday of President Brigham Young, June 1, 1915. I feel impressed to dedicate this ground for the erection of a Temple to God, for a place where the peoples of the Pacific Isles can come and do their temple work. I have not presented this to the Council of the Twelve or to my counselors; but if you think there would be no objection to it, I think now is the time to dedicate the ground." I have heard President Smith pray hundreds of times. He has thrilled my soul many times with his wonderful spirit of prayer and his supplications to our Heavenly Father. But never in all my life did I hear such a prayer. The very ground seemed to be sacred, and he seemed as if he were talking face to face with the Father. I cannot and never will forget it if I live a thousand years.[8]

At the general conference in Salt Lake City the next October, President Smith presented the Laie temple proposition to the Church. He said it was being built

> so that the good people of these islands may reach the blessings of the House of God within their own borders, and that the people from New

> Zealand, if they do not become strong enough to require a house to be built there also, by and by, can come to Laie, where they can get their blessings and return home and live in peace, having fulfilled all the requirements of the Gospel the same as we have the privilege of doing here. . . .
>
> I want you to understand that the Hawaiian mission, and the good Latter-day Saints of that mission, with what help the Church can give, will be able to build their Temple. They are a tithe-paying people, and the plantation is in a condition to help us. We have a gathering place where we bring the people together, and teach them the best we can, in schools and under the various auxiliary organizations of the Church.[9]

When the plans for the temple were announced, Polynesian members of the Church all over the Pacific began making preparations to attend the temple. In New Zealand, Tonga, Samoa, and French Polynesia, mission presidents encouraged members to work, earn, and save, and look forward to the time when they could partake of the blessings of the temple.

THE IOSEPA COLONY

One group of Hawaiian Saints whose fascinating story was brought to a conclusion by the announcement of the forthcoming erection of the Hawaiian temple was the band of native Hawaiians who had migrated years before to Iosepa, Skull Valley, Utah.[10] The concept of gathering had been taught to the Hawaiian Saints from the early 1850s. Laws of the Hawaiian kingdom, however, forbade the natives from leaving the country, particularly from leaving permanently. For this reason two different gathering places, Lanai and Laie, were chosen and established for the Hawaiians in the kingdom.

But as political matters changed and the kings became more friendly to the Church, one by one a few Hawaiian Saints were allowed to leave for Salt Lake City. The first Hawaiian Saint to visit Zion was Jonatana H. Napela. He went there in 1866 and stayed for some time; he attended general conference, received his own endowments, was ordained a seventy in the priesthood, and in general had a wonderful time. He gave many talks about Utah to his fellow believers when he returned home.

In the mid-1870s, when David Kalakaua gained the throne, some Hawaiians were allowed to emigrate to Utah. They did not go in large numbers, most likely because they could not afford it or because of close family ties, but gradually a trickle of emigrants began to flow toward the center of the Church. The attraction of the temple is usually put forward as an important motivation. It should be remembered, however, that the Salt Lake Temple was not completed until 1893. Endowment work was undoubtedly the major motivation for gathering to Zion. The Hawaiian Saints desired to obtain their endowments and be sealed together as families. This ordinance was solemnized in the Endowment House, which functioned in Salt Lake City from 1855 until 1889.

But gathering itself was also important. The members from Hawaii, like converts from other parts of the world, wanted to be with the Saints at the center of the Church. They also wanted more economic opportunities and adventure. Another factor was that the missionaries in Hawaii regularly encouraged their Hawaiian friends to go to Utah. This fact was apparently not known to President Wilford Woodruff, who told Hawaiian government representatives that the Church had not encouraged the Hawaiians to come to Utah. But as early as 1878 there are references in Hawaiian mission conference minutes indicating that certain Hawaiian Saints had been called to gather to Utah when the next missionaries were released and could take the Hawaiian Saints safely there with them.

By the late 1880s there was a small colony of approximately seventy-five Hawaiians living in the northwest section of Salt Lake City. Because of their lack of education and their different cultural background, they were not well integrated into the city's community life. They were generally limited in their employment to unskilled labor, working as hod carriers and ditch diggers, and at other unskilled jobs. When winter came they were the first to be put out of work and thus the first to be placed on the rolls at the tithing office, where assistance was given to them.

The returned missionaries from Hawaii became concerned about their Hawaiian friends. Perhaps the most concerned leader of the Church was President Joseph F. Smith. On 16 May 1889 the First Presidency organized a committee to find a suitable place for the Hawaiians to work together in a productive economic endeavor. The committee members, Harvey Harris Cluff, William W. Cluff, and Fred A. Mitchell, all former leaders of the Hawaiian mission, suggested the Hawaiians settle on a farm or ranch. Leaders of the Salt Lake City Hawaiian community supported the plan ardently. Three Hawaiians were appointed to the committee, and together the body of men searched for the best place for the Hawaiian group to settle. The Hawaiian committee members were J. W. Kaulainamoku, George Kamakaniau, and Brother Napeha. (Napeha should not be confused with J. H. Napela who had died at Kalaupapa, Molokai.)

During the first two weeks of June a number of properties in Tooele, Utah, Weber, and Cache counties were inspected. After considering all the proposed sites, the committee selected the ranch of John T. Rich in Skull Valley, Tooele County. The ranch consisted of 1,280 acres of clear-title property and another 640 acres of government land that had been set aside for a school. Two hundred acres were under cultivation; there was water available, and even a large pondlike portion of a stream where fish could be raised. The ranch was in a rather desolate area, but it was not so different from other parts of the state that had been made to "blossom as the rose." According to the report sent to the First Presidency, "winters are said to be milder than in Salt Lake or Tooele Valleys." Although other reasons for selecting the site may have existed, the records do not reveal them. Certainly Skull Valley presented a very different geographical setting from Hawaii. The land was priced at thirty-five thousand dollars and the livestock cost an additional twelve thousand dollars.

A proposition to buy the land was placed before the First Presidency, which, with the support of the committee, voted to purchase the Rich property. The action was approved 21 June 1889.

The economic arrangements of the settlement reflect the problems of the Church during these years because of the raging polygamy issue. Passage of the Edmunds–Tucker Act in 1887 reinforced the restriction of the Morrill Act that the Church could not own more than fifty thousand dollars worth of real estate. Rather than openly violate the law and risk forfeiture of the land to the U.S. government, the Iosepa property was not purchased directly by the Church. A corporation was set up with shareholders and officers in the standard manner of such a legal entity. It was the Church, however, that made all payments on the property and it was commonly known to own the land. The new legal corporation was called the Iosepa Agriculture and Stock Company.

The initial payment for the land was made on 16 August 1889. Eleven days later the first group of fifty Hawaiian pioneers traveled by train to the Garfield junction and then by wagon to Grantsville. The next day they arrived at the place where the Hawaiian Saints in Utah would spend the next twenty-eight years. This day, 28 August, became Hawaiian pioneer day in Iosepa and was celebrated as a holiday every year thereafter. The name chosen for the community, Iosepa, meant "Joseph" in Hawaiian. It honored President Joseph F. Smith.

Today, when the Iosepa colony is mentioned and its location discussed, there is almost universal amazement and frequently disappointment that the leaders of the Church would place the Hawaiian Saints in such a desolate spot. It is impossible to defend this action completely, but some facts concerning this venture should be remembered:

1. The leaders of the Church loved the Hawaiians and honestly sought to act in their best interests. The decision to purchase land in Skull Valley was not made by the First Presidency, but by a committee, three of whom were Hawaiians. They must have felt good about the decision.

2. Many of the Hawaiians were not especially happy in Salt Lake City. Their economic situation there was unstable. The Iosepa ranch did make it possible for them to earn a steady living. It also brought the Hawaiians together in a situation where they could speak their own language and live more in accord with their own life-style. It is true, however, that their life-style was modified by their new environment.

3. Although many people imagine that Hawaiians spend most of their time on balmy beaches or walking through fern grottos, the truth is that they have to work to survive. In the 1890s most Hawaiians in Hawaii worked at jobs that were not pleasant. Whereas most did not care for plantation work, they often seemed to enjoy ranching. Large portions of the Hawaiian Islands, particularly on the Big Island, are typical ranch country. In fact, one of America's largest ranches, the Parker Ranch, is on that island. The Iosepa ranch provided the kind of work that many Hawaiians enjoyed doing.

4. The Iosepa colony gave the Hawaiians the opportunity to own their own homes and lots. Very few of the Hawaiian Saints had been able to acquire their own property while in Salt Lake City, but most of the families were able to buy their homes at Iosepa because the company (the Church) loaned them the land and the money to construct homes without interest. All they had to do was pay off the mortgage in modest installments.

5. It should be remembered that Mormon pioneers settled many other places in the Mountain West that were as inhospitable as Skull Valley. The Saints, whether Caucasian or Hawaiian, have usually been willing to do what was possible during their own times of struggle.

When the Hawaiian Saints settled at Iosepa, they faced the same problems that all other settlers have faced. They had to make such decisions as where the town would be located, where to place the school and church, where each family would live, and how to procure potable water. All this was done. Like other pioneers in these valleys, the Hawaiians adjusted to a new physical environment. They learned to like, or at least live with, new foods; they learned to can and preserve fruits and vegetables; in short, they learned to do whatever was necessary to be comfortable in the Utah desert.

Iosepa colony had an unusual ecclesiastical status. It was a mission and therefore directly under the supervision of the First Presidency. The leadership of the Iosepa branch and supervision of the company were always vested in the same man. The first leader was Harvey H. Cluff. He served from the beginning of the colony until 1 November 1890. He was succeeded by William King, whose term as branch president and manager was cut short by his unexpected death in February 1892. At this point Cluff was recalled. His second term lasted until March 1901, when he was followed by Thomas A. Waddoups, who managed the colony until it closed in 1917. These men were assisted by both Hawaiians and haole missionaries who had served in the islands.

In addition to the building of the Hawaiian temple, three reasons have been suggested for the close of the colony: continued sickness, financial problems, and general discontent and unhappiness among the Hawaiians. None of these factors seem to be substantiated. The first problem, sickness, was real until about 1900. There were some cases of Hansen's disease (leprosy) that frightened other Utahns when discovered. This was not a widespread problem, however, and it was certainly no worse than the situation in Hawaii. It is highly unlikely that the Hawaiians in Utah were any less healthy than their brothers and sisters at home. Mission records in Hawaii during the same years frequently mention worries about cholera, smallpox, and other diseases.

Nor were financial problems a significant reason for the settlement's closure. The company did not make a profit for its first eighteen years, but then it was a self-supporting institution that continued for another ten years. Some Hawaiians were unhappy during the early years because they were paid in goods from the company store or in script to use at the store. But even this was not a serious problem. When necessary, cash could be obtained by any worker, and once the company began to make a profit, in 1907, the employees were paid in cash. Another part of the financial situation was the continued acquisition of land. Land was purchased until 1915. By that time there were 5,273 acres in the ranch property. If the project had been failing financially it is doubtful that the directors would have approved these purchases. When the property was finally sold, it brought $175,000. The total amount spent for land had been $58,300. In the final analysis, in addition to paying the residents a fair wage, the company also made a fine profit.

The third reason that has been given for closing Iosepa is that the Hawaiians were unhappy there. The fact that the colony reached its greatest size, 228 people, in 1915 seems to discount this argument. It should also be pointed out that a large number of the inhabitants of Iosepa were born there. They did not miss Hawaii because they had

Hauling goods from Timpie Station, Utah, to the Hawaiian settlement of Iosepa. (Collection of John and Maggie Broad, courtesy Iosepa Historical Society)

Iosepa Orchestra members were: (seated l–r) George Alapa (face faded), second violinist; John E. Broad, orchestra leader; William Pukahi, cellist; (back row l–r) Moses Alapa, banjo; John Makakau, guitar; David Makuilima, guitar; Maggie K. Broad, vocalist; Abraham Nahulu, guitar; Henry K. Nawahine, Sr., ukulele; and John Kealoha Pauole, mandolin. (Collection of John and Maggie Broad, courtesy Iosepa Historical Society)

Presiding Bishop Charles W. Nibley and Church President Joseph F. Smith are seated left and right in the center of the front row. Elder Reed Smoot, an apostle and U.S. senator, stands between them on the back row. Samuel E. Woolley is on far right. Photo was taken in 1915 when President Smith dedicated the ground for the Hawaii Temple. (Courtesy LDS Church Archives)

The Hawaii Temple under construction, around 1918. (Courtesy BYU–Hawaii Archives)

The Hawaii Temple in 1922, three years after its dedication. The architects, Pope and Burton, were influenced by Frank Lloyd Wright. (Courtesy BYU–Hawaii Archives)

President Heber J. Grant's party arrives in Honolulu on 23 November 1919 for the dedication of the Hawaii Temple (l–r): Arthur Winter, Church financial secretary; Sarah Cannon, widow of George Q. Cannon; Rudger Clawson, second counselor in the First Presidency; Anthon H. Lund, first counselor in the First Presidency; President Grant; Charles W. Nibley, presiding bishop; and Stephen L. Richards, apostle. (Courtesy BYU–Hawaii Archives)

A group of Church dignitaries at the creation of Oahu Stake, 1935: (seated l–r) Sister Grant; President Heber J. Grant; Sister Clark; J. Reuben Clark, Jr., first counselor in the First Presidency; general board visitors Edith G. Young, Anna G. Midgley; Sister Richards; and Preston D. Richards; (standing l–r) Joseph Anderson, secretary to the First Presidency; Sister Musser; J. B. Musser; Olivia Waddoups; William Waddoups, Hawaii Temple president; Verna Murphy; Castle H. Murphy, Hawaiian Mission president; Romania Woolley; Ralph Woolley, Oahu Stake president; and his counselors, Edward L. Clissold and Arthur K. Parker. (Courtesy LDS Church Archives)

The Oahu Stake Tabernacle on Beretania Street, Honolulu, was dedicated in 1941. (Courtesy LDS Church Archives)

President Hilton A. Robertson of the Japanese Mission in Hawaii, center second row, sits among Japanese-American members, investigators, and missionaries in 1937 or 1938. (Courtesy LDS Church Archives)

Hawaii's Adney Y. Komatsu was the first person of Japanese ancestry to become a General Authority of the Church. (Courtesy LDS Church Public Communications)

Members of the Central Pacific Mission work at the welfare cannery shortly after World War II. (Courtesy LDS Church Archives)

Laie Elementary School, northeast of the temple, was the place where David O. McKay conceived the idea of a college in Laie. (Courtesy BYU–Hawaii Archives)

Breaking ground for the Church College of Hawaii were (l–r): D. Arthur Haycock, Hawaii Mission president; Clifford E. Young, assistant to the Council of the Twelve; Edward L. Clissold, Oahu Stake president; James Uale, Laie Ward bishop; President David O. McKay; George Kekauoha, counselor in the Oahu Stake presidency; Reuben D. Law, Church College of Hawaii president; Ralph E. Woolley, former Oahu Stake president; and Benjamin F. Bowring, Hawaii Temple president. (Courtesy BYU–Hawaii Archives)

This group of Tongan labor missionaries helped build later additions to the Church College of Hawaii campus. (Courtesy LDS Church Archives)

Entrance to the David O. McKay Building foyer, after the college's name was changed to Brigham Young University—Hawaii Campus in 1974. (Ron Safsten, 1989, BYU–Hawaii Publications Office)

Polynesian Cultural Center under construction, 1963. (BYU–Hawaii Archives)

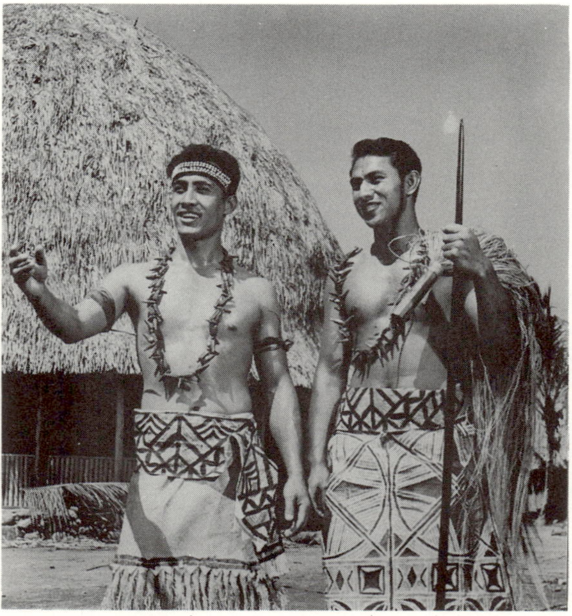

Students Vave Leauanae (l) and Eni Hunkin in Samoan village during the Polynesian Cultural Center's early days. (Courtesy BYU–Hawaii Archives)

never been there. Furthermore, most of the residents had grown to love their homes, their land, and their way of life at Iosepa.

The real reason for the closing of Iosepa was clearly the prospect of having a temple in Hawaii. If they returned home, they could seek out their genealogies and do vicarious ordinance work in the new temple. Many Iosepa Saints did contribute labor and financial resources to the temple when they returned.

When the Saints at Iosepa learned about the temple plans, they wondered what their role would or should be in the undertaking. President Smith was asked his opinion. His answer was that they were welcome to return to Hawaii or stay at Iosepa, whichever they desired. Many of the colonists wanted to go back to Hawaii and began making plans to return. The idea caught hold, gained momentum, and finally swept all but one family back to Hawaii. The Church bought their homes and property and even paid any expenses that could not be met by the Hawaiian Saints. The exodus began, and by early 1917 the last group had departed. The ranch was sold soon after.

FROM GROUNDBREAKING TO DEDICATION

Temples are the most sacred structures of the Latter-day Saints. Because its architecture must meet specific requirements, designing a temple is a demanding task. The firm of Hyrum E. Pope and Harold W. Burton was chosen to design the Hawaiian temple, the same architects who had designed the temple in Alberta, Canada, already under construction.

Pope and Burton evaluated the situation in Hawaii to determine the types of building materials available there. They discovered that few local materials could be used; however, there was an abundant supply of lava, which could be ground into aggregate for use in concrete. It was therefore decided to construct the entire building of concrete and steel.

How long the architects and First Presidency expected construction to take is not known. But President Woolley wanted the temple completed within a year from groundbreaking. It was not finished, however, until 15 July 1919, over three years from the official groundbreaking in early February 1916. Many difficulties were encountered in the construction process. First, a plant had to be built for crushing lava to use in the concrete. Then a foundation had to be dug through soil and coral to as deep as fifteen feet. After this the labor proceeded quite smoothly until the finishing work on the building began. Because of high humidity, particularly during the rainy season, a fungus or mildew that was very difficult to cope with grew on the canvas-covered walls of the interior. After nearly completing three rooms, the builders had to remove the canvas and treat the walls with a damp-proof preparation. This took considerable time. The interior construction work was finished by April 1918, but the fountains and gardens required more than another year to complete.

The principal people involved in the building process were Pope and Burton, architects; Ralph E. Woolley (son of President Woolley), construction supervisor; Leo and Avard Fairbanks, sculptors; and LeConte Stewart, the artist who painted the scenes in the various rooms. His work was not actually completed until July 1919.

Most of the materials in the building were brought from San Francisco, which caused frequent delays. Also, there were some problems finding skilled workmen for certain jobs. Care was taken to complete every detail in a first-class fashion. The end product was immediately recognized as the most beautiful structure in the islands. It can be said that the Hawaiian temple is a monolith, adorned with beautiful friezes and lovely fountains and gardens. It was early proclaimed by newspapers and public relations people to be the Taj Mahal of Hawaii.

Perhaps the delays were good for the Saints in Hawaii. The added time made it possible for them to raise their share of the $250,000 the building finally cost. They also had time to make the needed spiritual preparation before entering this sacred house.

The last year and a half before the temple was dedicated brought several changes in Church leadership. On 19 November 1918 President Joseph F. Smith passed away. The Saints in Hawaii were deeply saddened by his death. He, more than any living man, had been their advocate within the councils of the Church. Every active member of the Church in Hawaii had looked forward to the day when he would come among them again and dedicate the temple. He was succeeded by President Heber J. Grant, who dedicated the temple.

Two other changes occurred in Church leadership positions in Hawaii. In July 1918 President William M. Waddoups, then forty years old, who had been called as the first president of the new temple, arrived in Hawaii. He had maintained a close relationship with the Hawaiian Saints in Utah after completing his first mission in 1900–1903. He was called as an ordinance worker in the Salt Lake Temple in 1917 and was in this way prepared to direct the operation of the temple in Hawaii. He immediately began teaching the members how to prepare their genealogies and to understand the purposes of the temple. He toured the islands, holding training sessions and speaking in the mission branches.

A new mission president was also appointed, which came as a shock to some of the Saints. President Woolley had been in office so long that some members had been born, reared, educated, and married during his tenure. He too felt regret in having to relinquish his calling. Although he was released as mission president, he continued to manage the plantation until 1921 when Antoine R. Ivins was hired by the Church to handle that responsibility.

Woolley's replacement was E. Wesley Smith, a son of President Joseph F. Smith and his wife Julina. E. Wesley had been born at Laie on 2 April 1886. He filled a mission to Hawaii from 1907 to 1910. When he arrived in Honolulu on 25 June 1919 he established the mission headquarters in that city. Honolulu, now grown to a population of between forty-five and fifty-five thousand, was rapidly becoming the location of the greatest concentration of Mormons in the islands. It was also the most convenient place for transportation and other aspects of mission administration. From 1919 on, Honolulu and Laie became respectively the administrative and spiritual centers of the Church in Hawaii.

The Hawaii Temple was dedicated on 27 November 1919, Thanksgiving Day. Church President Grant had journeyed from Salt Lake City to preside at the services, accompanied by his counselors, Anthon H. Lund and Rudger Clawson. Other General Authorities of the Church present included Stephen L. Richards of the Quorum of the Twelve, Presiding Bishop Charles W. Nibley, and Elder Arthur Winter. Great preparations, both physical and spiritual, had been made for this most important of events in Hawaiian mission history. Grant expressed his deep personal regrets that President Smith could not be there to conduct the services. His dedicatory prayer was one of thanksgiving to the Lord for his mighty hand in caring for his Saints and restoring the gospel. He expressed gratitude to the Lord for George Q. Cannon, Joseph F. Smith, and Jonatana H. Napela. He gave thanks "that thousands and tens of thousands of the descendants of Lehi, in this favored land, have come to a knowledge of the gospel. . . ." He prayed that the way would be opened for the natives in Hawaii as well as in New Zealand and the other island groups of the Pacific to come to "this holy house and become saviors unto their ancestors."[11] On 2 December the temple was opened for baptismal work for the dead. Soon, within the week, the full services of its facilities were offered to worthy Saints.

The completion of the temple symbolized in many ways the ending of a major era of Church history in Hawaii. Joseph F. Smith, who represented the first generation of missionaries, was now gone. Samuel Woolley, who had worked so diligently to create a beautiful and productive Laie, had been released. The mission headquarters was now moved from

Laie to Honolulu, and a different kind of administration was about to begin.

Perhaps more than any other event, the death of Ma Manuhii represented the passing of the old era. She was a very old lady by 1919. She had taken care of Joseph F. Smith when he was deathly ill while serving his first mission in the 1850s. When he returned to the islands, he had shown his warm love for her, treating her as though she were his natal mother. Ma Manuhii was present at one of the five dedication services at the temple. Blind and unable to walk, she had to be carried. The week following the dedication, she was given the privilege of going through the temple and receiving her own endowments. Elder Wilford W. King, mission clerk, reported the touching event in this way:

> She had to be carried and helped all the way. While in the temple she testified she heard President Joseph F. Smith say "aloha" ("love to you") to her and it caused her to weep for joy.
>
> The next week she returned to her home in Honolulu and shortly after took sick. She called for Pres. E. Wesley Smith to come and see her. On his entering the room she sat up in bed and said, "Auhea ke keiki" (meaning "where is the boy?" the son of President Joseph F. Smith). President Smith took hold of her hand. She clasped it to her breast, kissed it and wept. Then she said in her own tongue, "It is enough, I am satisfied and ready to go now." She had been to the temple, a thing for which she had lived and she had now felt the hand of the son of the man she loved so much and she was ready to return to her Maker.[12]

Ma Manuhii passed away the next morning, 11 December 1919. With her passed an era of the history of the Church in Hawaii.[13]

–PART IV–

1920–1950

STEADY DEVELOPMENT

THROUGH

DIFFICULT TIMES

–11–

INSTITUTIONAL AND CULTURAL DEVELOPMENTS

THE NEW era signaled by the completion of the Hawaii Temple is reflected in the historical sources. Prior to 1920 missionaries felt they were adventurers in a foreign land. They wrote letters to the *Deseret News* and other Church periodicals giving the impression that the particular elder writing was the first to set foot in the exotic territory where he was now preaching the gospel. After 1920, however, communications from Hawaii became more matter-of-fact. Much space in Church periodicals continued to be devoted to Hawaii during the 1920s and 1930s, but the feeling that Hawaii was a primitive land was largely gone. Instead, missionaries reflected a new-found enchantment with an island paradise.

It is probably correct to say that the "aloha spirit," that is, the feeling of warmth, love, generosity, and kindness shown by the Hawaiian people toward visitors and friends alike, developed during the years when the temple was under construction. After that time Hawaiians are almost always referred to as kind, affectionate, and generous. LDS missionaries had previously expressed a love for a people who were naive, slow to harken, difficult to tutor, but very devoted if they happened to be in that phase of their frequently unstable emotional, social, and religious cycles. LDS perceptions of Hawaii and Hawaiians were not so different from those of other observers in the islands. It seems evident that the temple was built at an appropriate time in Hawaiian history. The territory was entering a new era of maturity. The Hawaiian people themselves had lived through the destruction of their way of life, and they were now in the process of finding a comfortable place in the new Hawaii of the twentieth century.

CHANGES IN THE HAWAII CHURCH

It was not the Hawaiians alone who were finding their place in Hawaii's economic and social system. Since the 1850s Chinese had inhabited the islands. In 1868 they were joined by laborers from Japan. Still later, Portuguese, Filipinos, Koreans, and a smattering of other racial and cultural groups were imported into the islands as plantation laborers, recruited by the Hawaiian Bureau of Immigration because of the inability of Hawaiians to adjust to farm discipline.

By 1900 Hawaiians represented only one fourth of the total population (see table 3). More impressive is the large percentage of Japanese among the islanders. It is understandable, yet to a degree regrettable, that the missionaries to Hawaii considered themselves called to teach primarily the Hawaiian people (interestingly, the first elders had thought themselves called only to the whites). As late as 1948 a mission president

TABLE 3 **Population of Hawaii, 1900–1940**

	1900	1910	1920	1930	1940
			Number		
Japanese	61,115	79,675	109,274	139,631	157,905
Caucasian	26,252	39,158	49,140	73,702	103,791
Hawaiian and Part-Hawaiian	38,254	38,547	41,750	50,860	64,310
Filipino	—	2,361	21,031	63,052	52,569
Chinese	25,762	21,674	23,507	27,179	28,774
Puerto Rican	—	4,890	5,602	6,671	8,296
Korean	—	4,533	4,950	6,461	6,851
Other	2,618	1,071	658	780	834
Total	154,001	191,909	255,912	368,336	423,330
			Percentage		
Japanese	39.7	41.5	42.7	37.9	37.3
Caucasian	17.1	20.4	19.3	20.0	24.5
Hawaiian and Part-Hawaiian	24.8	20.1	16.3	13.7	15.2
Filipino	—	1.2	8.2	17.1	12.4
Chinese	16.7	11.3	9.2	7.4	6.8
Puerto Rican	—	2.5	2.2	1.8	2.0
Korean	—	2.4	1.9	1.8	1.6
Other	1.7	.6	.2	.3	.2
Total	100.0	100.0	100.0	100.0	100.0

Source: Gerrit P. Judd IV, *Hawaii: An Informal History,* 132, 133.

encouraged his missionaries to put more effort into mastering the Hawaiian language. This notwithstanding, more could have been done to attract the Japanese before the 1930s, when serious efforts were made to proselyte them. The Church was known as a Hawaiian church, yet Hawaii no longer belonged to the Hawaiians.

Hawaiian mission records occasionally reported the baptism of a Japanese or, more frequently, a Chinese, before the turn of the century. Before the 1930s more Chinese converted to the Church than any other non-Hawaiian group, primarily because Chinese men occasionally married Hawaiian women and were then introduced to the Church. The Japanese usually married among themselves, frequently by obtaining mail-order picture brides. The first known Portuguese to enter the waters of baptism was Abraham Fernandez. He was actually half-Hawaiian, but was generally referred to as a Portuguese. Fernandez, a prominent Honolulu businessman and an active political figure during the reign of Liliuokalani, was a close friend and associate of the queen. He served the Church with all of his extensive resources. President Cannon stayed at his large home, as did President Joseph F. Smith. Fernandez served under President Woolley for many years as a member of the mission presidency. After his death in 1915 his wife continued the tradition of being the official host for the Church in Honolulu. President Grant spent time at her home when he visited Hawaii to dedicate the temple. Edward Fernandez, her son, was the first Hawaiian to attend and graduate from Brigham Young University.

In 1920 the Church in Hawaii was primarily Hawaiian, with a smattering of other peoples. But by 1950 the racial mixture had changed greatly. This happened for two primary reasons. First, the second generation, and in some cases the third generation, of Chinese and Japanese in Hawaii was becoming totally American. Those of the first generation still had strong ties to their native lands, but the children born in Hawaii were Americans: by 1930, 75 percent of the 139,631 Japanese in Hawaii had been born there. By the 1920s most people in Hawaii thought and acted somewhat like mainstream Americans. This fact made it possible for LDS missionaries to teach the gospel to these people in English.

The first recorded instance of proselyting among Hawaii's Japanese appears in the mission records of 12 October 1919: proselyting work had begun among the Japanese of Kauai. By the early 1930s Sunday School classes were being held in Japanese in Honolulu. In 1936 the Japanese Mission in Hawaii was organized. This development will subsequently be related in great detail.

The second reason for significant racial change in the Church between

1920 and 1950 was the influx, beginning in the 1920s, of a fairly large number of Samoans. They came to Hawaii to work in the temple, but for various reasons many chose to stay permanently.

Together these two processes—the expanded work among the Japanese and other Asian peoples and the immigration of Samoan members of the Church—transformed the racial composition of the Church in Hawaii.

The conclusion of World War I allowed more missionaries to enter the field than had been possible for several years. The Hawaiian Mission received an ample share of elders and sisters during most of the 1920s. The first six years averaged sixty-three missionaries per year; and from 1926 to 1930 there were usually fifty-one elders and sisters in the field. Church membership passed the fourteen thousand mark in 1926. Strangely, however, the number of members did not grow appreciably until after World War II. This is not easy to explain; however, two forces were involved during these years that made progress more difficult. In the 1930s the number of missionaries dropped to an average of thirty-three per year, for the Great Depression caused the number of missionaries to decline everywhere in the world. Again, Hawaii was subject to the same international forces affecting the rest of the Church. World War II brought about even more serious reductions. By late 1944 no young men were serving missions in the Pacific area. In that year the Hawaiian Mission was staffed by four older couples, one couple per island. This is not an entirely accurate picture, however, because a number of local part-time and full-time missionaries were called in Hawaii and they contributed to the growth of the Church. The foreign elders, however, ceased to come. Transportation to and from the islands was a critical problem once the war was underway.[1]

Another problem related to growth was the inaccuracy of Church records, particularly on the outer islands. During the late 1920s and again during the next decade, careful membership censuses were taken. In each survey it was discovered that many people had died, could not be found, or for some other reason should no longer be counted among the members of the Church. The worst discrepancy came to light in 1931, when it was found that 1,720 members could not be accounted for. Thus, in 1931 total membership stood at 12,735.

Migration also played a part in the reduction of the membership. In the late 1930s, but especially during the war years, many members left their homes on the outer islands to take jobs on Oahu. Those who were not active in the Church sometimes failed to become active in their new branches or wards after they moved. There was also some migration of members to the mainland.

Teaching the gospel in Hawaii during these years was not very different from teaching it in California or New York; the same methods were used. The missionaries seldom had set lesson plans to follow such as those that came into use after World War II. Tracting was a regular method of finding prospective investigators (potential converts). Often the missionaries found that it was too easy to spend time in the homes of the members. This was a problem in two ways. The Hawaiian members loved the elders. In many cases they felt deeply hurt if the missionaries insisted that they could not continue calling on them. On the other hand, the elders found it easy to fritter away their time learning to play the ukulele or listening to stories about the old days in the islands. It would be wrong to imply that a majority of the missionaries wasted their time in such pursuits, but the relatively high percentage of Latter-day Saints among the population made it fairly easy for missionaries to involve themselves in the nonreligious lives of baptized members.

After the temple was completed at Laie, many tourists visited there. A bureau of information was established for the distribution of tracts and other information to visitors. Different mission presidents held varying views of the information bureau. Most felt that a great missionary work was being performed there; in fact, it was sometimes considered the highest honor in the mission to be sent to the temple. In at least one instance, however, a mission president felt that he would rather have his missionaries doing active proselyting. In summary it can be said that the temple brought much acclaim to the Church in Hawaii, and it was a great aid to the missionary cause.

The methods used by the missionaries to spread the gospel changed to meet the circumstances of the times. Once in a while radio stations were used for special purposes, such as broadcasting tabernacle choir recordings or as a means of greeting an honored guest such as Church President Grant upon his arrival in Honolulu in 1935. Even though the special radio greeting was intended for Grant and his party, all of the islands were made aware of the Church through this means. Basketball teams were used to good advantage in making the public aware of the Church and its programs. The basketball program also brought many young people into the large Church amusement halls of the Honolulu area. The Mutual Improvement Associations (MIAs) appealed to young people, and many youths were brought into the Church through the athletic programs, drama, music, speech, and other activities of the MIAs.

After 1920 various mission presidents made frequent references in their reports to the honored place the Church held in the minds of most people in Hawaii. This was a change from the past, and it was also different from the attitude that existed in many other parts of the world during the 1920s and 1930s.

There were sixty-two branches and eight districts (previously called conferences) in the mission in 1929. Some of these branches were very small and were combined with other units as the decades passed. The movement of the branches was in the direction of consolidation more than division. As attempts were made to operate the branches in complete accord with the patterns suggested by the general boards of the various auxiliaries, it became evident that larger branches were often an advantage to Church members even if they had to travel greater distances to attend them.

The natural desire of the people to have the missionaries directly involved in their branch organizations was in conflict with the wishes of the mission presidents, who wanted to see the local Saints grow through holding offices. Several statements were made by mission presidents in their reports of the late 1920s, the mid-1930s, and again in the early 1940s to the effect that the missionaries were being pulled out of positions in the branches or districts, or that such action was planned for the near future. To the extent that this was accomplished, the local units benefited. It was recognized by mission presidents and adult local leaders alike that the young men who were serving as missionaries simply did not have the experience or the expertise of the mature Hawaiians and others who lived and served there.

Mission-owned homes were both a boon and a bane to the mission. They were a boon in the sense that they provided free housing to the missionaries. But they were also a bane because they were in most cases located near the branch chapels, and it was natural for the missionaries to act as resident pastors of a sort. They were generally available to branch members when help was needed or to give advice on how to organize a dance or other activity. This problem has persisted into the 1980s in some parts of the mission where new homes have been constructed to house missionaries. During the 1920s and most of the 1930s, most missionaries in the Honolulu area lived in one large mission home, along with the mission president and his family. This arrangement helped to develop fellowship but sometimes led to a spirit that was more like that of a fraternity house.

There was a desire among the Saints to operate the Church as nearly as possible according to the pattern of Salt Lake City. In addition to the regular effort made to teach the Saints about the basics of gospel life, the mission presidents and other leaders stressed the necessity of paying tithing and fast offerings. There was improvement in these areas almost every year during this entire period.

The Saints were organized into districts in much the same pattern that was followed in the stakes of Zion. In 1927 President Waddoups, who was temple president and mission president at the same time, organized mission boards and presidencies for all the auxiliaries—Sunday School, Relief Society, Primary, and Mutual Improvement Association. These boards traveled with their presidencies to the semiannual district conferences and directed, encouraged, and guided the efforts of the mission.

In 1928 the Laie District was combined with the Honolulu District. This paved the way for President Castle H. Murphy to organize the Oahu District Council at the all-mission conference of April 1931. Selected from members on the entire island of Oahu, the new district council was patterned after the high councils of the stakes of Zion (see appendix B). President Murphy was excited about the prospect of having a stake in Hawaii and predicted that the time would soon come when a stake would be organized.

What was good for Oahu was considered by President Murphy to be good for the outer islands as well. Within a few months after the Oahu District Council was organized, President Murphy established similar councils in each of the eight other districts of the mission. The time was definitely right for the Oahu council. Four years later, in June 1935, a stake was organized on Oahu. Because of the experience gained in the Oahu District Council, the change to a stake was fairly easy.

The period 1920–1940 was to some degree a time of transition. The older Hawaiians frequently understood little English or at any rate preferred to speak and read in the Hawaiian language. The young people, however, who had been schooled in English since childhood, had no interest in the Hawaiian language at all. This led to a problem in providing the right lesson materials for each group. Most of the classes and organizations were carried on entirely in English with materials provided from Salt Lake City. But it was still necessary as late as 1930 to provide translated lessons and instruction books for the older Hawaiians.

Closely related to the matter of lesson materials was that of proper management in the various auxiliaries. It was standard operating procedure for the mission president to tour the mission regularly to determine how organizations were functioning. Mission presidents frequently sent specialists, such as the mission president of the MIA, Sunday School, Primary, or Relief Society, to visit the districts and branches and "tune them up" by teaching proper methods and procedures. An example was a six-week mission tour of all MIA organizations made by Harry V. Brooks in the spring of 1930. Such tours were common to all the organizations through these years.

In their continuing effort to remain abreast of Church programs, the

Hawaiian Saints followed the counsel of the Church leaders in Utah when the welfare program of the Church was instituted in 1936 by planting papaya groves and taro patches and by storing goods and necessities for a time when they might be needed. They were needed and used during the early days of World War II, when even grocery stores were closed by military order.

Some efforts in the welfare area were undertaken during the war years, but in 1947 one of the most creative welfare projects anywhere in the world was begun. A monthly *hukilau* was held to attract visitors to Laie, but more particularly to raise money for a new chapel and later for welfare purposes. The term derives from the Hawaiian form of fishing in which people on the beach pull *(huki)* a fish net with leaves *(lau)* attached to it from the sea. Following this activity, in which the tourists participated, a Hawaiian dinner and program were presented. The hukilau brought a steady and considerable amount of money into the welfare savings of Laie. This project was continued well into the 1970s when it was eclipsed by the Polynesian Cultural Center and discontinued.

Visits by General Authorities and general board members became quite frequent during the years from 1920 to 1940. Each visit was a special spiritual occasion. The peoples of Hawaii, all of whom share the aloha spirit, withheld no effort to make these visits memorable for both themselves and their guests. In 1935 President J. Reuben Clark, Jr., of the First Presidency wrote these thought-provoking words concerning his visit, along with President Grant, to the islands:

> As one witnessed day after day and night after night among the Saints congregating together to meet him, the spontaneous upwelling and outpouring of their affections and reverence for President Grant, displayed as only people with deep feelings and great spirituality can show them, when their every word and look evidenced that to them President Grant was indeed the Prophet of the Lord, the Seer and the Revelator, one was shocked and saddened in the contemplation of how poor and destitute we Anglo–Saxons are in real depth of feeling, and how inhibited and niggardly we are in showing the feeling we have, in contrast with the overwhelming richness of the sentiment and emotion which the Hawaiians possess and with the understanding prodigality with which they shower these blessings upon others. Truly we feel little and show less; they feel much and show all.[2]

One of the high points among visits of the General Authorities was that of Elder David O. McKay and his traveling companion Hugh J. Cannon, a son of George Q. Cannon, in 1921. While in the islands

McKay was informed of the need many Church leaders felt for a Church academy, that is, a college. It was at this time, then, that the idea of a Church college for Hawaii was first considered by Elder McKay.

But the spiritual highlight of the visit was one in which only a few people participated. While on the island of Maui, McKay and the party visited Pulehu in the Kula district, where George Q. Cannon had baptized his first converts and organized the first branch of the Church in Hawaii in 1851. This was sacred ground to Elder McKay and the others present —Hugh J. Cannon, mission president E. Wesley Smith, Elder Samuel H. Hurst, and a Hawaiian elder, David Kailimai. President Smith recounted the event in these words:

> While there Elder McKay felt impressed with a desire to offer a prayer to the Lord in the spirit of thanksgiving for the privilege they had of being there, and for the many . . . who had embraced the Gospel. We bowed in prayer, Elder McKay being mouth. It was a moment never to be forgotten, for indeed the spot is sacred. Elder McKay said, "I feel certain that President Cannon and President [Joseph F.] Smith are near for the veil was very thin." Elder [Hugh J.] Cannon was deeply impressed, and with tears filling his eyes and in a choked voice said, "There was no veil."[3]

This incident was told to a group of assembled Saints at the Wailuku chapel that night, 8 February 1921. J. Pia Cockett, who later became one of the grand old men of the Church, wrote of the event in his notebook and added more details: "While he [Elder McKay] was praying, the Hawaiian Elder [David Kailimai] was privileged to see in a vision two hands clasped in the form of greeting. He thought Cannon and Hurst were shaking hands. He opened his eyes and saw they were apart. He closed his eyes again and after the prayer he told what he had seen. [At that point Elder McKay made the statement quoted above.]" For many years Elder Cockett was under the impression that the clasped hands of the vision were those of George Q. Cannon and his son, Hugh. But in 1936 on a subsequent visit to Hawaii the story was retold to President McKay. He corrected Cockett, saying, "Those hands were the hands of the two fathers, George Q. Cannon and Joseph F. Smith, in the presence of the two sons, Hugh J. Cannon and E. Wesley Smith."[4]

The site of the little chapel in Pulehu is still considered sacred ground. Perhaps this incident brought to the minds of the Hawaiian Saints the great labors of the early missionaries, especially those of George Q. Cannon. Late in the 1920s a monument was erected to mark the spot where these early events had taken place. On 26 October 1930 the Kula monument was dedicated by temple president William M. Waddoups, under the direction of mission president Castle H. Murphy. A bronze marker on the granite shaft tells its purpose.

The creation of the Oahu Stake in 1935 brought about more frequent visits by General Authorities. Before this their visits were occasional and according to special need. After June 1935 quarterly stake conferences necessitated four visits by General Authorities each year. It is impossible to document all visits of the Church leaders from Salt Lake City because they became so frequent. The Saints of Hawaii, however, looked forward to and appreciated every visitor as though he were the first.

Providing appropriate chapels and meeting facilities was a constant challenge for the mission presidents and the members. Chapels on the outer islands were seldom more than one-room, single-wall frame structures. Classrooms, if any, were usually small extensions on the side of or under the main hall. In most instances the chapel served for both worship and recreation. On MIA nights the benches were pulled back to the walls so that activities could take place. Some branches were not fortunate enough to have even such simple buildings. In some cases long established but small branches met in homes, borrowed halls, or rented facilities. As leaders became more conscious of the Church's image and became cognizant of the impossibility of providing the full Church program in makeshift chapels, a considerable amount of money and effort was put into chapel construction. During the 1920s the record was especially impressive. Three new chapels were completed in 1921, four in 1923, four in 1926, and seven small chapels were built in 1928.

The most impressive before 1940 was the Kalihi chapel in Honolulu. It was a large and commodious structure capable of holding several hundred people for meetings or conferences. It was a simple rectangle in shape, with a *lanai* (terrace) in front that served as a foyer and no spire. It had a meeting hall upstairs and classrooms and offices in the basement. The Kalihi chapel was constructed between 15 April 1922 and January 1923. President Anthony W. Ivins of the First Presidency dedicated the edifice on 3 August 1924. Over seventeen hundred people were in attendance on this special occasion. The Kalihi chapel was used until the early 1960s, when it was razed.

In 1925 an amusement hall, that is, a basketball gymnasium, was completed in Honolulu at a cost of twelve thousand dollars. Two years later a similar but smaller structure was completed in Hilo for six thousand dollars.

Construction slowed during the depression years. But in 1935 property was purchased at 1560 South Beretania Street in Honolulu. Six years later a new tabernacle was completed. It was impressive then and remains a beautiful architectural attraction. The tabernacle on Beretania Street, as it is generally referred to, did much to enhance the image of the Church both among members and nonmembers. It has often been called a temple by visitors to the islands. Nothing similar in size or appearance had been constructed by the Church in Honolulu before. Below its stately spire the concrete building included two chapels—one very large for stake conferences—a large hall for athletics and dramatic productions, numerous classrooms for Sunday School and other auxiliary meetings, and a baptismal font. Over the main chapel door was placed a large mosaic of the Savior with his arms outstretched as though to accept all peoples. An administration building, which also served as an information bureau, was situated on the grounds. A large home already on the property served as the mission home for a number of years.

This tabernacle was the headquarters for the Oahu Stake. The architects for the tabernacle were Hyrum Pope and Harold Burton, the same men who had designed the temple in Laie. Ralph E. Woolley, the stake president, was the contractor; he had supervised construction of the temple over twenty years before. The cost of the building was approximately $275,000, over $70,000 of which was raised by Hawaiian Saints. President David O. McKay, counselor in the First Presidency, dedicated it on 16 August 1941.[5]

Four months after the dedication of the tabernacle, the Japanese bombed Pearl Harbor. The war halted all subsequent building efforts until after the hostilities ceased in 1945.

LAIE AND THE PLANTATION

When E. Wesley Smith was called as mission president in 1919, the mission and the plantation were made separate responsibilities. Samuel E. Woolley remained plantation manager until May 1921, when Antoine R. Ivins was sent to Laie to preside. The plantation manager's responsibility was a secular one. The role the plantation had played in earlier history diminished to one of little significance. It was simply a business proposition that employed many Latter-day Saints. This is not to say that the Church suddenly turned its back on Laie and its people, but times were changing, and the concept of a gathering place was no longer stressed.

The Laie and Koolau plantations continued to expand over the years, by 1921 comprising 6,928 acres of land (789 of which were planted in sugarcane and 220 in pineapple); another 608 acres were leased, making a plantation of 7,634 acres. By Hawaiian standards this was still a fairly small operation.[6]

The plantation could not hold its own in the world sugar market, and by 1927 it was falling into debt. In an effort to recover its losses, Ivins decided to sell some beachfront property. But the $275,000 brought in by this sale failed to meet the plantation debts and the sale also angered some Laie old-timers, who did not believe the Zion's Securities Corporation, set up by President Grant in 1922 to manage all nonreligious properties of the Church, had the right to sell the land. Apparently some of Laie's residents did not believe that any property could be sold without their approval. The impression had grown that the land belonged to the people who lived on it, or at least that they had a right to direct its use. This was proved to be incorrect in a court case brought before the land court of the Territory of Hawaii, which was decided in favor of Zion's Securities Corporation on 28 February 1928.[7]

Economic problems continued for the plantation until 1931, when Ivins entered into a lease arrangement with the Kahuku Plantation Company to have it take over all the sugar lands. This arrangement was renewed from time to time down to the late 1960s. Essentially, in 1931 the Church got out of the management end of the sugar business. After Ivins' release to become a General Authority of the Church in 1931, several others managed the residential portions of Laie. The Church still maintains control of a major portion of Laie, but has not assumed the responsibility to provide employment for the Saints of Laie since that time.

One other institution passed from Church control during this time. The elementary school in Laie had been the pride of the mission for many years. Many missionaries had taught school there, most of them sisters during the later years. In 1927, however, the territorial government was given control of the institution. Church leaders determined that missionaries could better spend their time in full-time proselyting. Furthermore, the territory had sufficient money available to pay the cost of educating Laie's children.

THE SAMOAN MIGRATION TO LAIE

Another change in Laie was the growth of a small settlement of Samoans. The Samoan Mission, officially founded in 1888 (but unofficially in 1863 by two missionaries sent by Walter Murray Gibson), had grown to 2,647 members in 1920. The precise date of the first pilgrimage of a Samoan

Saint to the Hawaii Temple is not known. As early as 1922, however, President E. Wesley Smith noted in his yearly report the presence of one Samoan family living in Laie. A year later President Eugene J. Neff, the new mission president, noted that "a number of Samoan Saints have immigrated to Hawaii. . . ." He found it necessary to create a Samoan society "in order to keep them together and active in Church work."[8] After 1923 it is difficult to trace the development of the Samoan community. However, by 1929 there were 125 Samoans living in Laie. How many lived elsewhere, if any, is not known. Although 125 people seems a relatively small number, it was approximately 24 percent of Laie's 1930 population of 521.

Apparently the Samoan population in Hawaii did not grow during the depression years or during World War II. After 1951, because of an unusual arrangement with the U.S. government—which made it possible for American Samoans to travel to Hawaii free of charge on one voyage of the U.S.S. *President Jackson*—the population grew quickly again. Residents of American Samoa, a U.S. territory since 1899, were U.S. nationals, but not citizens. This rapid influx brought the permanent Samoan population of Laie to around three hundred in 1955.[9]

As implied above, the main attraction of Laie for Samoans was the temple. Hawaii also offered a more pleasant, perhaps even more luxurious way of life than Western or American Samoa. When migrants came, they cooperated to help bring other members of their families to the Hawaiian mecca. This phenomenon was strongly discouraged by most presidents of the Samoan Mission.

Once in Hawaii, Samoans found work on the Laie plantation or did whatever labor they could find. During World War II they found work in various war-related installations. The Samoan tradition of family ownership and cooperation has been both a help and a hindrance to them in adapting to an American setting. In Samoa almost nothing belongs to any individual, and the Western idea of personal property was difficult for many Samoans to grasp. Non-Samoans in many cases have been angered by the casual lack of respect shown for personal property. Even legal problems sometimes occurred.

Cultural adjustments notwithstanding, the Samoan Saints have added greatly to the Church in Hawaii. They, like the true Hawaiians, are full of the aloha spirit.

–12–

THE JAPANESE MISSION

THE 1930s and 1940s were difficult times for the Pacific missions of the Church. The Great Depression brought financial problems for many members and reduced the number of missionaries. In Hawaii, though, changes were underway that lifted spirits, as the first stake outside continental North America was organized. And missionary work among Hawaii's Japanese and Chinese began in earnest, resulting in a mission among island Japanese. The creation of that mission helped form a bridge for further missionary work in Japan following World War II.

THE OAHU STAKE

Halfway through this period, President Heber J. Grant organized the Oahu Stake. Today this seems a small matter, considering the present rapid growth of the Church, but in the 1930s the creation of a new stake was a matter of some weight and concern to the highest councils of the Church.

Perhaps the most serious question concerning the proposed Oahu Stake was whether the mission and a stake would each have sufficient workers to succeed after a division took place. The General Authorities surveyed the Church to find a precedent for a stake and mission operating in the same area and found a similar case in California where the mission and the stakes created there were able to work effectively. On 20 November 1934, the First Presidency wrote to Hawaiian Mission President Castle H. Murphy to find out his feelings on the matter. They told him the idea had been discussed for over a year among members of the First Presidency and Quorum of the Twelve and they agreed that a stake should be organized in the islands.[1]

Murphy was elated by the suggestion, for he had worked steadily in that direction ever since 1931. By 1934 he had placed the mission firmly on a stakelike basis. He was sure Hawaii was ready for a stake and told the First Presidency so.

On 20 June 1935 President Heber J. Grant, J. Reuben Clark, Jr., first counselor in the First Presidency, and a number of other dignitaries were welcomed to Hawaii with one of the most lavish greetings the Hawaiians had yet mustered. Music, leis, feasts, tears, and laughter blended into a spiritual occasion still remembered by many *kamaainas* (old timers) today. Ten days later, 30 June 1935, after the First Presidency and their party had visited Kauai, Molokai, Maui, and Hawaii, a special conference was held. That was an important day not only in Hawaii but also throughout the Church. The new unit was named the Oahu Stake. The first stake to be organized outside continental North America, it signaled the continuing expansion of the Church beyond the confines of the Mountain West.

The first stake president was Ralph E. Woolley. The son of Samuel E. Woolley, he had spent most of his life in the islands and before that among the Hawaiian Saints at Iosepa colony. He selected as his counselors Edward L. Clissold and Arthur K. Parker. Clissold was a former Hawaii missionary who had been living in Honolulu for the previous ten years. Parker, a native Hawaiian, was a local member.

The progress of the Church in Hawaii pleased President Grant greatly. He and President Clark believed that after eighty-five years of experience in the Church, "the Hawaiians had earned the right to the gift of a greater power and fuller local responsibility in the administration of Church activities upon the islands."[2] It was a source of deep satisfaction to them that the distribution of Church offices among various racial groups in the new stake, in the wards and branches, "was essentially proportionate to their relative numbers." This was a matter of particular concern to Grant for he felt the Hawaiians were entitled to a large share of the callings both because of their numbers and because of their long years of faithfulness and training. In addition, he was cognizant of their blessings as descendants of Lehi. In Clark's words, "the organization of the Oahu Stake gave the opportunity to demonstrate that in the Church . . . all who are entitled to the Priesthood, without distinction to race or color, stand on an equality." President Grant also believed that the organization of the stake would have an "almost coercive effect upon the launching of the Gospel in the Eastern hemisphere."[3]

THE CENTRAL PACIFIC MISSION

President Grant was no stranger to the peoples of Asia. In 1901 he and several other missionaries opened Japan to the preaching of the restored gospel. Although he remained in Japan for several years, it was not a totally satisfactory experience for him. He was diligent in studying the language and worked at acquiring a taste for Japanese food. But, because of the slow progress of the mission, Grant did not leave Japan with the feeling of satisfaction that missionaries, and especially apostles of the Lord, wish to have.

Over the years Grant observed the snail-like progress of the mission in Japan. Although many elders and sisters served there, after twenty-three years only 176 baptisms had been performed. Relations between the United States and Japan were strained in 1924 when the Oriental Exclusion Law was passed. This, in addition to many other difficulties, finally made it advisable for Grant, now president of the Church, to close the mission. He considered it a temporary measure and did not feel comfortable with the action. Nevertheless, Japanese ultranationalism in the 1930s and World War II proved his decision to be a wise one.[4]

When President Grant arrived in Hawaii to organize a stake on Oahu, he was introduced to nine Hawaii Japanese, generally called Americans of Japanese ancestry (AJAs), who had been baptized members of the Church the day before. Brother Edward L. Clissold, then a member of the district council who was working closely with the Japanese Sunday School, asked President Grant to confirm these people members of the Church. Afterward, he said he had not confirmed so many Japanese during his entire mission in Japan.[5]

President Grant's entire Hawaiian experience seemed to point him toward the conclusion that work had to be seriously undertaken among the Japanese and other Asians in Hawaii. The Japanese members in Honolulu hosted a beautiful dinner for him, as did the Japanese at Laie. The president was told of the various ethnic Sabbath schools in Honolulu, but the Japanese organization, which held all of its meetings in the Japanese language, seemed to impress him most. The organization of both the Japanese and Chinese Sunday Schools had resulted from the inspiration of Castle H. Murphy. He called Clissold and Elwood L. Christensen to work with these special units of the church. Both Grant and Clark had prophetic visions of the role Hawaii was to play in the expansion of the Church into Asia. President Clark wrote,

> . . . it would seem not improbable that Hawaii is the most favorable place for the Church to make its next effort to preach the Gospel to the Japanese people; and it would further appear that a strong colony of Japanese Saints in Hawaii could operate from there into their homeland in a way that might bring many Japanese to a knowledge not only of Christianity, but of the restored Gospel. There are evidences that the fields are ripening; if so, they will be ready sooner or later for the harvest to begin.[6]

The same reasoning was applied to the Chinese, Filipinos, and East Indians of Hawaii. To a remarkable degree this vision of things to come has been fulfilled.

At the time of Clark's statement, a number of AJAs were maturing in various parts of the islands. Among those not yet touched by the gospel were Adney Y. Komatsu, later to become the first AJA mission president and then a General Authority of the Church; among other mission presidents to Japan would be Tomosue Abo, Kenji Akagi, Russell N. Horiuchi, Kotaro Koizumi, William Nako, Arthur Nishimoto, Edward Okazaki, Ray Sasaki, Satoru Sato, Ralph Shino, and Walter Teruya. Many other Hawaii Japanese have served in Japan as missionaries.

While President Grant was in the islands, he talked with mission president Murphy and others about reopening the Japanese Mission in Hawaii. Over a year passed, and then, in November 1936, Hilton A. Robertson and his wife Hazel, both of whom had served missions in Japan (he was mission president when the mission closed), were called to open the Japanese Mission in Hawaii. They arrived in Honolulu on 24 February 1937.

The following Sunday the Robertsons met with the little band of Japanese Saints and investigators (those studying the restored gospel). Among the thirty-five people present was Isune Nachie, now very old, who had joined the Church in Japan prior to the mission's closure. She came to Hawaii in 1923 to do temple work, living at Laie most of this time. Edward L. Clissold described her as a true Saint. Also there were Dr. Tomizo Katsunuma, who had been converted to the Church while attending Utah State University (the Utah Agricultural College), and Kay Ikegami, who proved to be a faithful leader. At the time of the Robertsons' arrival the Japanese group was only holding Sunday School. The first Sunday in March they began to hold sacrament meetings. From that time on steady progress was made toward instituting the full program of the Church.

The first three missionaries to the Japanese Mission in Hawaii arrived in October 1937. They were Melvyn A. Weenig, Preston D. Evans, and Roy W. Spear. Weenig was later called as mission president in 1946. By the end of the first year the total membership of the mission was seventeen, nine men and eight women; but four converts had been baptized and a good beginning made. The number of missionaries increased fairly rapidly after 1937, and the number of members began to rise steadily as well (see table 4). During 1938 work was expanded to the Big Island of Hawaii, and in January and February 1939 to Maui and Kauai, respectively. From the beginning the greatest success came among the young

AJAs. The older generation, who still thought in Buddhist and Shinto terms and spoke mostly Japanese, never did join the Church in significant numbers. Sunday Schools, Primaries, and MIAs were organized wherever the missionaries worked. The first Japanese Primary in Honolulu had a regular attendance of over a hundred children before the end of 1938. Boy Scout troops were very successful in Honolulu and Hilo.

During the entire duration of the mission, elders and sisters were encouraged to learn the Japanese language. In retrospect this seems almost unnecessary since nearly all converts were young people, but it was considered wise at the time. The hope was that when the youths had been influenced by the missionaries, they would want to introduce them to their parents. An ability to speak Japanese would help to influence the older people, if only to convince them that their children should become Latter-day Saints.

Another reason for learning Japanese was the hope that the Japanese Mission in Hawaii would some day become the base of operations for the reopening of Japan. Although this did not happen, the missionaries of Hawaii did teach Japanese to the first missionaries called to reopen Japan. In 1948, while waiting for permission to enter Japan, five elders studied the Japanese language on Oahu under the tutelage of Paul V. Hyer and a companion, both of whom had learned to speak Japanese while missionaries in Hawaii.

TABLE 4 **Growth Patterns, Japanese / Central Pacific Mission**

Year	Missionaries	Baptisms	Total Membership
1937	5	4	17
1938	19	13	30
1939	32	26	60
1940	54	37	101
1941	55	48	150
1942	18	156	302
1943	13	72	375
1944	7	48	437
1945	4	34	484
1946	34	30	522
1947	66	15	532
1948	89	52	604
1949	77	67	671

Source: Adapted from J. Christopher Conkling, "Members Without a Church," 210. Conkling's data are from Mission Financial and Statistical Reports, Hawaiian Mission, 1937–1948; I have added data for 1949.

The Robertsons were released in September 1940, and Jay C. Jensen and his wife were called to direct the work. Jensen had been a missionary in Japan during the early mission. He continued the patterns of proselyting established by the Robertsons.

As the missionary force increased, it became necessary to coordinate the work of the Japanese Mission, the Hawaiian Mission, and the Oahu Stake. Guidelines were established to avoid duplication and interference, so that when elders of the Hawaiian Mission contacted AJAs interested in the Church, they could be smoothly transferred to the care of the Japanese Mission, and vice versa. Mission president Jensen wrote, "Racial lines are being forgotten and we are all bearing our testimonies every time we can regardless of race and are trying to break down what prejudice there may be. Such an attitude means greater success in future work."[7] Jensen fell ill with a malignant tumor during the latter part of 1942. He left the mission field on 13 December, and died in Utah early in 1943. But before he was released, he saw a period of tremendous growth. Several factors came together to produce the large number of baptisms performed in 1942.

On 7 December 1941, Pearl Harbor was bombed by Japan. Although Pearl Harbor was severely damaged, the rest of the islands were virtually untouched—physically at least. As a result of the Japanese attack thousands of AJAs in California and Oregon were immediately suspected of disloyalty to the United States. They were eventually placed in internment camps in California, Utah, Wyoming, Arizona, and elsewhere. This action caused great loss of property and earning power during the war years. The pathetic truth, however, was that almost no Japanese in America were guilty of sabotage or other disloyal activities.

In Hawaii it would have been impossible to place all AJAs under arrest because they were the largest racial group in the islands. Nevertheless, there were incidents of open character assassination and verbal abuse directed toward the Hawaii Japanese. This notwithstanding, the older Japanese proved to be intensely loyal to the United States, and no cases of sabotage were ever detected among them; the young people had never known another home and considered themselves Americans. This was their home; they loved Hawaii and the United States.

The AJAs in Hawaii proved their loyalty through service in war plants, at war installations, and in many other ways. The most decorated combat units of the entire war were the famous 100th Infantry Battalion and the 442nd Regimental Combat Team. Both were made up entirely of Americans of Japanese ancestry, most of whom were from Hawaii. But those who had to stay home also wanted to show that they were real Americans. Statistically all churches of Hawaii grew during the war. Many of the new members were AJAs. This does not discount the validity of their conversions. They, like many others, found themselves turning more to religion in a time of trouble. It is fortunate that the LDS Church had developed an organization ready to benefit from this new interest. As can be seen in table 4, the Japanese Mission membership more than doubled during 1942, the first year of the war.

Another factor may have contributed to the rapid growth of the Church during 1942. The missionaries were going home, and no new elders were on their way to replace them. It is probable that the missionaries put more pressure on their prospective converts to make the decision to be baptized than they might have done otherwise. Whatever the reasons, the number of converts expanded rapidly during 1942 and continued to grow throughout the war, even though the missionary force was greatly diminished.

Edward L. Clissold, first counselor in the Oahu Stake presidency, was called to replace President Jensen. He remained acting president until 1944, when his assignment as a naval reserve officer took him away from Hawaii. He was also temple president during these years.

One of the first changes President Clissold made was the name of the mission. Because the term "Japanese" was held in derision, Clissold felt that a more innocuous name would benefit the image of the mission; thus it became known as the Central Pacific Mission (CPM), from 1943 until the Japanese and Hawaii missions were combined in 1950.

By the end of 1942 the missionary force had dropped to eighteen (see table 4). Over the next three years the number plunged to thirteen, seven, and finally four full-time missionaries from outside the field. Clissold had to encourage the Japanese members to combine with the long-established branches. In 1944 Castle Murphy was again called to Hawaii, this time to act simultaneously as president of the Hawaiian Mission, the Central Pacific Mission, and the Hawaii Temple. He knew Hawaii better than almost any other man in the Church and was thus well prepared to handle the responsibilities placed upon him. Murphy called local missionaries into service; in 1945 there were twelve full-time and nineteen part-time missionaries called from among the members in Hawaii. He organized councils among the Japanese members on each island and in this way placed much of the responsibility for their branches upon them.

The conclusion of the war brought marked changes to the mission. In 1946 Melvyn A. Weenig and his wife were called to preside over the CPM, and before the year was over there were forty-five missionaries serving the mission. But Weenig felt he needed at least seventy-five missionaries to accomplish all that could be done in the mission. Over the next two years the mission force increased, although the number of baptisms did not grow accordingly. Weenig noted a change in the attitude of AJAs toward Christian churches: there seemed to be a shift back toward things Japanese. Perhaps with the passing of the war crisis there was simply a reversion to earlier social and religious patterns. But even though the number of converts did not grow rapidly after the war, the AJA converts of earlier times remained loyal. They were total converts to the gospel and were assuming responsible positions in their own branches and districts. An indication of the strength of the Japanese members was their faithfulness in paying tithing. According to J. Christopher Conkling, they "were the most faithful [Saints] in the world." He writes, "In 1945, for example, over 97% were tithe payers, which compares with only 61% paid in the non-Japanese Hawaiian Mission, and less elsewhere [in the world]."[8]

President Weenig was an enthusiastic leader. Shortly after he arrived in Hawaii, he recognized that little was being done in the welfare program of the Church. Although missions were not required to have welfare projects, he wanted to encourage welfare work and decided to build a cannery. He directed the construction of the cannery on the tabernacle grounds on Beretania Street. When the factory was ready to operate, Weenig led his Saints into the pineapple fields to glean what was left behind. Other foods were also preserved at the cannery. In this way he not only taught members of the CPM about welfare but also taught all the Saints of Hawaii and some nonmembers as well.[9]

One of the aspirations of Weenig and his missionaries was to establish a mission in Japan. They saw themselves as a force that could move into Japan when the time was right. This, however, did not prove to be the destiny of the CPM. It was the source of many missionaries who were called to Japan—in fact, eight were recommended in 1948—but it turned out to be only a training ground for the Church's preparations to work in Japan again. If matters had developed differently, it is probable that Weenig would have had a larger role to play in Japan.

What did develop was that Edward L. Clissold was assigned to Japan as a member of the occupation forces at the end of the war. When he returned to Hawaii in 1946, he reported to Church president McKay concerning the missionary work of the LDS servicemen among the Japanese. In 1948 it was decided that Clissold and Weenig should go to Japan together, but because of restrictions set up by the occupation forces, only one man could be sent. Clissold was already familiar with conditions in Japan and knew many of the important men it would be necessary to work with; thus it was decided that he would be the man to reopen the mission in Japan. He was sent there in the spring of 1948. The story of the Church's growth there must be told elsewhere. Suffice it to say that by 1987 there were eighty-five thousand church members there.

WORLD WAR II AND THE CHURCH IN HAWAII

It was several years after the beginning of World War II in Europe that its direct effects were felt in Hawaii. The leaders of the Church in Salt Lake City were much concerned about the war and watched its development carefully. In October 1940 the First Presidency ordered all LDS missionaries home from New Zealand, French Polynesia, Tonga, Samoa, and Australia. Some were transferred to the Hawaiian Mission. In fact, there was a sudden increase in missionary numbers from 58 in 1939 to 85 by the end of 1940. But in the years that followed, the number decreased to 67, 31, 15, and finally a low of 5 missionaries in 1944. By the end of 1945, however, the number of missionaries had increased to 16. In 1946 it jumped to 51, and by the end of 1949 there were 98 in the field. The great increase in 1946 and the years following of course reflects the conclusion of the war and the availability of young men to fill missions.

With the exception of the loss of the full-time foreign missionaries and the more restricted way of life, the war did not significantly slow down the Church's progress in Hawaii. Because of military restrictions, no Church meetings were held during January and part of February 1942. After that there were blackouts for a time that made night meetings impossible, but for the greater part of the war the Church was able to carry on as usual. A curfew hampered evening activities for a while, but even this restriction was short-lived.

Most of the Saints prospered financially during the war. The large military installations created work even for the unskilled. The migrations of the prewar years continued, but at a faster pace. The outer islands lost members to Oahu. In 1945, for example, 653 Saints moved to Oahu from the outer islands. In 1942 President Eldred L. Waldron of the Hawaiian Mission reported that tithing and fast offering contributions were up more than 100 percent over the previous year. Such contributions continued to rise during the war years but dropped in 1949 when war industries diminished in number.

Not only did financial contributions increase, but temple activities grew as well. Excursions were planned, and Saints were brought from the outer islands as well as from Oahu. In an effort to strengthen the young people against temptations introduced into Hawaii as a result of the war, a series of youth conferences was held on Oahu and on the outer islands. Here the young people were encouraged to remain close to their parents and avoid the evils of the day.

The Church cooperated with the war effort by leasing the two large amusement halls in Honolulu to war agencies. Concerning the contribution of the Church to the war effort, President Waldron wrote:

> Our church gained great respect from the military and the government officials in Hawaii at the time of Pearl Harbor for we were prepared to render much needed aid. In the organization of Civil Defense, our priesthood quorums and missionaries gave needed assistance. Our Boy Scouts worked in the vital communication system, and the Relief Society helped the Red Cross care for the wounded and sewed and rolled bandages for the hospitals.[10]

The missionaries made a significant contribution to the defense effort. A special historical issue of *Ka Elele O Hawaii,* titled "Hawaiian Mission Review" and published in late 1942, contained a number of photographs of missionaries on police patrol and acting as air-raid wardens, communications operators, fingerprinting specialists, and gas-mask instructors. Others were assigned to guard duty. The editors wrote:

> Our elders were pressed into service as policemen, armed guards on vital bridges and highways, communications operators to send and receive important military messages, air-raid wardens, first-aid instructors, observation-post watchmen, ship-charters, and grave diggers. Many missionaries were donating as much as eighteen hours a day to emergency duty! Even today, after a year of warfare, many missionaries are still taking their regular turns at the switchboards of "Communication Headquarters." Others are permanent "Block Wardens," assigned to check on blackout restrictions, to keep track of all people living within certain districts, and to go into active duty in case of air-raid alarm.[11]

The Church also stressed the welfare program and "victory gardens" as means of better caring for the needs of the people.

The war brought hundreds of LDS servicemen and women to the islands, who not only participated in the activities of the Church but also contributed to its operation in many ways. No special programs were needed for them; they simply attended the regular wards and branches of the Oahu Stake or branches of the mission. One special facility, however, was prepared for the service personnel. A large home located on a lot adjoining the new tabernacle became a recreation and rest center for LDS service people and their friends. The place was named Malamakoa, meaning "take care of the soldier." In addition to recreational and inspirational facilities, there were rooms for sleeping.

One important result of the war was the calling of more local people to hold responsible positions in the Church. By 1944 virtually all positions were held by permanent residents of Hawaii. Thus, many good Saints were given the opportunity to develop leadership skills.

Although World War II was a trying experience for the Saints of Hawaii, it was not an unhappy time from a spiritual point of view. Many people grew because they were given new or greater responsibilities and because of their efforts to serve one another. The servicemen and women helped local Saints to realize that it was possible to be in the world and not of it. Together the Saints moved forward during a time when degeneration could have taken place.

THE END OF THE ERA

In May 1947 Castle and Verna Murphy were released from their fourth and last mission to Hawaii. They had begun their service in Hawaii in 1909 and had served over fifteen years as missionaries, mission president and mission mother, temple president and matron, and as friends of the people of Hawaii. Their service stands as an example of the selfless devotion of LDS members to their fellow men.

The man who replaced President Murphy was E. Wesley Smith, who as mission president had begun this era of missionary and Church history. Once again while he presided, the number of missionaries grew rapidly, emphasis on active missionary work was reinforced, and the number of convert baptisms increased. By 1950 Hawaii was well into a new phase of its history, and the Church was ready for an important transition as well.

The need for a separate Japanese mission in Hawaii was questioned in 1948. Church leaders finally decided that, considering the general compatibility of all the peoples of Hawaii and the fact that virtually everyone could speak English, the Hawaiian Mission and the Central Pacific Mission should be combined into a new entity, the Hawaii Mission. The name was to denote its geographical location, not a particular race of people. The merger took place on 1 April 1950. Edward L. Clissold was called as acting mission president during the transition. At Clissold's request, Ernest A. Nelson, a missionary companion of Clissold's many years before, was called from Salt Lake City to act as first counselor. He served in some capacities as mission president and was soon called as president of the mission.

The actual consolidation of the two missions on the outer islands took a little over two months to effect, but it was completed by June. In President Clissold's words, "Many of the districts and branches were reorganized with the members of both former missions being represented in the officer and teacher assignments of the new mission." The consolidation process did not take place on Oahu until 10 December, when a combined Oahu Stake–Hawaii Mission conference occurred in Honolulu. At that time the merger of all mission branches on Oahu with the stake was announced. Also, the jurisdictional boundaries of the stake and mission were explained to the members of the Church. The Oahu Stake was to take charge of all Church organizations and units on Oahu; the mission would be responsible for the outer islands.[12]

December 1950 marked the centennial of the Hawaiian mission. The ceremonies and festivities celebrating this event, however, had been held the previous August when President George Albert Smith visited Hawaii. They included a pageant, feasts, and much rejoicing in song and dance. Newspapers and special programs recounted the accomplishments of the Church in the islands. Marvelous progress had been made during the Church's first hundred years.

–PART V–

1950–1987

FULFILLMENT

IN THE

CONTEMPORARY WORLD

–13–

NEW STAKES AND THE DEVELOPMENT OF RELIGIOUS EDUCATION

IN 1951 Ralph E. Woolley was released as stake president after having served for sixteen years. Edward L. Clissold was called as his replacement. Few stake presidents in the Church have assumed the office with as many years of administrative experience as Clissold brought to the post. His knowledge was much needed during the next two decades. Although Clissold served as stake president for twelve years, he did not give up some of his important Church assignments until he returned to his home in Salt Lake City in 1970.

Woolley had been faced with many problems during his tenure. Under the mission, the Hawaiian Saints had never been given the responsibility for their own Church financial affairs. Because he was concerned about the accuracy of the tithing and other financial reports and records, Woolley decided to handle all financial matters in the Oahu Stake on a stake level. This remained the practice until 1951, when he was released.

When President Clissold was called to preside, he, his counselors, and the stake high council concluded that the Saints within the stake had made sufficient progress in administrative matters to be given the financial responsibilities as well as all other parts of their stewardships. By placing the tithing and budget records in the hands of the bishops, the stake leaders helped to teach many men the order of the Church.

Not long after he became president, Brother Clissold observed another problem in his stake: a concentration of leadership in the Waikiki Ward at the expense of other wards and branches. World War II had brought many haole servicemen and women from the mainland to Hawaii. The number of haole Church members, probably only 150 or 200 before the war, increased rapidly during and after the war, and many of them gravitated to the Waikiki Ward even if they lived elsewhere on Oahu. Because this situation developed over several years, it had not been considered a serious problem. President Clissold, his counselors, and the stake high council, however, recognized that a large share of the most experienced leaders and potential leaders of the stake were concentrated in one ward. To eliminate the problem they asked all members to attend the wards in which they lived. This suggestion, however, was not well accepted by some haole members of the stake. The problem was ultimately solved when Elder Marion G. Romney visited the stake for quarterly conference and asked the Saints to follow the order of the Church. Most haole members followed the counsel of the Church leaders, but a few persisted in attending Waikiki Ward at least into the 1970s even though they lived outside the boundaries of the ward.

During the 1950s a number of Americans of Japanese ancestry emerged as important Church leaders in Hawaii. Many had been too young to assume major leadership responsibilities before this time, but after 1950 they became more conspicuous in bishoprics and high councils. The same was true of Hawaii's Chinese. Thus the Church began to move ahead at a desirable pace, at least on Oahu. All the programs of the Church were being followed according to the patterns and instructions of the leaders in Salt Lake City.[1]

When President Clissold was sustained in his calling, there were sixteen wards and branches and nearly eleven thousand members in Oahu Stake. After only four more years it was time to divide the stake again. Clissold wanted three stakes, but the General Authorities suggested a single division for the time being and the creation of a third stake later. On 28 August 1955 the Honolulu Stake was organized, with Bishop Jay A. Qualey, Jr., as the first president. Continued progress and expansion made it possible to reorganize once again on 4 February 1962, forming the Pearl Harbor (presently the Honolulu Hawaii West) Stake with George Q. Cannon as stake president. He had formerly been a member of the Hawaii Mission presidency.

The development of stakes in Hawaii since 1962 has been steady, with ten stakes organized since that time. The Hilo Stake, the first one on an outer island, was organized on 15 December 1968, with Rex Alton Cheney as its first president. On 21 November 1971, Robert H. Finlayson was called to preside over the newly organized Kaneohe Hawaii Stake on Oahu. Pearl Harbor West, now the Waipahu Hawaii Stake, followed on 20 February 1972, with William E. Fuhrimann as president.

Perhaps the greatest success story of all is that of the Kona Hawaii Stake. Its organization on 24 November 1974 proved that even the most underdeveloped areas of the islands could become recipients of all the blessings of the Church. The president of the new Kona stake was Haven

J. Stringham. The organization of stakes on Maui and Kauai symbolized the further development of local leadership. The Kahului Hawaii Stake was created 9 November 1975, with Evan A. Larsen, a Church construction supervisor, as president. This occurred almost exactly 125 years after George Q. Cannon and his companions first began teaching the gospel on Maui. With the creation of the Kauai Hawaii Stake, organized 24 July 1977 with Garner W. Wood as the first president, all of the islands were encompassed by stakes.

On 23 January 1977, six months before the Kauai stake was organized, the BYU–Hawaii Stake was created with Eric B. Shumway as president. Until that time campus church activities had been under the direction of the Laie Stake. As BYU–Hawaii continued to grow, a matter discussed in the following chapter, the BYU–Hawaii 2nd Stake, for married students and their families, was organized 22 November 1981 with H. Kamaka Sproat as president.

The most recent nonstudent stakes are both on Oahu. Mililani Hawaii Stake was created 3 February 1980 with Kotaro Koizumi as its first president. And the thirteenth stake, Laie North, was founded 16 January 1983. Willard K. Kekauoha was its original president.[2]

In one sense the purpose of the mission had been fulfilled. From this time on the president of the Hawaii Mission had no direct administrative responsibility over any branches or districts. Nevertheless, in another very real sense the goals of the mission had not been met. Only 3 percent of the total population of the islands were members of the Church. Further proselyting was still needed.

Saints of the outer islands have long held a special place in the hearts of the missionaries to Hawaii. "Honolulu is okay," said a missionary in 1960, "but you have to go to the outer islands to get the real aloha spirit." This is not wholly true, but the Saints of Kauai, Molokai, Lanai, Maui, and Hawaii have retained the feeling of old Hawaii more than have the better organized and generally more affluent Saints of Oahu. The Saints of the outer islands have been slower than their counterparts on Oahu in learning the administrative skills required by the Church organization of the 1960s, 1970s, and 1980s. Other aspects of Church development have also lagged behind Oahu. For example, during the 1950s and into the 1960s many branches on the outer islands were still meeting in old frame meetinghouses ill-equipped to handle the contemporary programs of the Church. Each of the mission presidents during these years made great efforts to rectify this situation, but money was scarce among the outer-island Saints, and the number of members in some branches was small.

The organization of the Hilo, Kona, and Maui stakes indicates, however, that by around 1975 the Saints there were prepared to handle their own administrative responsibilities. Aside from the blessing of having high priests and bishops in their midst, a stake actually offered them little not found in a well-organized district.[3] Nevertheless, in the hearts and minds of the members, stakehood was almost the same as having full citizenship.

The Effects of Statehood

The Congress of the United States passed a bill on 12 March 1959 admitting the Territory of Hawaii as the fiftieth state of the union. The words of a multiracial native son captured the feelings of most Hawaii residents as they became in a full sense part of the United States of America: "Now we are all haoles." The direct effects of statehood could not be seen immediately, but during the 1960s changes became evident. Statehood spurred the development of the already important tourist industry. As a Honolulu banker remarked, "Statehood had the effect of a multimillion-dollar advertising campaign—for free. Everyone suddenly discovered Hawaii."[4]

Concurrent with the growth in the tourist trade, and partly because of it, many mainland-based corporations began establishing offices in Honolulu and other parts of the islands. Many Latter-day Saints were among the men and women sent to the new state by corporations and small businesses, and they have made great contributions to the Church in Hawaii. In fact, several have been called as stake presidents. Some kamaainas have complained that their rightful positions have been usurped by strangers from the mainland. There is an element of truth here, but these problems have generally been short lived.

Educational Developments

The most important developments in the Church in Hawaii during the last twenty-five years have been in education. The crowning achievement in this field is Brigham Young University–Hawaii, formerly called the Church College of Hawaii (CCH). This institution will be discussed in chapter 14.

LDS education in Hawaii developed in several stages. The first schools in Hawaii were established by the early missionaries, and Hawaiian children were included in these schools from the beginning. As years passed, the school at Laie took on the elements of a mission school—that is, it was used by the missionary teachers as a proselyting tool. Over the years a fair number of nonmember children were always in attendance. The school was continued into the twentieth century, but in the 1920s the need for the school was questioned by mission leaders. Earlier missionaries had insisted that a means of teaching LDS children in a Church environment was needed, but now it was asked whether the school could be justified on a cost-benefit basis. For this reason the Church finally got out of the education business at Laie. From 1927, when the Laie elementary school was turned over to the territory, until 1955, when CCH began, the Church did not operate any schools in Hawaii.

The Church was much concerned, however, with the religious education of its children. Church leaders made efforts to give the young people a solid foundation in doctrine as well as character training. In 1929 the territorial legislature passed a law that allowed students one hour per week of free school time to attend religious education classes taught by the denomination of their choice. A decade passed before LDS missionaries recognized the teaching and proselyting possibilities provided by this law. In 1938–1939 principals and superintendents of schools of the Kohala area of Hawaii were surveyed to ascertain their attitudes toward religious education classes in their schools. They were universally in favor of such a program.

That same academic year, the first religious education (RE) classes of the Church were started at Kohala. Once underway, the program expanded rapidly. The Hawaiian and Japanese Missions as well as the Oahu Stake participated in and supported the teaching efforts. Because special lessons were needed for different age groups, Elder Don W. Conover, mission RE supervisor, prepared a series of materials. Mission area supervisors were called to direct the work. In September 1940 thirty-one RE classes were started, but the number increased until by the end of the school year there were eighty-five classes in seventy-one different schools. Average weekly attendance by the spring of 1941 was 1,468. Approximately half of these students were not members of the Church.[5]

Because of the success of the program, stake president Ralph E. Woolley suggested to Church president David O. McKay that a full-time appointment be made to take charge of it. In August 1941 President McKay visited the islands and decided that the idea was worth acting upon. That month the Church Board of Education, on the recommendation of Church Commissioner of Education Benjamin L. West, decided that the Church seminary program should be initiated in the islands. In

November 1941 Alfred C. Nielsen, who had been principal of Cyprus High School Seminary in Magna, Utah, was sent to Hawaii to act as supervisor of RE classes in the elementary and high schools. He was also made director of an institute of religion to be organized at the University of Hawaii. Unfortunately, two weeks after his arrival the attack on Pearl Harbor occurred, schools were closed until February 1942, and in general the RE program fell into disarray.

Despite these difficulties, Nielsen and the missionaries pursued the RE program during the war years. As the missionary force gradually dwindled, it became more difficult to carry on, but the program was never suspended. It was finally necessary to call for volunteers to teach the classes, but Nielsen and his replacement, Frank W. McGhie, who arrived in the summer of 1945, succeeded in filling most of the posts on Oahu. In this manner the program was carried on until the war ended.

In 1946 missionaries returned to the islands in fairly large numbers. With their return, the RE program received new emphasis. Two new textbooks by Nielsen, added during 1947–1948, helped the program's effectiveness. Over thirty-two hundred students participated during this school year.

In April 1948 the Supreme Court of the United States handed down a decision that religious education classes that met in public schools on school time were unconstitutional. Immediately, the commissioner of schools in Hawaii decided that the RE classes had to cease. However, he finally decided that schoolrooms could be used for RE purposes thirty minutes after classes ended for the day. This delay allowed students to leave for home instead of staying for RE class, thus making it almost impossible to continue the program.[6]

The major effectiveness of the RE program ended in 1948, but classes were continued in some parts of the islands into the early 1960s. An example is the RE program in South Kona, which was still directed by missionaries in 1960. There, the schools were dismissed an hour early one day each week and classes were held away from public facilities.

The early morning seminary program of the Church was introduced in Hawaii in 1953. It began in Honolulu, where it was supervised by Frank W. McGhie. During the early years, seminaries were generally manned by part-time or volunteer teachers who taught early morning classes in chapels or homes for a small remuneration. Much expansion has come over the years.[7] By the 1963–1964 school year, 927 students were registered in seminary classes in Hawaii.[8] And by 1975 there were 1,133 students enrolled in regular seminary classes.

The first coordinator of seminaries in Hawaii was also designated as the director of the institute of religion, a new organization for LDS students attending the University of Hawaii. The program of the early 1940s had not succeeded. This new program floundered until 1959 when arrangements were made by Trevor Christensen to hold classes in the Atherton House, a university-owned home next to the Manoa campus. Prior to this, classes had been held in the evening at the tabernacle on Beretania Street. Neither the time nor the place was convenient for the students. After 1960 the number of students at the institute continued to be small (in 1963 there were still only twenty-four young people involved), but since that time enough growth has taken place to justify the construction of a new building near the campus.

–14–

BRIGHAM YOUNG UNIVERSITY–HAWAII

THE CHURCH College of Hawaii was President David O. McKay's school. It was his idea; it was born of his vision and persistence.

THE VISION

During McKay's tour of Hawaii in 1921 as a member of the Quorum of the Twelve, he visited the temple, the plantation, and the elementary school at Laie. On the morning of 7 February he, along with Hugh J. Cannon and mission president E. Wesley Smith, attended a flag-raising ceremony at the school. Many children participated in the ceremony, but three boys—a Hawaiian, a haole, and a Japanese-American—had the principal parts. Elder McKay was deeply moved by the event and wrote:

> As I looked at that motley group of youngsters, and realized how far apart their parents are in hopes, aspirations, and ideals, and then thought of these boys and girls, the first generation of their children, all thrown into what Israel Zangwell has aptly called the "Melting Pot" and coming out Americans, my bosom swelled with emotion and tears came to my eyes, and I felt like bowing in prayer and thanksgiving for the glorious country which is doing so much for all these nationalities. But more than that, when I realize that these same boys and girls have the opportunity of participating in all the blessings of the Gospel which will transform the American into a real citizen of the Kingdom of God, I feel to praise His name for the glorious privileges vouch safed to this generation. We held short services in the school room in which all—American, Hawaiian, Japanese, Chinese, Filipino—participated as though they had belonged to one nation, one country, one tongue.
>
> America and the Church of Christ will truly make of all nations one blood. May God hasten the day when this is accomplished.[1]

With these thoughts, Elder McKay, his host President Smith, and his companion, Brother Cannon, traveled by boat to Maui, arriving there the next morning. It was on this day that the vision of the fathers shaking hands occurred. But it was also on this day, after many hours of meetings and discussions among the visitors and the Maui-based missionaries, that Elder McKay made the decision to recommend the founding of a new college for the young Saints of Hawaii, to be built at Laie. Elder Samuel H. Hurst recorded this event in his journal: "Following the reports and this discussion, Elder McKay said that he was very strongly impressed that such a church school was the big need of the mission, and that before many days he would write a letter to the First Presidency recommending that one be built. . . ."[2] Elder McKay never faltered in his conviction that the school should be built at Laie.

On a number of occasions during the next thirty years President McKay, a counselor in the First Presidency since the 1930s, spoke to the leaders of the Church in Hawaii concerning his school in Laie. In 1936 he visited the islands and "reiterated his vision, his faith that this was to be the center of education." When he came again in 1941 and dedicated the tabernacle, he said to the stake leaders, "Don't forget Laie. This is the educational center and the spiritual center of our people in these Islands."[3]

The war years made the building of a school impossible, but in 1949 stake president Ralph E. Woolley organized a committee to survey the educational needs of the Saints in Hawaii and to make recommendations for the future. A year later another survey was made. Although these reports and other relevant data were forwarded to McKay, they did not seem to reflect the vision he had for the Laie school.

CHURCH COLLEGE OF HAWAII

When he became president of the Church in 1951, McKay immediately took action. Until then he had suggested, proposed, recommended, and encouraged stake leaders in Hawaii and the First Presidency on this matter. Now he directed that steps be taken to establish the school.[4] Four surveys were taken between 1951 and 1954, some by local people and others by groups from the mainland. Finally, on 21 July 1954 the establishment of a college in Hawaii was officially announced by the First Presidency. Dean Reuben D. Law of the College of Education at Brigham Young University was appointed the first president of the school.

Hundreds of decisions had to be made by Law and others before the college could open its doors, among them where the school should be situated, what it should be called, how many years of formal study should be offered, and what the curriculum should be. Buildings also had to be designed, a faculty hired, and students recruited. A group of advisors was appointed to oversee the creation of the school. This body, known as the Continuing Committee, was composed of Edward L. Clissold, chairman, president of Oahu Stake; Ralph E. Woolley, past stake president and a successful businessman, contractor, and civic leader; D. Arthur Haycock, president of the Hawaii Mission; George Q. Cannon, counselor in the mission presidency and later president of the Pearl Harbor Stake; and Lawrence Haneberg, later a counselor in the Honolulu Stake presidency. This group, which later became the board of trustees of the institution, met regularly with President Law to approve plans and advise him concerning the needs of the school.

During the summer of 1954 Law and two associates, Dean Clarence Cottam of the College of Biological and Agricultural Sciences at BYU, and Kenneth Bennion, director of LDS Business College in Salt Lake City, spent a month in Hawaii studying the educational needs of the young Latter-day Saints, looking at possible sites for the college, and surveying other relevant information. The committee noted a number of advantages if the school were placed in or near Honolulu, among them convenience of travel, more work opportunities for students, and a much larger population base. Because of these attractions, Law and the committee proposed that the school be erected at Kaneohe, a fifteen-minute automobile drive from Honolulu. But McKay rejected this plan. He wanted the school to be at Laie.

It was suggested to the First Presidency that the college be named "Central Pacific College of The Church of Jesus Christ of Latter-day Saints." Although this name had merit, the First Presidency countered with the simpler name "Church College of Hawaii," which was chosen. In some ways the name became a problem. Outsiders frequently asked, "Which church?" or "Who runs the college?" Nevertheless, CCH came to stand for a special educational institution with unusual purposes.

These purposes and goals were made clear by President McKay when he dedicated the land on which the college is built. Only a year after plans for the college were announced, he journeyed to Laie to preside at the ground-breaking ceremonies of CCH. During the services he recalled his vision, thirty-four years before, of a school at Laie. He spoke not only of the role Laie and the school were to play in the lives of the Hawaiian race, but also of the influence the college would have on the peoples of the South Pacific and Asia. He praised God that Laie had been dedicated "as a gathering place for the Hawaiians and other races on these cherished islands." After speaking about the importance of education among Latter-day Saints, he delineated some of the purposes for which the college was being built. First in importance was the acquisition of knowledge "pertaining to God and His kingdom." The second purpose followed the first: those who obey and follow the precepts of the gospel should "develop manhood, character, and make noble men and women." Concerning the people who would teach in the college President McKay said:

> No man or woman should teach in this college who doesn't have in his or her heart an assurance, not a mere belief, an assurance, that God has had a hand over this entire valley, that that dedication offered years ago was inspired, that this land is a choice land. It's part of America, part of Zion. . . .

Then, in a spirit of prophecy, he spoke of the destiny of the Church College of Hawaii.

> You mark that word, and from this school, I'll tell you, will go men and women whose influence will be felt for good towards the establishment of peace internationally. Four hundred and fifty million people waiting to hear the message over in China, a noble race. I've met them. I don't know how many million over in Japan. You prepare to go and carry that message. Three hundred and fifty million down in India. We have scarcely touched these great nations, and they're calling today as the people's voice over in Macedonia called, "Come over to us, come over to us."[5]

The principles and purposes proposed by President McKay remain as a challenge to the people who affiliate themselves with the school. Contrary to the popular understanding that CCH was created to serve only the needs of the Polynesian peoples, it is clear from President McKay's discourse that it was created to serve the educational, missionary, and spiritual needs of all the people of the Pacific and Asia. The missionary purpose of the college was a priority with President McKay. In his prayer dedicating the land for the college he said, "We dedicate our actions in this service unto thee and unto thy glory and to the salvation of the children of men, that this college, and the temple, and the town of Laie may become a missionary factor, influencing not thousands, not tens of thousands, but millions of people who will come seeking to know what this town and its significance are."[6]

At the time of the ground-breaking, President McKay met with the

Continuing Committee and asked when the college would open. He was told that the target date was September 1956. To this President McKay replied, "I would like it to begin in the fall of 1955." In Edward L. Clissold's words, "There was a feverish several months of labor, but the school opened its doors on September 26, 1955, according to [President McKay's] wish."[7] In order to do this it was necessary to move war surplus buildings from Wheeler Air Force Base near Honolulu. At one time thirty-six sections of buildings were on the road to Laie at once. A temporary campus was formed near the existing chapel so that its facilities could be used for devotional meetings and other gatherings of the student body.

There were 153 students and 20 faculty and administrators on hand when the first day of classes began. Since that time CCH, now BYU–Hawaii, has grown to around two thousand students with almost ninety faculty members on the staff. The administrative organization and curriculum were quite broad for a new two-year school. There were nine divisions: Agriculture and Industrial Arts, Art and Music, Business Administration and Secretarial Training, Education, Home Living, Language Arts, Religion, and Social Sciences. Within these divisions were twenty-three departments.[8] In addition to academics, the new school also provided a full slate of athletic and recreational activities. Emphasis was placed on intramural and inter-club competition.

Unlike most secular schools, which are constructed by hired contractors, the Church College of Hawaii was erected by building missionaries called by the Church to contribute two or more years to the construction project. The building missionary system of the LDS Church was first conceived in Tonga as an emergency measure to complete the Liahona High School. It was later used in Samoa and New Zealand, and it was in New Zealand that the program was brought to fruition. Credit for the method belongs to many people, but it was Wendell B. Mendenhall who developed the system into first a Pacific and then a worldwide program of the Church. Mendenhall was appointed chairman of the Church Building Committee in 1955.

When the needs and costs of construction at CCH became known, President McKay asked Mendenhall and the Continuing Committee to use building missionaries to construct the college. President McKay's request was that the cost of building be cut by $1,300,000. This was a large demand, but when the school buildings were completed in 1958 Mendenhall, Clissold, and others close to the work believed that the savings goal had been met and even exceeded.

Although the land for the college was dedicated in February 1955, construction of permanent buildings did not begin until December. The entire undertaking was directed by Joseph E. Wilson. At the height of the work, over fifty mainland missionaries or supervisors and their wives were working on the job. An additional seventy-five to eighty local building missionaries from all parts of the islands also participated. Local Saints from Laie also helped in different phases of the work. The wives of the builders contributed much moral support, and they also cleaned all the windows and laid around 174,000 square feet of floor tile.

The completed buildings cost around four million dollars. Brother Wilson figured the cost per square foot to be about twelve dollars, which was far below that of similar construction in the islands. The new campus provided every need for a student body of between one thousand and twelve hundred. Since 1958 a number of dormitories, the beautiful Joseph F. Smith Library, the Aloha Center, the George Q. Cannon Activities Center (the second largest indoor seating facility in Hawaii), and the new Lorenzo Snow Administration Building have been completed. The original administrative and classroom building was renamed the David O. McKay Building in 1980.

Dedication services for the initial college buildings were held on 17 December 1958. President David O. McKay presided at this well-attended meeting. Dignitaries from Hawaii and the mainland were in attendance, and many other important people from government, education, and religious groups sent notes of congratulation. Elder Marion G. Romney of the Quorum of the Twelve gave an address concerning the LDS philosophy of education. Edward L. Clissold recounted the history of the college first proposed by President McKay in 1921. Several other dignitaries also spoke. But the highlight of the program was President McKay's sermon and prayer. The white-haired prophet talked at length to the multiracial throng about the purposes of education. He suggested that economic and social advancement were legitimate objectives for a person seeking a higher education. "But," he said, "education for a livelihood is not the highest purpose of education." He emphasized this point by quoting from Robert M. Hutchins of the University of Chicago, who said in part, "What education can do, and perhaps all it can do, is to produce a trained mind. It is principles, and everlastingly principles, not data, not facts, not helpful hints, but principles which the rising generation requires if it is to find its way through the mazes of tomorrow." President McKay went on to say that the "paramount ideal permeating all education . . . should be more spiritual than economic for the good of our country."[9]

In his dedicatory prayer President McKay stressed the missionary nature and purpose of the college. He paraphrased and quoted from the Doctrine and Covenants (section 88, verses 77–81), wherein the Lord outlines the kinds of knowledge men should seek, and then tells them why they should have this knowledge:

> This large assembly of thy children, the program rendered in sermon and song, all buildings erected, equipment furnished, the instruments and mechanical devices that are in these buildings—all are in use and action because of divine instruction from thee to the end that thy children shall teach one another the doctrines of the kingdom, and all things that pertain to the kingdom of God that are expedient to understand; things both in the heaven and in earth, under the earth, things which have been, things which are, things which must shortly come to pass, things which are at home, things which are abroad, the wars and perplexities of nations and the judgements which are on the land, and the knowledge of countries and of kingdoms—all this and more that thy saints may be prepared in all things to magnify their callings where unto thou hast called them and the mission to which thou didst commission them.
>
> Thou hast emphasized the responsibility which rests upon thy people to carry the message of the restoration of the gospel to all nations. Thus doth thou emphasize the fact that it is not sufficient merely to testify to the world of the restoration, but to present the principles of the gospel in an intelligent manner that the honest in heart may be convinced of the truth, and may be led from paths of error into the way of righteousness.
>
> To this general and glorious purpose, therefore, our Father, we unitedly assemble and authoritatively dedicate The Church College of Hawaii.[10]

Later, he again mentioned the missionary responsibility and purpose of the school, saying, "May there radiate from these buildings an aura of light as tangible as personality radiates from each individual, influencing all to live clean and upright lives, to seek truth diligently, to be inspired so to live that others seeing their good deeds may live to glorify thee, our creator, our Father, our God."[11]

ADMINISTRATION AND CURRICULUM

The Church College of Hawaii began as a two-year institution that granted associate degrees. In October 1959, after visits from evaluation teams, CCH was fully accredited as a two-year college. In that same year the Pacific Board of Education authorized the expansion of the college to a four-year teacher-training institution. Emphasis in the four-year course of study centered on the liberal arts curriculum.

One of the problems encountered by CCH has been the mushrooming of majors offered for graduation. Although the faculty was relatively small even in the early 1970s (around eighty in number), over sixty different degree programs were offered.

Changes in administration have been relatively frequent at CCH. This applies not only to the office of president but also to the governing boards. The college was first directed by the Continuing Committee, which was later made the board of trustees of the institution. Then in 1957, President McKay formed the Pacific Board of Education, which was responsible directly to the First Presidency and which had responsibility for CCH and all Church schools in New Zealand, Samoa, Tonga, Fiji, and later in French Polynesia. Wendell B. Mendenhall was chairman of the board, with Owen J. Cook as executive secretary. The other members of the board were D'Mont Coombs, former president of the Tongan Mission; Edward L. Clissold; and Ermel J. Morton, former principal of Liahona High School in Tonga. In January 1965 the Pacific board was dissolved, and responsibility for all schools in the Pacific was turned over to the Unified Church School System.

The Church College was administered by four presidents during its nineteen years of existence separate from Brigham Young University. Reuben D. Law served during what was probably the most difficult and the most rewarding years. Law had the problems of designing a new institution and working with an advisory board that was at times difficult to please, but he also had the satisfaction of seeing his ideas and theories about education brought to reality.

Dr. Richard T. Wootton became the second president in June 1959. He had previously been a member of the faculty and director of the counseling center. He served until August 1964. During his tenure the college experienced much growth. CCH gained accreditation and status as a four-year college; the student body more than quadrupled and the faculty tripled; new dormitories were added and two student wards of the Church were organized. In addition, the Polynesian Cultural Center opened. Although it was not Wootton's direct responsibility, he was much involved in its planning and construction.

The third president of the college was Dr. Owen J. Cook. During his years as president the school was placed on a firm financial foundation. The students remember him for his contributions to their welfare. He was instrumental in obtaining approval for the Aloha Center (a student center) and also for the construction of a number of married-student dormitories. Under his direction the first summer school was held in 1966. By the fall of 1970, CCH had reached an enrollment of 1,307 students,

60 percent of whom were from Hawaii. Cook left CCH during the spring of 1971.

One other development occurred during Cook's term as president. In January 1969 the First Presidency announced the establishment of a Language Training Mission (LTM) at CCH. The purpose of the mission was to teach Asian and Polynesian languages to men and women going to East Asia and the South Pacific as missionaries. Concerning the influence the LTM had on the college, Harvey L. Taylor has written:

> The establishment of the mission on campus played an important role in the growth of the college. It not only brought a large number of young men [and women] to the campus who had a marked influence on the total morale of the school, but because of the missionary efforts of the young people trained at the Language Training School, a number of students from the Far East and the South Pacific came to the college.[12]

The Language Training Mission remained at CCH until 1975, when it was consolidated with all other language training programs at BYU in Provo, Utah.

The fourth president of the college, Dr. Stephen L. Brower, came to CCH in July 1971, having recently been released as mission president for the Church in Columbia and Venezuela. Although he had not been a college administrator prior to his assignment at Hawaii, he had spent a number of years as district director of extension services in Utah and as a manager and executive consultant for large development projects in South America. During his tenure the college reached a crossroads where it was necessary to determine the direction, goals, priorities, and programs of the school. President Brower envisioned a college in which the sacred and secular parts of life were closely integrated. He was also concerned about the kinds of training programs and majors available for the students from Polynesia. He believed that too much emphasis had been given to the liberal arts and that the students needed training in specific technical skills. In his effort to make the curriculum more practical, he apparently infringed on the established domains of some faculty members, who seriously opposed his efforts.

Curriculum was not the only problem he was forced to confront. Unfortunately, influences of student radicalism, the drug culture, and other elements of that era's "counter culture" had filtered into the campus; it was Brower's task to rid the school of such disharmony. Brower studied the prophetic statements of President McKay concerning the purposes of the school and concluded that CCH had an important role to play in the missionary work of the Church. He did not see, however, any organized or planned efforts in this important area. After unsuccessfully attempting to enlist the cooperation of the student body officers in an effort to create a higher standard of behavior on campus, Brower disbanded student government and asked the local stake officers to call student body leaders through the priesthood to plan and direct student programs and activities. He was sharply criticized for his action, but during the next two years the student body united under the new system, which brought about many good results.

Another area of concern for Brower was the composition of the student body. Although the number of students was large when he assumed his post, many were marginal achievers, employed and taking only one or two classes a year; some were wives of faculty members. Brower, with the support of the board, established a planned admissions program that required students to justify their admission to the college on the basis of set criteria. Students were required to establish definite purposes for attending CCH. He also emphasized their "returnability" to the countries from which they came. That is, he stimulated the faculty and administrators to create programs that would help to insure the return of the foreign students to their native lands. During President Brower's administration the emphasis upon returnability was such that students were forced to consider their admission to CCH somewhat in the light of a missionary call. As a result, enrollment at CCH dropped. Brower made another contribution by clarifying the formal relationship of CCH with the Polynesian Cultural Center. Again his concern was with the missionary role of the college as it related to the center.

In summary, Brower's presidency was a period of turmoil and change. He felt that he was a catalyst that brought the purposes and objectives of the school into focus and helped the faculty and student body see and understand their responsibilities as members of an LDS institution.

On 1 July 1974 the Church College of Hawaii became a satellite branch of Brigham Young University, and its name was changed to the Brigham Young University—Hawaii Campus. The school was administered by a dean, although this title was soon changed to executive vice-president and then to president. The head of BYU–Hawaii was responsible to the president of BYU. The newly designated Hawaii campus was not a branch college; it was an administrative unit of the Utah school. Faculty members and administrators at the Hawaii campus continued to determine the school's curriculum and to administer a separate budget.

Much prestige came to the school as a result of its new name. Many people in Hawaii and elsewhere who had only a vague idea of what the college stood for realized that it was supported by the Church and that it was part of Brigham Young University.

The first dean and then president was Dr. Dan W. Andersen, a specialist with many years of experience in international education. During his tenure Andersen provided stability and a spirit of trust. Enrollment began to climb once again. He initiated the construction of the 5,400-seat Cannon Activity Center and the Snow Administration Building.

Andersen was succeeded on 1 August 1980 by Dr. J. Elliot Cameron, a vice president at BYU in Provo. He completed several building projects, strengthened the faculty, and created a generally higher level of academic achievement. Many faculty members from his era appreciated his maintenance of a peaceful university climate.

In early 1986, President Cameron was chosen as commissioner of the Church Education System, a new assignment that required relocation to Salt Lake City. A presidential search resulted in the selection of Dr. Alton L. Wade, president of Dixie Junior College in St. George, Utah, as the seventh president of BYU–Hawaii. He assumed office on 1 July 1986. A "students' " president, Wade has emphasized improved teaching, quality student activities, and a caring attitude throughout the university community.

BYU–HAWAII TODAY

BYU–Hawaii has a ceiling of two thousand students. Close to that number have attended each fall semester for the past several years, principally from Hawaii, the South Pacific, East Asia, and the U.S. mainland. The mixture of nationalities has created an interesting sociological "chemistry" on campus. Mainland students provide language models for the over eight hundred students for whom English is a second language. Students from countries that have a tradition of animosity toward each other often find themselves sharing not only classes but also dorm rooms and religious assignments. The two campus stakes help to blend students with multiple cultural backgrounds into a cooperative student body.

Being a closed and somewhat isolated institution has advantages and disadvantages. Laie is a controlled environment and as such is much less worldly than Honolulu and Waikiki. However, its small size can create problems. Faculty members live close together and not only work together on campus but also in their wards and stakes. Rumors are common and tend to cause friction between various factions and groups. There exists a certain amount of friction between "town and gown," but not as much as is frequently found in small academic communities. Most Laie residents recognize the necessity of a close working relationship among Laie's various groups.

During the Andersen–Cameron–Wade eras, BYU–Hawaii matured greatly. Faculty tensions subsided significantly. The goals of the institution were clarified and new and higher academic standards implemented. And the concern of the faculty, staff, and administration for the student with great language, educational, and cultural deficits to overcome was never greater.

–15–

HAWAII: AN INFLUENCE ON MILLIONS OF PEOPLE

The Polynesian Cultural Center

In 1951 Elder Matthew Cowley, who was at that time presiding over all Asian and Pacific missions of the Church, visited Laie during one of his frequent visits to the Hawaiian Islands. While there, he and stake president Edward L. Clissold discussed the needs of the Maori Saints who regularly came to Laie to do temple work. Their living costs were high. To counter this problem Elder Cowley suggested that the Maoris build a large Maori house, a communal dwelling, where they could live inexpensively while at Laie. Also, he thought they might do some entertaining, attract some tourists, and thus make a little money to sustain themselves. President Clissold felt that if the idea was good for the Maoris, it should be good for all the island peoples. They could build houses typical of their homelands, perform their own songs and dances, and demonstrate their cultural arts and heritage.

At the stake conference in Honolulu two weeks later, Elder Cowley told those assembled that he could envision the time when there would be many villages at Laie. He said he could see a carved house from New Zealand and a Samoan village and a Tahitian village.[1] But for nine years nothing came of these early discussions or of Elder Cowley's vision of Polynesian villages at Laie.

When the college was established and students from the South Pacific began to attend, President Clissold wanted to help them find ways to support themselves. In his capacity as manager of Zion's Securities Corporation and also as stake president, Clissold talked to new faculty members and community leaders as well as to a number of businessmen and encouraged them to establish businesses and industries in the Laie area. Some did, but they did not provide enough jobs to take care of the students' needs. At about the same time, 1955, a community association was proposed, to be called the Hui Lau Lima o Laie. Its objective was the town's general welfare. But little was done until 1958, when several CCH faculty members decided to inject new life into the organization. Jerry K. Loveland was elected president.

After a visit to the mainland, Clissold met with Loveland, Joseph R. Smith, President Richard Wootton, and Wylie Swapp and enthusiastically told them about a Boy Scout undertaking in Colorado in which scouts performed Indian dances for the entertainment of visitors. If they can do it there, Clissold asked, why not in Laie? "Joe and I put our heads together," Loveland later remembered, "and decided to see if the college couldn't organize an entity that could do this kind of thing as well as perform an academic function. (Big dreams for a junior college!) Wootton agreed to form a Polynesian Institute, with me as the director. The Institute was to organize a performing troupe to take to Honolulu and also to collect for sale some handicraft items."[2]

Swapp, a CCH art teacher, trained a group of Hawaiian, Samoan, Tongan, Maori, and Fijian dancers, singers, and musicians and by 1960 they were ready to perform at the Dome in the old Kaiser Hawaiian Village in Waikiki. Their performance garnered rave reviews. The all-male dances—rare and unusual—received an especially warm response.

Tourists continued to come to Laie, visiting the temple grounds and information center. As Church and CCH leaders struggled to fulfill needs of the students, they thought about their special talents and conceived a plan to create a living center of Polynesian culture and entertainment. In 1960 Loveland proposed to President Clissold that the college sponsor the Polynesian village that had been seriously discussed for two or three years. Clissold contacted Wendell Mendenhall in Salt Lake City and before long the Polynesian Cultural Center (PCC) was underway. Although there was opposition to the project in Honolulu and some General Authorities of the Church were skeptical about the project's success, Church president David O. McKay liked the idea and gave it full support. The college, however, never controlled the PCC. That function was given to a new board created to oversee its operation.

A large number of the employees for the proposed center were to be students, and thus their financial needs could be met. The original plan to provide homes and employment for island Saints visiting the temple was superseded. The idea of having people live in villages that were being visited by thousands of tourists proved impractical. Also, it was not possible to meet zoning and health standards while carrying on normal village life. The PCC had to become a living museum, but without the inhabitants actually living there.

In addition to the acclaim given the CCH dance troupe, earlier successes in two similar endeavors gave Clissold and his people confidence that the PCC could succeed. There were already two Samoan *fales* (houses) in Laie where many tourists were entertained by Samoans who performed dances and songs and gave demonstrations of their culture. In addition, for a number of years the Laie wards had been giving a luau and hukilau as a money-raising activity. All of this experience was combined to create the PCC.

President Clissold was in a strong position to accomplish the task of building the center. He was stake president, manager of Zion's Securities Corporation in Laie, and a member of the Pacific Board of Education, which directed CCH. He was able to move the work along quickly. The First Presidency gave formal direction of the endeavor to the Pacific Board of Education, chaired by Wendell B. Mendenhall.

Nevertheless, the PCC did not come into existence without a few problems. One of the most serious setbacks concerned the original site for the Center. Work was started on land between the college and the temple; in fact, much underground pipe had been laid when the First Presidency asked the leaders in Hawaii to relocate the Center on its present site, *makai* (toward the sea) of the school. The new site, previously taro land, proved to be a wiser choice; better waterways for canoes and water-related activities could be constructed, and it has more recently allowed easy expansion of the entire facility. It is also far enough from the temple to keep that sacred edifice separate from the less serious atmosphere of the Center.

The original Center was constructed almost entirely by building missionaries, many of whom were artisans brought from the South Pacific. It consisted of a cluster of huts with a lagoon winding among them. There were six different villages—Hawaiian, Samoan, Tongan, Fijian, Maori, and Tahitian—and the complex covered over sixteen acres of land. Native craftsmen constructed the buildings to insure their authenticity; the landscaping, too, was as authentic as possible.

Construction of the Center began in early 1962 and continued for almost two years. On 12 November 1963, over a thousand people gathered at the Center to hear President Hugh B. Brown, counselor in the First Presidency, dedicate the facilities. Although the directors of the undertaking, Clissold and Mendenhall in particular, were sure the new operation would be successful, many skeptics in Honolulu, some of whom held high positions in the tourist industry, prophesied failure. An eighty-mile round-trip journey from Honolulu to Laie and back is too far, they argued. Tourists don't really want an authentic cultural experience, particularly if the dancers are dressed modestly, other critics claimed. But Church leaders were right and the skeptics were wrong. Within four years of its official opening, the Center was being hailed as a grand success by Honolulu newspapers and leaders of the tourist industry. During 1975 more than 850,000 people visited the Laie complex. By that time the show had been sold out each night for seven years. Tickets had to be ordered well in advance. Only two attractions in Hawaii, both free, drew more visitors—the Honolulu Zoo and Volcanoes National Park on the Big Island. In 1975 about half of Hawaii's tourists visited the PCC. Tours are conducted in twelve different languages. Since its expansion, over one million people a year visit the Center.

The Center is a nonprofit organization of the Church. Its principal purpose is to provide employment for students at the college and to generate money to help support that institution. The Center has been successful in doing both. In addition, the PCC was able to make a sizeable contribution to the large expansion project completed during the summer of 1976 and dedicated on 4 July of that year. The expanded facilities cover more than forty-two acres and include a new 2,772-seat theater, a dining pavilion the size of a football field, a number of new cultural attractions, and service and administrative buildings. The head offices are now in the Snow Administration Building, BYU–Hawaii. Before the expansion over three-quarters of the Center's employees were students, but the ratio of students to outside employees dropped slightly as the new facilities came into greater use. Nevertheless, the fact that 50 percent of the Center's employees were students (600 out of 1,200) in 1987 indicates that one of its original purposes is being accomplished.

As with all large institutions, the PCC has had both internal and external critics. Employees have complained that wages and salaries are too low. Some full-time workers especially have expressed concerns about the long hours they devote and the relatively low level of remuneration. Many of these people, often unskilled immigrants, have no other employment options. During the mid-1970s organizers tried to create a union among PCC workers; the attempt failed, probably because of the workers' loyalty to the PCC as a quasi-branch of the Church.

Outsiders, particularly union entertainers and Waikiki show promoters, have complained that if the PCC had to pay union wages it would close because it would have to charge prohibitive entrance fees. Obviously, such people would prefer to see tourists remain in Waikiki and spend their money there. Nevertheless, they are probably right. Luckily, the Center has not been put to such a test. The students at BYU–Hawaii need the Center and the Center needs the students. It is a cooperative effort of the highest order.

Of all the attractions within the Center, the night show has been criticized most frequently over the years. Viewers familiar with Polynesia have sometimes been disappointed with the Hollywood style of the show. Some tourists, also, think they want to "go native"—at least until they experience something really authentic. The PCC show has tried to strike a balance, and the vast majority of visitors come away feeling wonderfully well entertained.

Most of the credit for the success of the PCC must be attributed to the men who conceived the plan and to those who have directed its operations. Its board of directors was originally headed by Howard W. Hunter, a distinguished lawyer and businessman before he became an apostle and General Authority of the Church. "Some of the brightest, sharpest business heads in the U.S.," according to Stephen Brower, have made up the board over the years. They include Howard B. Stone, first head of the operation; Bill Gay and Howard Anderson of the Hughes Corporation; Wendell B. Mendenhall; Edward L. Clissold; George Q. Cannon; J. Willard Marriott, Jr.; and the various presidents of CCH. In 1976 Marvin J. Ashton of the Quorum of the Twelve replaced Elder Hunter as chairman of the PCC Board. And in 1987 Elder Dallin H. Oaks was assigned to the board, becoming chairman in 1988. The most recent PCC presidents, Ralph G. Rodgers, Jr. (1983–1988) and James P. Christensen (1988–present), have improved and refined the quality of the Center. Rodgers concentrated on theatrical matters while Christensen has focused on financial concerns.

During the early years the Center's main purpose was to provide student employment and financial support for the school. In 1973, however, when the new expansion was approved, the First Presidency modified the role of the PCC. The Center's highest priority was now seen as a major missionary function in giving large numbers of people favorable contact with the Church. This priority calls to mind the words of President McKay as he dedicated the ground for CCH:

> We dedicate our actions to this service unto Thee and unto Thy glory and to the salvation of the children of men, that this college, and the temple, and the town of Laie may become *a missionary factor, influencing* not thousands, not tens of thousands, but *millions of people* who will come seeking to know what this town and its significance are.[3]

In an effort to make the Center a better missionary tool, management has placed renewed emphasis on appropriate appearance and deportment among guides, entertainers, and other employees. The objective of employees at the Center is to demonstrate through their conduct the high standards and principles of the Church.

Another missionary tool, conceived and developed by Norman Nielsen and Steven Bennett of the PCC staff, is a free guided tour of Laie, the University campus, and the temple grounds. To make the experience interesting, two replicas of 1910 Honolulu trams were purchased; a monologue recounts the history of Laie plantation, the purposes of the college, and reasons why Latter-day Saints construct temples. The final stop on the tour is the temple bureau of information. By 1975 thousands of PCC visitors were participating in these free tours. Every year about ten thousand copies of the Book of Mormon are distributed at the temple information bureau, most to people on the PCC tours. About 10 percent of those taking the tour ask for missionaries to be sent to their homes. In 1975 this amounted to eight thousand "golden contacts," that is, individuals who seemed willing to study the gospel. "Millions of people" now visit Laie, as was President McKay's prayer, and are influenced by the PCC, Brigham Young University–Hawaii, and the temple.

THE BUILDING MISSIONARY PROGRAM IN HAWAII

The contributions made by the building missionary program at the college and the Polynesian Cultural Center are only part of the accomplishments of the men and women who gave up years of their lives to build up the Church in Hawaii. The builders completely remodeled and enlarged the visitors' center (information bureau) at the temple and constructed homes for missionaries and workers who served at the temple and for the temple president. They also built homes for the faculty at CCH and constructed a number of maintenance and other auxiliary buildings for the college. Between 1960 and 1963, the big years of the building program, building missionaries constructed seven chapel complexes on Oahu and another seven smaller chapels and cultural halls on the outer islands. More chapels were built during the remaining two years of the building missionary program. The modern homes built for the full-time proselyting missionaries in many parts of the islands have contributed much to the comfort of the missionaries and to the good image of the Church. The new chapels have gone far to change the image of the Church from one of poverty, embodied by the old frame chapels on the outer islands, to one of success and progress.

LAIE, THE PLANTATION, AND ZION'S SECURITIES CORPORATION

Laie, with its temple, schools, cultural center, and plantation, has received much of the attention of this book. This is appropriate because this little community has been not only the spiritual center of the Saints in Hawaii, but also the economic and social center of the Church in the islands during the years from 1865 to around 1920. The story of Laie, and its relationship to the Church and Zion's Securities Corporation (ZSC), now needs to be completed.

One of the last official acts of Antoine R. Ivins, manager of Laie plantation from 1921 to 1931, was to lease the cane lands to Kahuku Plantation Company for an extended period. After Ivins left, the plantation and community lands held by Zion's Securities Corporation (ZSC, see p. 152) were managed by William Waddoups, Frank and Ralph E. Woolley, and then, after 1951, by Edward L. Clissold. Clissold served as manager and then chairman of the local ZSC board until 1970. The manager of ZSC's Laie lease lands from the late 1950s through the 1960s was Howard B. Stone, who had served as mission president in Samoa.

The original lease between ZSC and the Kahuku company expired in 1953. Bishop Thorp B. Isaacson of the Presiding Bishopric was assigned by President McKay to negotiate a new lease with Alexander & Baldwin Company, owners of the Kahuku company. The new lease arrangement included an escalation clause that increased the lease payment from Alexander & Baldwin if the price of sugar rose beyond a certain level. Because the price of sugar did rise past that point, ZSC and the Church benefited greatly from the new lease. The lease arrangement with Alexander & Baldwin ended in the late 1960s. Since the Kahuku mill was producing a marginal profit for its mother company, its owners decided to suspend the relationship with ZSC. Since that time the Church has been out of the sugar business. The sugar business of the Church in Hawaii lasted almost exactly one hundred years. Since the late 1960s the cane lands have been leased to various private interests for the grazing of cattle and other uses.

The closing of the sugar mill caused an even greater reliance on tourism. According to anthropologist Max Stanton, "About half the workers in Laie depend directly on tourism for their jobs and most who work at the PCC are not skilled for other jobs. They are very dependent on the Center."[4] The community of Laie is primarily owned by the Church. Most of the property belongs to ZSC; the exceptions are a hundred or so house lots that have been sold since 1984 and the school and lands used for Church purposes such as chapels. In recent years the economic and social functions of Laie have changed. Laie was originally purchased by the Church as a place where the Hawaiian Saints could be taught the arts of civilization, moral behavior, and good work habits. It later became a gathering place, similar in purpose to Utah. In other words, the original objective of the community as a place where the Hawaiian people could be upgraded had been accomplished, and Laie was to be simply a place where the Saints could gather out of the world. From the time of Presidents Noall and Samuel E. Woolley, the main purpose of the endeavor seems to have been to provide employment for the families living in the little village. During all this time the leaders of the mission continued to encourage the Hawaiian Saints to gather to Laie.

The building of the temple changed the nature of Laie to some extent. The spiritual purposes of the community became more evident. The main function of the Church in Laie was now to support temple work. After Antoine R. Ivins negotiated the lease with the Kahuku company, the Church through ZSC no longer provided jobs for the people of Laie. The only real economic relationship that existed between the citizens of Laie and the Church was through the land lease-rent agreements the people held with Zion's Securities. Church leaders in Hawaii stopped trying to persuade the Saints from the outer islands to move to Laie. There was no work for them there. Laie's main immigrants after the temple was completed were Samoans and a smattering of Maoris, Tahitians, and later a fairly large group of Tongans. By mid-century the Church's attitude concerning gathering to Zion was firmly set against movements of people from their homelands. For several decades the First Presidency had been asking Saints throughout the world to remain in their own areas and build up the Church there.

By the early 1950s the Laie community had run the full gamut from a paternalistic sociological experiment to a modern, up-to-date, 100 percent business proposition. Rents for house lots in Laie had been as small as twenty-five cents a year in early days. Later they were only one dollar a month. When President Clissold took over ZSC in 1951, he found many thousands of dollars on the books in overdue rents, taxes, and other debts to the corporation. After evaluating the situation, Clissold and his associates decided that the best course of action would be to have all the Laie properties appraised and then to assign rental prices according to the value of the land. They established three rent rates in accordance with the services provided to the various lots. The less valuable property continued to be leased at approximately the same low rate as before, but better lands were charged higher rents. At this time ZSC also instituted a policy of rewriting all leases every five years. In this way rent rates could be adjusted to reflect changing economic conditions. Unfortunately this arrangement has made more enemies than friends for ZSC. The new higher rents have placed a greater burden on older members of the community with fixed incomes than on others.

Laie has continued to change over the years. Each racial-cultural group has contributed to the interest and variety found there. The Samoans mentioned earlier, who migrated to Laie during the 1920s and in 1950, wanted to be close to the LDS temple and to other Latter-day Saints. Since then others have come whose objectives are not so clear. Among the reasons for coming are education and employment. Some Samoans and other relatively recent settlers in Laie came as labor missionaries, stayed to get an education, and have remained as part of the community.

Some critics have suggested that too much power was vested in the hands of E. L. Clissold for the good of the community. But at worst he was a benevolent leader who had to make difficult decisions. At best he was a man with clear vision of what Laie was becoming. In a way, he was the last of the old-style Church leaders in Hawaii. In earlier times the mission president held almost all the power in Laie. But since the 1960s Laie has grown and its institutions—BYU–Hawaii, the PCC, the two campus stakes and the two regular stakes, and ZSC—have distributed power into the hands of a number of people. There is no longer a single central leader in Laie. Max Stanton observed,

> There have been some allegations made in the community that even with the present diversification of power, the Caucasians still control the religious affairs of the village. Some substance to such an accusation might have existed in the past, but recent events have dispelled this problem. The past stake presidents have both been Samoans along with large numbers of Polynesians and Orientals in the stake and ward organizations.[5]

The leaders of the Laie Community Association, a nonchurch group, represent the various racial groups in the village.

One hundred years ago Laie was needed as a gathering place where Saints could come together and gain strength. But by the 1980s the Church was strong everywhere in the islands. Laie still offered blessings to the Saints of Hawaii through the temple, the university, and the missionary influence of the Polynesian Cultural Center, but it could not be considered Zion. Zion was appropriately in the stakes and wards.

In August 1973 the First Presidency of the Church, Harold B. Lee, N. Eldon Tanner, and Marion G. Romney, counseled the Saints of Laie concerning their role in the Church. They explained that as temples were built and stakes organized, the gathering spoken about in earlier days had come to a close.

> As time goes on, it is more important that members of the Church living in different areas throughout the world accept their responsibilities and help carry the load and not be dependent on the Church for financial assistance. This applies to the Saints in Laie. It is important that we realize that the original concept concerning gathering has now been fulfilled.[6]

The First Presidency went on to explain that if there were needy among the members in Laie, the regular welfare services of the Church were to be used to take care of the problems.

GUAM AND THE TRUST TERRITORY OF MICRONESIA

Latter-day Saints have lived on Guam since World War II. At that time, many of the islands of Micronesia—the Marshalls, Carolines, and Marianas, with their tiny islands of Majuro, Kwajalein, Ponape, Truk, Yap, and larger Saipan—were forever engrained on the minds of Americans and the world as Allied troops fought their way across the Pacific. Since World War II, servicemen's groups and branches of the Church have continued on Guam.

Guam, a territory of the United States, is America's westernmost outpost. It played a large role in U.S. defense during the Korean and Vietnam conflicts and remains strategically important to the United States. In 1970 Guam's total population was 86,926, but current estimates place the number much higher, around 120,000. Military families are much in evidence, but the local people, the Chamorros, number well over 60,000. English is the official language of the island, but the Chamorro tongue is still widely spoken. Guam was controlled by the Spanish for over two hundred years. During that period the local people were converted to Roman Catholicism, which remains the predominant religion.

The LDS presence on the island has been evident since 1945, when the first servicemen's group was organized. On 25 August 1955, President Joseph Fielding Smith visited Guam and dedicated it to the preaching of the gospel. In January 1957 the first full-time LDS missionaries arrived. Mark E. Petersen of the Quorum of the Twelve dedicated the first chapel in 1959. Until the 1970s, however, the missionaries confined their efforts almost entirely to Americans interested in the Church.

Guam has been part of many different missions—the Japanese, the

Northern Far East, the Southern Far East, and the Hawaii missions and the Kaneohe stake—even though Guam is separated from Hawaii by 3,300 miles of ocean. The Hawaii Mission sent missionaries to Guam in 1970, and soon after the Church there grew from a branch to two wards. During the mid-1970s missionaries broadened their proselyting base to include the Chamorro people. In January 1975 President Robert E. Crandall of the Hawaii Honolulu Mission sent elders to Saipan in the Mariana Islands, headquarters of the U.S. Trust Territory. This was the first real move into Micronesia proper.

Through the enthusiastic encouragement of Elder John H. Groberg, executive administrator for Hawaii and the South Pacific, President William W. Cannon of the Hawaii Mission led the expansion of the mission into all seven districts of what was called the U.S. Trust Territory until the early 1980s. Many missionaries, half of whom are from Tonga and Samoa, proselyte on or near Saipan, Palau, Yap, Truk, Pohnpei, Kwajalein, and Majuro. In March 1979 there were five hundred members of the Church in these islands, and by 1983 membership had grown to around three thousand.[7]

In the spring of 1980 Guam and Micronesia became a separate mission with Ferron C. Losee as president. The entire population of the mission, which is estimated to include approximately three hundred thousand people, is spread over several thousand islands in millions of square miles of ocean. In no island group does the population much exceed thirty thousand. There are nine distinct cultural groups and at least as many different languages. Considering these facts, the Church cannot expect to bring large numbers of people into the Mormon Church. Nevertheless, through programs such as seminary and schools, the Church can expect to greatly enrich the lives of many people in this far-flung part of the world.[8]

The Changing Role of the Mission President

Little has been said in this history about the mission presidents who have served since 1950. This omission does not mean that they have not accomplished as much as their predecessors; rather, it is indicative of the progress that has been made in Hawaii since 1950. Prior to that date there existed in Hawaii, as well as in many other mission areas of the world, what might be called the "cult of the mission president." This term does not necessarily have a negative connotation. But it does imply that the mission president was the most powerful Church official in the islands and that virtually any occasion when he was present was considered almost hallowed by many members and missionaries. This was both good and bad. In a Church that provided leadership through a basically vertical authority structure, it was good to have a strong Church authority. But sometimes it led to a near adoration of the presidents themselves, something they did not desire.

Two factors have helped to change the nature of the mission president's calling in Hawaii. First and most important has been the organization of stakes. The focus of authority is now directed toward stake presidents rather than toward mission presidents. Second, the Church has standardized the role of mission presidents everywhere so that with rare exceptions they are called to fill three-year missions. They administer their areas of responsibility in accordance with the *Mission President's Handbook,* and their major stewardship is now directed toward the young men and women who are filling missions under them.

The mission presidents since 1950 have been among the strongest leaders the Church has ever had in Hawaii. They have focused their attention primarily on the teaching of the gospel to prospective converts. Some older members of the Church have missed the casual teaching methods of earlier times when the elders frequently dropped in to chat and strum the ukelele. Although missionaries are still learning to play the "uke" and sing songs of Hawaii, the pressure of reports, tracting time, scripture study, and everything else that is required by the worldwide missionary program of the last four decades has made filling a mission in Hawaii much like performing the same service in California or elsewhere in the world. But it has been the mission presidents who have implemented this important change in missionary work.

The improved teaching methods of recent years have resulted in greater numbers of convert baptisms than in earlier times. President D. Arthur Haycock, who served as president from 1954 to 1958, was instrumental in raising the average number of convert baptisms per missionary so that the Hawaii Mission ranked among the top missions of the world. President Harry V. Brooks, who served from 1958 to 1963, maintained the high standards of missionary work that President Haycock had established. Both Haycock and Brooks also served for a number of years as presidents of the Hawaii Temple.

Still other developments have tended to reduce the importance of the mission president. Significant changes in Church organization since the late 1960s have made other leaders more visible and more important. Hawaii has its own resident Regional Representatives. In addition, two General Authorities reside in Hawaii and direct affairs there and in the

South Pacific as area executive administrators. For a period the office of the director of temporal affairs for Hawaii and the South Pacific was in Honolulu, as was the Church education system office that administered seminary and institute work as well as other area administrative affairs for Church schools in the South Pacific.

THE CHURCH IN HAWAII: AN INFLUENCE FOR GOOD

To many Church members in Hawaii, June 1978 stands out as a singular time in recent Church history. In that month President Spencer W. Kimball presided over rededication ceremonies of the Hawaii Temple (13–15 June) following extensive remodeling, and also directed an area conference for members throughout the Hawaiian Islands (18 June). Media covered both events and the Saints were thrilled to again have the Lord's Prophet among them. But the news event that captured the most television and radio time and the most newspaper space was the revelation on the priesthood. On 9 June the First Presidency announced that henceforth priesthood blessings would be available to "all worthy male members" regardless of "race or color."[9] Most Hawaiian Latter-day Saints heaved a sigh of relieved gratitude that they could feel freer to associate fully with all races. One Latter-day Saint observed that as he walked down King Street that day he felt for the first time in his life the full freedom to extend his love to the blacks of the world. A television reporter, expecting a different response, was surprised to hear his black LDS interviewee say that his only reaction to receiving his long-awaited blessing was his fervent hope to be worthy to receive the priesthood when it was bestowed upon him. All Latter-day Saints who loved their fellow men felt joy and some wept that the Lord had seen fit in his tender mercies to speak to his prophet.

The first 139 years of Church history in Hawaii have passed. But the end of every history is in reality but the beginning of a new chapter that must be written at a later time. The Church in Hawaii in the 1980s is a mature organization, 45,000 members strong.[10] Many families have been members of the Church ever since the time of George Q. Cannon. Such people are strong in their faith and well schooled in the purposes, practices, and doctrines of the Church. The number of Church members in Hawaii is not large, yet the Saints there appropriately see themselves as a vital part of a worldwide Church.

APPENDIX A

MISSION PRESIDENTS

HAWAII HONOLULU MISSION

This mission was originally organized as the Sandwich Islands Mission. The name was officially changed to Hawaiian Mission in 1900, to Hawaii Mission in 1950, and to Hawaii Honolulu Mission in 1974.

1. Hiram Clark	1850–1851
2. Philip B. Lewis	1851–1855
3. Silas Smith	1855–1857
4. Henry Bigler	1857–1864
5. Lorenzo Snow	1864
6. Ezra T. Benson	1864
7. Joseph F. Smith	1864–1865
8. Alma L. Smith	1865
9. George Nebeker	1865–1873
10. Fred A. H. F. Mitchell	1873–1876
11. Ward E. Pack	1876–1878
12. Simpson M. Molen	1878–1879
13. Harvey H. Cluff	1879–1882
14. Edward Partridge	1882–1885
15. Enoch Farr	1885–1887
16. William King	1887–1892
17. Matthew Noall	1892–1895
18. Samuel Edwin Woolley	1895–1919
19. Elias Wesley Smith	1919–1923
20. Eugene Jefferson Neff	1923–1926
21. William Mark Waddoups	1926–1931
22. Castle Hadlock Murphy	1931–1936
23. W. Francis Bailey	1936–1939

24. Roscoe C. Cox	1939–1942
25. Eldred Logan Waldron	1942–1944
26. Castle Hadlock Murphy	1944–1947
27. Elias Wesley Smith	1947–1950
28. Edward LaVaun Clissold	1950–1951
29. Ernest Alfred Nelson	1951–1954
30. David Arthur Haycock	1954–1958
31. Harry Vernal Brooks	1958–1963
32. George William Poulsen, Jr.	1963–1966
33. Orin R. Woodbury	1966–1969
34. Kenneth N. Gardner	1969–1972
35. Robert E. Crandall	1972–1975
36. William W. Cannon	1975–1978
37. Daniel B. Crawford	1978–1981
38. Robert J. Martin	1981–1984
39. William Perry	1984–1987
40. Yoshihiko Kikuchi	1987–1989
41. Waldo Perkins	1989–

JAPANESE MISSION (1937–1944)
CENTRAL PACIFIC MISSION (1944–1950)

1. Hilton A. Robertson	1937–1940
2. Jay C. Jensen	1940–1942
3. Edward LaVaun Clissold (acting)	1942–1944
4. Castle Hadlock Murphy (Hawaiian and CPM)	1944–1946
5. Melvyn A. Weenig	1946–1950

APPENDIX B

CHURCH ORGANIZATION

Clergy

Latter-day Saints define the word *priesthood* as the authority and power to act in the name of God. The Church is founded upon the belief that certain angelic messengers visited Joseph Smith and various of his associates and gave them, through the laying on of hands, the authority and power to act in the name of God the Father and Jesus Christ. This authority has in turn been given to other men. Worthy LDS males who are age twelve and older are ordained to the priesthood and may achieve positions of leadership.

Priesthood authority is of two kinds. The *Aaronic Priesthood* includes the offices of *deacon, teacher,* and *priest.* The higher *Melchizedek Priesthood* includes the offices of *elder, seventy,* and *high priest.* Other offices such as *bishop, patriarch,* and *apostle* are held by men who are ordained high priests.

All holders of the Melchizedek Priesthood are honored with the title *Elder.* It is always used to designate male LDS missionaries. Female missionaries are called *Sisters.*

Church Callings

Within the Church there are many positions or *callings.* For example, a woman might be *called*—that is, asked or assigned—to teach in the Sunday School. If she accepts her name will be placed before the congregation for a vote, which is usually unanimous; she is thus *sustained.* In a private setting, probably in the bishop's office, she will be *set apart.* The bishop and his counselors will place their hands on her head and set her apart, that is, give her a blessing that she may do well in her calling. In certain priesthood callings Church leaders may confer authority upon someone who has been called and sustained. Following a period of service an individual will be *released* from a calling. The person in authority interviews the person and formally releases him or her from that responsibility.

SCRIPTURES

The *Bible* is the Word of God as far as it is translated correctly and the *Book of Mormon* is also scripture. The *Book of Doctrine and Covenants (D&C)* is modern revelation, primarily to Joseph Smith. The *Pearl of Great Price,* which contains writings of Moses, Abraham, and Joseph Smith, is also scripture.

CHURCH ORGANIZATION

Church hierarchy is composed of men known as *General Authorities,* frequently referred to as the *Brethren.* The Church is led by a *President* who is also sustained by the members as a prophet, seer, and revelator. He is assisted by two *counselors,* also addressed as *President.* Together they make up the *First Presidency of the Church.* Immediately below the First Presidency is a *Quorum of Twelve Apostles,* also called the *Quorum* or *Council of the Twelve.* Members are also sustained as prophets, seers, and revelators. They and the members of the *First Quorum of the Seventy,* the next ranking quorum, are generally addressed as *Elder.*

Until the late 1970s seven men presided over missionary work as the *First Council of the Seventy.* Then the decision was made to expand the quorum, and sixty-six men now serve in the *First Quorum of the Seventy,* acting under direction of the Quorum of the Twelve Apostles. Presently the only other General Authorities are the three members of the *Presiding Bishopric,* who are responsible for the temporal affairs of the Church.

The *stake* is the basic geographical unit of the Church. The term derives from Isaiah 54:2–7, where "in prophetic imagery, Zion is pictured as a great tent upheld by cords fastened securely to *stakes.*" Elder Bruce R. McConkie explains that "the great areas of church population and strength, which sustain and uphold the restored Zion, are called *stakes.* . . . In area they cover from a few blocks to many miles; in membership they comprise from a few to several thousand saints" (McConkie, *Mormon Doctrine*).

Each stake is presided over by a *stake president* and two *counselors* who meet regularly with an advisory body of twelve men who compose a *Stake High Council* and are called *high councilors.*

Stakes are composed of several smaller congregations called *wards.* A *bishop* and two *counselors* oversee each ward.

Missions operate either in cooperation with stakes or independently in areas where stakes are not yet organized. They are presided over by a *mission president* and his two *counselors.* Units within missions are called *districts* (formerly *conferences*) and *branches,* both of which are led by presidents and counselors. Several branches comprise a district, just as several wards comprise a stake.

AUXILIARY ORGANIZATIONS

Present auxiliary organizations are: the *Relief Society,* the *Primary,* the *Sunday School,* the *Young Men* (formerly the Young Men's Mutual Improvement Association), and the *Young Women* (formerly the Young Women's Mutual Improvement Association). These organizations are auxiliary or addenda to the priesthood and are intended to support and sustain the general purposes of the Church. In a sense they are all temporary, but they have existed within the Church almost since its founding. Each organization has a *Presidency* of three individuals plus a staff of teachers, advisors, and other specialists such as musicians.

APPENDIX C

THE LATTER-DAY SAINT MESSAGE

The Church of Jesus Christ of Latter-day Saints (also known as LDS or Mormon) was organized on 6 April 1830. Even before the official founding of the Church, Joseph Smith sent his brother Samuel on a missionary journey in the eastern United States. Samuel took with him copies of the recently published Book of Mormon and proclaimed, as Mormon missionaries have done ever since, that the heavens, which had long been sealed, had been opened, that God the Father and his Son Jesus Christ had visited Joseph in a vision, wherein they revealed themselves in the form of perfected immortal men, and as a result of that experience Joseph Smith had been called as a prophet to reveal God's will to mankind and restore (not reform) the pristine gospel of Jesus Christ. Samuel Smith explained to his listeners that the Book of Mormon was a translation of ancient metal plates that contained a record of Christ's dealings with the people of the Americas. Within this book is the record of Christ's appearance to his "other sheep" following his ministry in Palestine. Much has been added by way of enlargement, instruction, and clarification of the message carried by the first Mormon missionary, but essentially the message is still the same today.

Because the doctrines of Mormonism are quite different from those of mainstream Christianity, it is appropriate to explain the LDS theological position here briefly.

GOD THE FATHER AND JESUS CHRIST

Mormons hold that *Jesus Christ* (Jehovah or Yahweh) is the God of this world and that he created this earth under the authority and direction of his Father, or Elohim. Jesus Christ was the firstborn in the spirit, the Only Begotten in the flesh, without blemish, a God in mortal form who atoned for the sins of humankind by dying on the cross. He was literally resurrected (John 20:19–20; 21:13). Christ now directs the affairs of this earth in his resurrected, perfected, immortal state.

WHAT IS HUMANKIND AND WHY WAS IT CREATED?

Human beings are the spiritual offspring of God the Father (Heb. 12:9; Acts 17:59). These spiritual offspring developed, thought, learned, and grew while in the pre-mortal stage (Jer. 1:1–7). When appropriate in the development of these souls, God the Father introduced the program of mortality to them. In essence, it was that a world would be prepared whereon the spirits would be placed in mortal, physical bodies (a closer stage to God's perfect immortal body) away from the presence of the Father. In this stage humankind would be tested and gain experience by faith (Heb. 11:6; Phil. 2:12). God promised that he would reveal a path by which mortals could purify themselves. It was expected that mortals would make mistakes and have trouble controlling their passions, appetites, and desires. Nevertheless, because no unclean entity could be allowed back into the presence of the Father, a Savior would be sent to take upon himself the sins of the world. Mortals could not give their own lives. They would have no such control; but a God could make this infinite sacrifice. Thus a Savior who was the Son of God would die of his own free will and meet the demands of eternal justice. Justice demands that every mortal pay the price for his or her own sins. The Father's program made it possible for mortals to repent and place their trust in Jesus Christ. Jesus agreed to pay the debt for the sins of humankind and did so. The responsibility placed on human beings was to obey God's laws, repent, perform the commanded ordinances, such as baptism, and remain faithful until death.

Latter-day Saints believe this plan was accepted and is in effect. They refer to it as the "Plan of Salvation." There is another important aspect of this, though. Lucifer, son of the morning, dissented and asked the Father and the spirit children to follow his plan, which was to limit human free agency and give the glory to Lucifer. Salvation would be assured, but growth would be limited. A war resulted (Isa. 14:12–15; Rev. 12:7–17) and a third of the spirits of heaven were cast down to earth, led by Lucifer who became the devil (Luke 10:18). The evil forces of the earth were created in this way. They remain here to tempt and try mortals.

Latter-day Saints believe the world was created as a testing ground for mortals. The only purpose of existence is to prepare humankind to be like God the Father and Jesus Christ. LDS scriptures (see p. 204) tell us that "Adam fell that men might be, and men are that they might have joy" (Book of Mormon, 2 Nephi 2:25). Further, "This is [God's] work and [his] glory, to bring to pass the immortality and eternal life of man" (Pearl of Great Price, Moses 1:39).

THE MORMON VIEW OF THE AFTERLIFE

Death is a sorrowful time for Latter-day Saints, but only because of the temporary separation of loved ones. Upon death, the spirit leaves the body and enters the spirit world. There a partial judgement occurs and the spirits of the righteous enter a realm called Paradise. Spirits of the wicked are sent to a spirit prison (1 Pet. 3:18–19). All spirits are conscious and have the ability to communicate with one another. Teaching goes on in this sphere, but mortal work cannot be performed. All spirits await the day of resurrection and final judgement (Rev. 20:5–6, 12–14). When this happens at the end of the Millennium, some souls will be crowned with glory and exalted in the Celestial Kingdom (1 Cor. 15:40–42). These souls, now having perfect resurrected bodies, will partake of the glory of the Father. They will live in eternal family units and produce spiritual offspring like God the Father. Souls who have not measured up to the same standard will be assigned to the Terrestrial or Telestial kingdoms. Almost all souls will be happy, but only those of the Celestial realms will have glory.

THE PRIESTHOOD AND SALVATION

Latter-day Saints not only believe God the Father and Jesus Christ appeared to Joseph Smith, they also affirm that many other heavenly messengers appeared to Smith and various associates. Among those who came from the other realm were John the Baptist; Peter, James, and John; Elijah; Moses; and Moroni, a Book of Mormon prophet. Each of these visitors gave Joseph Smith keys and authority relating to church organization, order, and ordinances (recorded in Doctrine and Covenants, and The Pearl of Great Price). This authority to act in the name of God is called the Aaronic and Melchizedek priesthoods.

Mormons believe that salvation (in the sense of exaltation) can be obtained only by faith in Jesus Christ, repentance, baptism, receiving the gift of the Holy Ghost, and through receiving other ordinances, such as marriage for eternity. These ordinances can be performed by men holding the priesthood. All humankind will be resurrected but only those who obtain the ordinances and obey the commandments will be exalted.

Temple Work and the Family

Mormons believe that Christ's admonition, "whatsoever thou shalt *bind* on earth shall be bound in heaven" (Matt. 16:19; italics added), applies literally to those who have priesthood authority. The highest ordinances available to rank-and-file Mormons are called the endowment (covenants, promises, and blessings), and marriage for time and all eternity. These blessings can be obtained only in a Latter-day Saints temple. Mormons teach that children born to couples who are sealed in the temple will be part of the eternal family of their parents.

In addition to ordinances for the living, Mormons also do proxy work for the dead in these temples; that is, ordinances for people who died without hearing the gospel of Jesus Christ while mortal. Baptisms (1 Cor. 15:29), endowments, and sealings of families are all performed for the dead. Latter-day Saints are especially concerned for their kindred dead; hence there is great interest in genealogy. Saving ordinances are mortal in nature and must be performed by mortals; nevertheless, Latter-day Saints believe that this work can be performed for the dead, who then have the right to accept or reject it.

In conjunction with this is the belief that missionary work is being carried on among the spirits of the dead, by those spirits of the dead who know and understand the gospel. This has obvious implications for souls who have died without a knowledge of Jesus Christ. The dead of all nations, Christian and non-Christian alike, are being taught the gospel in the spirit world. They are not beyond the hope of salvation.

NOTES

Full bibliographic information can be found in the bibliography.

CHAPTER 1

1. Samuel Eliot Morison, *The Oxford History of the American People,* 548.

2. Eugene E. Campbell, "The Mormon Gold-Mining Mission of 1849"; see also Henry W. Bigler, Journal, 25 September 1850; and William Farrer, Biographical Sketch, Hawaiian Mission Report and Diary, 25 September 1850.

3. Farrer, Mission Report and Diary, 13 December 1850.

4. The title "elder" is used by one of the lay priesthoods of The Church of Jesus Christ of Latter-day Saints. Latter-day Saints define the word "priesthood" as the authority and power to act in the name of God. See appendixes B and C for explanation of this and other LDS terms and concepts.

5. King James Version, James 1:5–6.

6. The Pearl of Great Price, Joseph Smith 2:17; see also Joseph Smith, *History of The Church of Jesus Christ of Latter-day Saints,* 1:3–8.

7. The information concerning Hawaiian history in this chapter is from Ralph S. Kuykendall, *The Hawaiian Kingdom;* Gavan Daws, *Shoal of Time: A History of the Hawaiian Islands;* and Gerrit P. Judd, IV, *Hawaii: An Informal History.*

CHAPTER 2

1. George Q. Cannon, *My First Mission,* 19.

2. William Farrer, Biographical Sketch, Hawaiian Mission Report and Diary, 13 January 1851.

3. Ibid., 18 January 1851.

4. Cannon, *My First Mission,* 22.

5. George Q. Cannon, Journal of Travels to the Hawaiian Mission Jubilee, 30 December 1900, p. 16.

6. Farrer, Mission Report and Diary, 26 January 1851.

7. Cannon, *My First Mission,* 27 (quotation); Farrer, Mission Report and Diary, 27, 30 January 1851.

8. Farrer, Mission Report and Diary, 2 February 1851 (and quotation); also Cannon, *My First Mission,* 29.

9. "Manuscript History of the Hawaiian Mission," 27, 28 February 1851, compiled by Andrew Jenson (hereafter cited as MHHM).

10. The Society Islands Mission was founded in 1844 and closed temporarily in 1852.

11. MHHM, 20 February 1851.

12. Cannon, *My First Mission,* 38.

13. Ibid., 38–43; also MHHM, dates as mentioned.

14. Cannon, *My First Mission,* 46.

15. MHHM, 6 August 1851; also Cannon, *My First Mission,* 46. The terms used to designate the organizational structure of the LDS Church are somewhat different from those used by other churches. Within a foreign mission—that is, an ecclesiastical area outside the organized stakes, similar to dioceses—the areas of the mission are divided into districts, which were called conferences until 1927. In this book the term appropriate to the time period will be used. Readers unfamiliar with Church organization should consult appendix B.

16. MHHM, 17, 18 August 1851.

17. Henry William Bigler, Journal, 12, 13 March 1854 (Cannon's speaking abilities were similarly mentioned by his other companions); Cannon, *My First Mission,* 44.

18. Farrer, Mission Report and Diary; MHHM, dates as mentioned.

19. The wife of Elder Woodbury had temporarily remained in California because of illness. The wives of all three elders were apparently not considered missionaries; they merely accompanied their husbands on their missions. The following quotation is from a letter from Parley P. Pratt to Brigham Young: "We have sent to those islands three additional missionaries who sailed on the sixth day of August for the Port of Honolulu." Parley P. Pratt, *Autobiography of Parley P. Pratt,* 386.

20. Farrer, Mission Report and Diary; Cannon, *My First Mission,* 47; MHHM, dates as mentioned; *Millennial Star* (Liverpool, England) 14:492–493.

21. MHHM, 22 August 1851.

22. Ibid., 22 September 1851.

23. R. Armstrong to R. C. Wyllie, Honolulu, 8 October 1851, Hawaii State Archives, Foreign Office, Box 15; also in Letters to Brigham Young, 1851. See also Margaret Comfort Bock, "The Church of Jesus Christ of Latter-day Saints in the Hawaiian Islands," 12–15.

24. Cannon, *My First Mission,* 50.

25. Farrer, Mission Report and Diary, 5 December 1851.

26. Philip B. Lewis to Brigham Young, 16 March 1853, Letters to Brigham Young, Box 21, fd. 13; see also Gerrit P. Judd, IV, *Hawaii: An Informal History,* 81.

27. Farrer, Mission Report and Diary, 13 December 1851.

CHAPTER 3

1. George Q. Cannon, *My First Mission,* 69. Cannon's comments on the beginning of this work are inconsistent. He states that he started translating in the last days of the month of January 1851. But this seems highly unlikely since he had been in the islands only six weeks at the time. On the previous page of *My First Mission* he states that the work of translation was begun after the branches at Wailuku and Waiehu had been organized, which did not happen until the fall of 1851. Cannon apparently remembered the process taking two and a half years, for he wrote: "The translation was finished on July the 22nd, 1853—about two years and a half from the time I commenced it" (p. 70). However, it is more likely that the work took only one and a half years to complete. This is confirmed by Andrew Jenson, who states that translation work began 27 January 1852. See Andrew Jenson, comp., *Church Chronology,* 45.

2. William Farrer, Biographical Sketch, Hawaiian Mission Report and Diary, 14 June 1852 through 6 August 1852.

3. Cannon, *My First Mission,* 68–70.

4. Conference Minutes of the Sandwich Islands Mission, 6 October 1852.

5. Cannon, *My First Mission,* 70–71.

6. In July the same subject had been discussed but not resolved. John Stillman Woodbury, Journal, 25 July 1853.

7. Ibid., pp. 124–126. Woodbury's notes appear to be a copy of the minutes of the conference. Henry W. Bigler, Journal, made notes that are almost identical. See dates around 6 October 1853 in both Woodbury and Bigler.

8. Farrer, Mission Report and Diary, 6 November 1853; Bigler, Journal, 5 January 1854.

9. Farrer, Mission Report and Diary, 2 December 1853.

10. Two references do indicate that the books were slow in coming. For example, in a letter to Brigham Young, written 13 April 1856, John T. Caine acknowledges the receipt by the missionaries in Hawaii of fifteen hundred copies of a letter from Cannon in the Hawaiian language. It gave "a brief history of the rise of the Church, the coming forth of the Book of Mormon &c." It was, according to Caine, "the first publication setting forth our principles ever issued in the Hawaiian language." Caine mentioned that Cannon had written to say the Book of Mormon had been printed but was not bound at that time. John T. Caine to Brigham Young, 13 April 1856, Letters to Brigham Young.

11. Bigler, Journal, 24 November 1857; Bigler to Brigham Young, 3 December 1857 and 21 May 1858, Letters to Brigham Young. Statistics of the last conference held while the foreign elders were still there listed "1800 copies Book of Mormon in Hawaiian, unbound." MHHM, 25 April 1858.

12. Farrer, Mission Report and Diary, 20 September 1852.

13. Woodbury, Journal, 9 April 1853.

14. Ephraim Green, Diary, 18 April 1853.

15. Farrer, Mission Report and Diary, April–May 1852.

16. Ralph S. Kuykendall, *The Hawaiian Kingdom, 1778–1845,* 1:351–360.

17. Notes on Conference between Mr. Armstrong and Certain Mormon Ministers, 20 August 1853, Hawaii State Archives, Foreign Office and Executive File; see also Margaret Comfort Bock, "The Church of Jesus Christ of Latter-day Saints in the Hawaiian Islands," 21.

18. Woodbury, Journal, 7, 8 May 1854.

19. Philip B. Lewis to Brigham Young, 16 March 1853, Letters to Brigham Young.

20. James B. Allen and Glen M. Leonard, *The Story of the Latter-day Saints,* 69.

21. Ibid., 170–171.

22. Ibid., 278–279.

23. Woodbury, Journal, 7 April 1853.

24. Ibid., 22 May 1853.

25. The polygamy issue is amply documented by Bock ("Church in the Hawaiian Islands," 25–27), who used numerous sources from the Hawaii State Archives; for further details see Woodbury, Journal, pp. 314–317, 320, 339–341, 345, 389. Before the ruling preventing Church officials from performing marriages had even been made public, Francis A. Hammond wrote that he had met with Levi Haalelea, a member of the privy council, who told Hammond "how he fought against a bill that has just been passed by the legislature and house of Nobles to have the power of marrying retained only in the hands of the Minister of Interior and make it a source of revenue by affixing a license to it &c. He said the bill was got up on account of our ordaining so many natives to the priesthood, and his fighting stoutly against it caused Armstrong, the framer of the bill, to call him a Mormon. They have also passed a law to have all ministers of the gospel taxed. This too was got up for our benefit as we had ordained many natives to the priesthood and under the old law they could all get clear from their taxes." Francis A. Hammond, Journal, 24 July 1854.

26. Benjamin F. Johnson, *My Life's Review,* 176–179.

27. Woodbury and Hammond both commented on this problem.

28. Bigler, Journal, 29 December 1853.

29. On one occasion, while performing this ordinance, Farrer and Lewis were assaulted by a bully—an Australian prisoner who had been released from jail to help bury the dead—who told them they were under arrest. This man, named Turner, insisted that he had been sent by the marshal and attempted to make the elders go to the fort on charges of breaking quarantine regulations and ministering as physicians contrary to law. They refused, insisting that they had done nothing wrong. He relented, but because of later difficulties they made an official complaint against him. The trial turned out to be more a trial of the elders than of Turner. Finally Elder B. F. Johnson took the case into his own hands, and the results were turned in favor of the Saints. Turner, incidentally, was so moved by Johnson's defense of the Church and the cause of the elders that he wept and asked forgiveness of the brethren he had assaulted. Johnson, *My Life's Review,* 158–161.

30. Bigler, Journal, November 1853.

31. Johnson, *My Life's Review,* 157–158.

CHAPTER 4

1. For more information on the LDS concept of gathering, see Leonard J. Arrington, *Great Basin Kingdom: An Economic History of the Latter-day Saints, 1830–1900,* 23–28.

2. John Stillman Woodbury, Journal, p. 125; Benjamin F. Johnson, *My Life's Review,* 164, 168–169. Francis A. Hammond noted in his journal that the decision was made to get a vessel as soon as possible. However, there was strong opposition to the idea. See Hammond, Journal, 5 October 1853.

Tanner's plan was impracticable because Hawaiian laws forbade any Hawaiian from permanently leaving the kingdom. The population was diminishing in the face of diseases to which the Hawaiians had little or no immunity, and the government did not permit anyone to leave. The elders did not take this law into consideration a year or two later when they tried to take a few Hawaiians home with them. They were refused passports, but thought the government was showing prejudice toward them. Tanner, apparently ignorant of this, continued to work for what one of his companions called his "hobby" until President Lewis permitted him to go to California to buy a ship. He sailed in late March, but his voyage ended abruptly when the ship was driven ashore on Kauai. He sailed from Honolulu again in April.

The story of Tanner's ship is rather tragic. He had raised more than a thousand dollars to help buy the vessel before he left Honolulu. When he arrived in California, he purchased an old brig for six thousand dollars. In time Elder Parley P. Pratt, still presiding over the Pacific coast and area missions, had to help, both financially and with encouragement, as did the new Hawaii-bound missionaries. A large sum of money was spent fitting out the old vessel and repairing it. When the boat was relatively seaworthy, the former owner, who had supervised the whole operation, took the missionary crew out for a shakedown cruise. It turned out to be a near disaster. Captain and crew did not work at all well together, for the captain was a rugged, worldly sort and the elders were unaccustomed to his manner and choice of words. Pratt decided that the whole idea would not work and sold the vessel back to its original owner at great loss to all who had invested in it. As a result the new elders were forced to go to work to earn funds to pay for their passage to Hawaii. Because of this they were delayed about two months, and the mission was short of workers from the end of July, when the first group left, until 27 September 1854, when they arrived. Johnson, *My Life's Review,* 183; Parley P. Pratt, *Autobiography of Parley P. Pratt,* 409. Other sources used concerning Tanner's boat project are Henry W. Bigler, Journal, 11, 18 March 1854; Woodbury, Journal, 1 March, 2 May, 25 July 1854; Philip B. Lewis to Brigham Young, 8 August 1854, Letters to Brigham Young; and Joseph Fielding Smith, Jr., *The Life of Joseph F. Smith,* 166–167.

3. Johnson, *My Life's Review,* 167–169.

4. Ibid.

5. F. A. Hammond to William Farrer, 24 February 1854, in Farrer, 2:81; see also Hammond, Journal, 23 February 1854.

6. Brigham Young to Philip B. Lewis and missionaries to the Sandwich Islands, 1 April 1854, Letterbooks, Ms f 219.

7. Lewis to Young, 8 August 1854, Letters to Brigham Young.

8. Ibid.

9. Sources vary on the number of years, but Haalelea finally allowed five years' use without rent.

10. Johnson, *My Life's Review,* 182.

11. Hammond, Journal, 17 August 1854.

12. Ephraim Green, Diary, various dates 1854–1855. Except when otherwise noted, the information on Lanai comes from this diary.

13. Hammond, Journal, 3 September 1854.

14. Green, Diary.

15. Ibid., 3 October 1854.

16. George Q. Cannon, *My First Mission,* 20–21.

17. Hammond, Journal, 8 October to 4 November 1854; Green, Diary, 14 October to 29 December 1854.

18. Green, Diary.

19. Ibid.

20. MHHM, 18 November 1854.

21. *Millennial Star* (Liverpool, England) 17:444.

22. Smith, *Life of Joseph F. Smith,* 183.

23. Woodbury, Journal, 8 August 1855.

24. Smith, *Life of Joseph F. Smith,* 183.

25. Hammond, Journal, 25 July 1855.

26. John T. Caine to Brigham Young, 13 April 1856; Silas Smith to Brigham Young, 13 May 1856, Letters to Brigham Young.

27. Silas Smith to Brigham Young, 3 July 1856, Letters to Brigham Young.

28. MHHM, 27 December 1856, 15 May 1857, and 4 September 1857; see also Smith, *Life of Joseph F. Smith,* 185.

29. The information in the preceding paragraphs was taken from the following letters from Silas Smith to Brigham Young, Letters to Brigham Young: 3 July, 31 July, 11 October, 6 December 1856; 17 May 1857.

30. Bigler, Journal, 13 September 1857. But he later enlarged this estimate to several hundred faithful Saints.

31. Ibid., 4 October 1857; and Manuscript History of Brigham Young (hereafter cited as MHBY), 4 October 1857.

32. Bigler, Journal, 4 October 1857.

33. MHBY, 20 November 1857.

34. Ibid.

35. Ibid.

36. Ibid., 22 December 1857.

37. Ibid., 4 February 1858.

38. Henry W. Bigler and John Stillman Woodbury to Brigham Young, 3 December 1857, Letters to Brigham Young.

39. Ibid.

40. *Directory: Church of Jesus Christ of Latter-day Saints, Hawaiian Mission,* 10.

41. MHHM, 25 April 1858; 6, 7, 8 October 1858.

CHAPTER 5

1. MHBY, 10 October 1858.

2. The most frequently cited books, articles, and theses concerning Gibson's Mormon years include: Gwynn Barrett, "Walter Murray Gibson: The Shepherd Saint of Lanai Revisited"; R. Lanier Britsch, "Another Visit With Walter Murray Gibson"; Gavan Daws, "The Shepherd Saint," in *Shoal of Time: A History of the Hawaiian Islands,* 220–225; Ralph S. Kuykendall, *The Hawaiian Kingdom,* vol. 2, *1854–1874: Twenty Critical Years,* 102–104, passim; Frank W. McGhie, "The Life and Intrigues of Walter Murray Gibson"; James A. Michener and A. Grove Day, "Gibson, the King's Evil Angel," in *Rascals in Paradise,* 120–154; Joseph B. Musser, "Walter Murray Gibson—Oceanic Adventurer"; Brigham H. Roberts, *Comprehensive History of the Church,* 5:97–100; Esther L. Sousa, "Walter Murray Gibson's Rise to Power in Hawaii"; Samuel W. Taylor, "Walter Murray Gibson: Great Mormon Rascal"; Lorrin A. Thurston, *Memoirs of the Hawaiian Revolution.* The newest books on Gibson are Paul Bailey, *Hawaii's Royal Prime Minister: The Life and Times of Walter Murray Gibson;* and Jacob Adler and Robert M. Kamins, *The Fantastic Life of Walter Murray Gibson: Hawaii's Minister of Everything.*

3. The one author who has taken a positive position regarding Gibson is Gwynn Barrett, whose article is mentioned in note 2. After careful investigation I have concluded that Barrett was not correct in his reassessment of Gibson. See my article mentioned in note 2.

4. *Deseret News* (Salt Lake City), 18 November 1860.

5. *Pacific Commercial Advertiser* (Honolulu), 17 October 1861.

6. Walter Murray Gibson, Diary, 5 November 1861. Gibson's diary is also reproduced as an appendix in McGhie, "Life and Intrigues."

7. Gibson, Diary, 31 January 1862.

8. Ezra T. Benson to George Q. Cannon, 12 April 1864, MHBY.

9. Joseph F. Smith to Cannon, 4 May 1864, MHBY.

10. Walter M. Gibson to Brigham Young, 7 April 1864, Letters to Brigham Young.

11. Captain Gibson remained in Hawaii until shortly before his death in 1888. Although he did not die a wealthy man, he enjoyed a considerable amount of financial as well as political and social success during the post-Lanai years of his life. He was a firm supporter of causes that were popular with the Hawaiian royalty. For several years, from 1882 until 1887, he was prime minister of the Hawaiian kingdom. He died in a Catholic hospital in San Francisco.

CHAPTER 6

1. Joseph F. Smith to Brigham Young, 5 July 1864, MHBY.

2. Brigham Young to Joseph F. Smith, 28 July 1864, Letterbooks.

3. MHHM, 1–4 October 1864.

4. Brigham Young to King Kamehameha V, 24 March 1865, Letterbooks.

5. Gavan Daws, *Shoal of Time: A History of the Hawaiian Islands,* 174–178.

6. Francis A. Hammond, Journal, 26 January 1865.

7. Brigham Young to Daniel H. Wells and Brigham Young, Jr., 28 February 1865, Letterbooks.

8. Brigham Young to William King, 29 March 1865; Brigham Young to Hammond and Nebeker, 29 December 1864, Letterbooks; Hammond, Journal, 9 March 1865.

9. Hammond, Journal, 1 May 1865.

10. Ibid., 7 May 1865.

11. Kamehameha V to Brigham Young, 10 May 1865, Letters to Brigham Young.

12. Nebeker to Brigham Young, 15 March 1867; Alma L. Smith and Benjamin Cluff to Brigham Young, 10 March 1867; Smith to Brigham Young, 16 March 1867, Letters to Brigham Young.

13. Brigham Young to George Nebeker, 30 May 1866, Letterbooks.

14. Nebeker to Brigham Young, 17 October 1865 and 19 November 1866, Letters to Brigham Young.

15. See Ralph S. Kuykendall, *The Hawaiian Kingdom,* 2:106–114.

16. "Sandwich Islands Conference Report," 6, 7, and 8 April 1866, MHBY.

17. MHHM, 7 October 1866.

18. Daws, *Shoal of Time,* 175–176.

19. Brigham Young to Nebeker, 16 July 1867, Letterbooks.

20. Daws, *Shoal of Time,* 176.

21. Brigham Young to Nebeker, 6 February 1868, Letterbooks; Nebeker to Brigham Young, 24 February 1868 and 15 March 1868, Letters to Brigham Young.

CHAPTER 7

1. Previous authors have generally devoted much space to the operation of the plantation over the years. Although Laie plantation was the physical location of Church headquarters in Hawaii, the history of the operations of the plantation are outside the central concern of this book. For more detailed treatment of the plantation operations, see Margaret Comfort Bock, "The Church of Jesus Christ of Latter-day Saints in the Hawaiian Islands," chap. 3; Joseph B. Musser, "Laie—Home Place of the Church in Hawaii"; and Antoine R. Ivins, "Laie Plantation."

2. Doctrine and Covenants, Section 89.

3. Leonard J. Arrington, *Great Basin Kingdom: An Economic History of the Latter-day Saints, 1830–1900,* 250.

4. Harvey Harris Cluff, Autobiography, 160.

5. Native Saints in the Sandwich Islands to Brigham Young and Counselors, 25 June 1874, Letters to Brigham Young. Mitchell was, in fact, more dictatorial than would normally be expected of a mission president. When he came to Laie, he came as part-owner of the plantation, having purchased one third of the farm from Nebeker while the latter was home in Utah taking care of business. (Nebeker returned home fairly regularly during the last four years of his eight-year mission.)

6. Edward Partridge, Jr., Journal, 15 June 1882.

7. Cluff, Autobiography, 123; Smith to Brigham Young, 9 November 1874; Pack to Brigham Young, 19 April 1877, Letters to Brigham Young.

8. MHHM, 23 February 1889.

9. MHHM, passim.

10. Alma L. Smith to Brigham Young, 14 October 1875, Letters to Brigham Young.

11. Ibid.

12. Ward E. Pack to Brigham Young, 19 April 1877, Letters to Brigham Young.

13. Gerrit P. Judd IV, *Hawaii: An Informal History,* 111.

14. Kamehameha V to Brigham Young, 10 May 1865, Letters to Brigham Young.

15. Cluff, Autobiography, 158.

16. Bock, "Church in the Hawaiian Islands," 68, 76–77; Partridge, Journal, 152.

17. MHHM, December 1882.

18. MHHM, March to May 1892.

19. Helena G. Allen, *The Betrayal of Liliuokalani, Last Queen of Hawaii, 1838–1917,* 388. Allen dates the baptism in 1916. The date is unclear on the baptismal record in the LDS Church Archives, the zero looking much like a one. However, Abraham Fernandez died in 1915, making the 1916 date impossible.

20. Gavan Daws, *Shoal of Time: A History of the Hawaiian Islands,* 291–292.

CHAPTER 8

1. Harvey Harris Cluff, Autobiography, 129; *Woman's Exponent* (hereafter cited as *WE,* Salt Lake City) 3, no. 12: 1, letter of 5 October 1874.

2. MHHM, passim.

3. *WE* 9, no. 10 (1 August 1880): 74.

4. Sister Noall died at the early age of thirty-three, in 1897. She had filled two missions with her husband totaling over seven years. After their return to Salt Lake City in 1895 she gave birth to a fifth child. Three children had been born in Hawaii.

5. References relating to the Relief Society are taken from *WE,* 1875–1895.

6. MHHM, 6 May 1877.

7. MHHM, 5 April 1883, 6 April 1885, and 6 April 1895.

8. *WE* 12, no. 11: 86; 23, nos. 3–4 (1 and 15 August 1894): 173; 24, no. 2 (15 June 1895).

9. Jerry K. Loveland, "Dedication of the Old Laie Chapel." The manuscript quotes at length from the original minutes of the dedication by William G. Farrell, conference clerk.

10. Ibid.

11. MHHM, December through March 1879–1880.

12. *WE* 3, no. 12: 1.

13. Ibid.

14. MHHM, 5 April 1883.

15. MHHM, 5 October 1887.

16. The Spaulding manuscript was published as *The "Manuscript Found:" Manuscript, Story, by Rev. Solomon Spaulding, Deceased* (Salt Lake City: Deseret News, 1886). For more sources on this subject see James B. Allen and Glen M. Leonard, *The Story of the Latter-day Saints,* 665.

17. It is probable that Saints at Laie were discouraged about the Laie plantation during the time when President Smith was among them. Yet some writers and speakers have implied that the continued existence of the Laie settlement was in serious question. (See David W. Cummings, *Centennial History of Laie.*) There is no evidence in the records of the mission or of the missionaries at that time that this might have been so.

On the other hand, there is little reason to doubt that President Smith made this prophecy. According to Castle H. Murphy, who was in Hawaii when Smith visited on several occasions after the turn of the century, such statements are in harmony with the kinds of things he said in Murphy's presence.

The principal problem is that Smith's words were recorded many years after the fact by a woman who had been young at the time. She stated that her memory had been reinforced by her grandparents' retelling of the event. Although her testimony lends authenticity to the belief that Smith did make the prophecy, the accuracy of statements remembered after so many years must be questioned.

18. Cummings, *Centennial History of Laie,* 13–15.

19. MHHM, February 1885 to 25 June 1887; Joseph Fielding Smith, Jr., *The Life of Joseph F. Smith,* 262–286; John J. Stewart, *The Life of Joseph Fielding Smith,* 39–44.

20. James Keeler to David O. Calder, 23 August 1877, MHHM.

21. *WE* 26, nos. 18–19 (15 February and 1 March 1898).

CHAPTER 9

1. Leonard J. Arrington, *Great Basin Kingdom: An Economic History of the Latter-day Saints, 1830–1900,* 409–411.

2. James B. Allen and Richard O. Cowan, *Mormonism in the Twentieth Century,* 7–18.

3. The information concerning the mission years of Matthew Noall, unless otherwise indicated, has been taken from MHHM (see appropriate dates). See also Matthew Noall and Elizabeth DeEtte Laker Noall, Journals, Reports, and Letters to the First Presidency, Etc.; and Matthew Noall, *To My Children.*

4. An incidental matter, yet one that sheds light on the situation during those years, was the installation in December 1893 of a telephone connected to Honolulu. Because Sister Noall was very ill during her pregnancy, it was considered advisable for the Noalls to move to Honolulu where better medical care was available. So for the next six months, until the baby was born, they lived in Honolulu, and Noall managed the plantation by occasional visits to Laie and frequent conversations on the telephone. He kept all of the accounts and records at Honolulu.

5. Matthew Noall, "Letter of Instructions to the Missionaries . . . Laboring in the Hawaiian Mission," April 1894, in Elders Improvement Association Minute Book, pp. 76–89.

6. The main source for the years 1895 to 1915 is Samuel E. Woolley, Journals.

7. MHHM, 4 November 1895.

8. Antoine R. Ivins, "Laie Plantation," 6.

9. Margaret Comfort Bock, "The Church of Jesus Christ of Latter-day Saints in the Hawaiian Islands," 90. The frequent and extensive references to the finances of the plantation may give the impression that the economics of the Laie plantation were the only concern of the mission president. It is unfortunate that missionary journals do not really portray the actual spirit and procedures of missionary work among members and prospective converts. It is important to know that nearly all of the twenty to twenty-five missionaries laboring in Hawaii during these years were out among the people teaching the gospel.

10. Joseph B. Musser, "Laie—Home Place of the Church in Hawaii," 12–13. See also MHHM, 22 August 1918.

11. Ivins, "Laie Plantation."

12. George Q. Cannon, Journal of Travels to the Hawaiian Mission Jubilee, 17 December 1900, p. 9. Other important sources for the Jubilee are the journals of Samuel Woolley and MHHM, by date.

13. Woolley, Journal, 23 December 1900.

14. Cannon, Journal of Travels, 30 December 1900, p. 16.

15. Ibid., p. 14; see also Woolley, Journal, 27 December 1900.

16. Woolley, Journal, 28 December 1900.

CHAPTER 10

1. Italics added. General Minutes, Hawaiian Mission, 6 April 1911, p. 8, fd. 3.

2. "Civic Pride Is Part of Mormon Policy as Evidenced by Settlement at Laie:

Homes, Roads and School Are Credit to the Territory," *Pacific Commercial Advertiser,* Sunday, 21 March 1920.

3. Moses Cowley, "Correspondence," *Liahona* 12 (26 August 1913): 159; MHHM.

4. General Minutes, Hawaiian Mission, April 1914, fd. 4.

5. Cowley, "Correspondence."

6. General Minutes, Hawaiian Mission, April 1916.

7. General Minutes, Hawaiian Mission, Conference, 3 April 1915, fd. 5.

8. Quoted in Joseph Fielding Smith, Jr., *The Life of Joseph F. Smith,* 421.

9. *Conference Reports* (Salt Lake City), October 1915, pp. 8–9. *Conference Reports* are the official record of the semiannual general conferences of the Church.

10. The principal source for this section is Dennis H. Atkin, "A History of Iosepa, the Utah Polynesian Colony." Some useful information concerning the Hawaiian government's attitude toward the colony is found in Margaret Comfort Bock, "The Church of Jesus Christ of Latter-day Saints in the Hawaiian Islands," 77ff.

11. Heber J. Grant, "The Dedicatory Prayer in the Hawaiian Temple," 284.

12. MHHM, 11 December 1919.

13. MHHM, by date. See also *The Improvement Era* (Salt Lake City) 19:79–80, 953–958; 23:149–153, 281–288; and 29:258–262. The *Era* was the official magazine of the Mutual Improvement Association until Church auxiliary periodicals were consolidated and replaced by the *Ensign* in 1970 as the principal periodical of the Church.

CHAPTER 11

1. Most of the information in this section is derived from the mission president's annual report, which was part of the Mission Financial and Statistical Reports of the Hawaiian Mission.

2. J. Reuben Clark, Jr., "The Outpost in Mid-Pacific," 532–533.

3. Mission Financial and Statistical Reports, Hawaiian Mission, 1921.

4. J. Pia Cockett, "Visit of President David O. McKay in 1921." See also Reuben D. Law, *The Founding and Early Development of the Church College of Hawaii,* 19–21. Law quotes a 1955 transcript of D. Arthur Haycock, president of the Hawaii Mission, in which President McKay retold this story.

5. Richard C. Harvey, "The Development of the Church of Jesus Christ of Latter-day Saints in Hawaii," 76–77.

6. MHHM, 5 June 1921.

7. MHHM, 28 February 1928.

8. Mission Financial and Statistical Reports, Hawaiian Mission, 1922, 1923.

9. Bernard Francis Pierce, "Acculturation of Samoans in the Mormon Village of Laie, Hawaii," 16–22.

CHAPTER 12

1. First Presidency to Castle H. Murphy, 20 November 1934, First Presidency Letterbooks.

2. J. Reuben Clark, Jr., "The Outpost in Mid-Pacific," 535.

3. Ibid. President Clark's assertion that the leadership positions of the Church were "essentially proportionate to their relative numbers" is difficult to assess scientifically. The main problem is correctly matching names to ethnic groups. A review of the rosters of branch, district, and mission leaders without the benefit of pictures or a living informant to identify the people involved would probably produce inaccurate conclusions. Many Hawaiian families have American or European surnames. Examples such as Cockett, Plunkett, Peters, Newton, Harrison, Cummings, Napoleon, and Ellis abound. But the same is true of Chinese names. As often as not individuals with such names as Ah Cook, Ah Sing, or Aki are more Hawaiian than Chinese. Thus it is difficult to demonstrate that the Church leadership really reflected the racial composition of the membership. However, careful study of the pictures of the district boards of each of the districts in Hawaii in 1934 leads to the conclusion that a very high percentage of the leaders at that time were Hawaiian or of Hawaiian extraction. Only the Oahu council seems different. Of the ten men shown in the picture, five are haole, four are Hawaiian, and one is Chinese. At least three of these haoles were native residents of Hawaii. See *Directory: Church of Jesus Christ of Latter-day Saints, Hawaiian Mission,* April 1934.

More study is needed to determine the ratio of race to Church leadership positions in the past and at present. Such a study must be done in Hawaii; it cannot be done from records.

4. R. Lanier Britsch, "The Closing of the Early Japanese Mission."

5. Edward L. Clissold, interview, 11 June 1976, Salt Lake City, Utah.

6. Clark, "Outpost in Mid-Pacific," 533.

7. Mission Financial and Statistical Reports, Japanese Mission, 1940.

8. Conkling, "Members Without a Church: Japanese Mormons in Japan from 1924 to 1948," 211.

9. Clissold, interview, 11 June 1976.

10. Eldred L. Waldron to R. Lanier Britsch, 15 June 1976, in possession of the author.

11. *Ka Elele O Hawaii,* December 1942, p. 38.

12. Mission Financial and Statistical Report, Hawaii Mission, 1950.

CHAPTER 13

1. Edward L. Clissold, interview, 11 June 1976, Salt Lake City, Utah.

2. The information in the preceding paragraphs was taken from "Stakes of the Church," *Deseret News 1989–1990 Church Almanac,* 210ff.

3. Bishops are ordained "common judges" and given greater jurisdiction over the affairs of their wards, both spiritual and temporal, than are branch presidents. High priests have the authority to minister in spiritual things and are expected to have a better knowledge of gospel principles and church administration procedure than elders.

4. Gavan Daws, *Shoal of Time: A History of the Hawaiian Islands,* 191.

5. Roscoe E. Cox, "Religious Education in Hawaii," 728.

6. William E. Berrett, interview, 23 June 1976, Provo, Utah; Frank W. McGhie, "Religious Education in the Hawaiian Islands."

7. Berrett, interview, 23 June 1976.

8. Leon R. Hartshorn, "Mormon Education in the Bold Years," 120.

CHAPTER 14

1. David O. McKay, Diary, 7 February 1921, quoted in Reuben D. Law, *The Founding and Early Development of the Church College of Hawaii,* 27–28; see also David W. Cummings, *Mighty Missionary in the Pacific: The Building Program of the Church,* 257–258; and Harvey L. Taylor, "The Story of L.D.S. Church Schools," 2:78ff. These three works are the principal sources relating to the history of CCH. Taylor's study is brief but useful. Law's work is primarily a stringing together of documents generated by himself and others during the years of his presidency. Cummings' book is written in a flamboyant, exaggerated manner. An in-depth scholarly study remains to be done on the founding and history of the institution.

2. Law, *Founding and Early Development,* 27–28. Law quotes from a letter from Hurst in which he gives the verbatim journal account as he wrote it in 1921.

3. Edward L. Clissold, "Address"; see also Law, *Founding and Early Development,* 37–39.

4. Clissold, "Address."

5. Law, *Founding and Early Development,* 66–69.

6. Ibid.

7. Clissold, "Address."

8. Taylor, "Story of Church Schools," 2:88.

9. Law, *Founding and Early Development,* 253.

10. Ibid., 256.

11. Ibid., 239–258, passim.

12. Taylor, "Story of Church Schools," 2:123.

CHAPTER 15

1. Edward L. Clissold, interview, 11 June 1976, Salt Lake City, Utah; *Building Missionaries in Hawaii,* 132.

2. Jerry K. Loveland to author, 1985.

3. Reuben D. Law, *The Founding and Early Development of the Church College of Hawaii,* 69; italics added.

4. "The Gates of Paradise," *BYU Today,* April 1982, p. 8.

5. Max E. Stanton, "Samoan Saints: Settlers and Sojourners," 29.

6. First Presidency to President Faaesea P. Mailo, 21 August 1973, copy in possession of author.

7. Alf Pratte, "Message Is Taken to the Pacific Isles: Gospel Is Taught to the Micronesians"; Farron C. and Fay Losee, interview, 23 February 1984, Provo, Utah.

8. Sources for this section include John H. Groberg Oral History, typescript, 1:26, 47 and 2:26–27, 51; John H. Groberg, interview by R. Lanier Britsch, 16 January 1979, Salt Lake City, Utah, in possession of R. Lanier Britsch; Alf Pratte, "The Gospel Moves to Micronesia"; Robert E. Crandall to R. Lanier Britsch, 25 June 1976, in possession of R. Lanier Britsch; Judy Tudor, *Pacific Islands Year Book,* 235–263, passim.

9. Doctrine and Covenants, Declaration 2.

10. *Deseret News 1989–1990 Church Almanac,* 121.

BIBLIOGRAPHY

This bibliography includes the major works used. It is not a complete bibliography of Hawaiian or LDS Church history. There are several fine single-volume histories of Hawaii available for general readers. Gavan Daws, *Shoal of Time: A History of the Hawaiian Islands,* is a good place to begin. For a comprehensive history of the Latter-day Saints in the Pacific, see R. Lanier Britsch, *Unto the Islands of the Sea: A History of the Latter-day Saints in the Pacific.* The best single-volume history of the Latter-day Saints is by James B. Allen and Glen M. Leonard, *The Story of the Latter-day Saints.* Russell T. Clement has compiled a useful bibliography, *Mormons in the Pacific: A Bibliography.*

PRIMARY SOURCES

Church Records and Manuscripts

The following items are found in the Archives of the Historical Department of The Church of Jesus Christ of Latter-day Saints, Salt Lake City, Utah, hereafter cited as Church Archives.

Conference Minutes of the Sandwich Islands Mission. CR 3695 11, Box 1, fd. 1. 1852.

First Presidency Letterbooks. 1934.

General Minutes, Hawaiian Mission. CR 3695 11, Box 1. 1911–1916.

Historical Reports of the Central Pacific Mission. 1942–1949.

Letterbooks. Letters of Brigham Young to various mission presidents and missionaries. 1854–1877.

Letters to Brigham Young. Ms d 1234. 1853–1877.

MHBY. Manuscript History of Brigham Young. 1857–1866.

MHHM. Jenson, Andrew, comp. "Manuscript History of the Hawaiian Mission." 1935.

Mission Financial and Statistical Reports, Hawaiian Mission. 1910–1955.

Mission Financial and Statistical Reports, Japanese Mission. 1937–1941.

Noall, Matthew. "Letter of Instructions to the Missionaries . . . Laboring in the Hawaiian Missions," April 1894. Elders Improvement Association Minute Book. CR 3695 11, Box 2, fd. 8.

Other Manuscripts

Foreign Office and Executive File, 1851–1853. Hawaii State Archives, Honolulu.

Unpublished Autobiographies, Diaries, Journals, and Oral History

Bigler, Henry W. Journal. Church Archives.

Cannon, George Q. Journal of Travels to the Hawaiian Mission Jubilee. Typescript of dictation taken by Clawson Y. Cannon. In possession of R. Lanier Britsch.

Cluff, Harvey Harris. Autobiography. Handwritten copy, Church Archives.

Farrer, William. Biographical Sketch, Hawaiian Mission Report and Diary, 1821–1906. 2 vols. Typescript in Special Collections, Harold B. Lee Library, Brigham Young University, Provo, Utah.

Gibson, Walter Murray. Diary. Church Archives.

Green, Ephraim. Diary. Typescript in Special Collections, Harold B. Lee Library, Brigham Young University, Provo, Utah.

Groberg, John H. Oral History. Vols. 1–2. Interview by Gordon Irving, 1978. James H. Moyle Oral History Program, Church Archives.

Hammond, Francis A. Journals, 1852–1884. Ms f 338. Church Archives.

Noall, Matthew, and Elizabeth DeEtte Laker Noall. Journals, Reports, and Letters to the First Presidency, Etc. Western Americana Collection, University of Utah Library, Salt Lake City, Utah.

Partridge, Edward, Jr. Journal, number 4. Church Archives.

Woodbury, John Stillman. Journal. 2 vols. Typescript in Special Collections, Harold B. Lee Library, Brigham Young University, Provo, Utah.

Woolley, Samuel E. Journals. Ms f 405. Church Archives.

SECONDARY SOURCES

Adler, Jacob, and Robert M. Kamins. *The Fantastic Life of Walter Murray Gibson: Hawaii's Minister of Everything.* Honolulu: University of Hawaii Press, 1986.

Allen, Helena G. *The Betrayal of Liliuokalani, Last Queen of Hawaii, 1838–1917.* Glendale, California: Arthur H. Clark Company, 1982.

Allen, James B., and Richard O. Cowan. *Mormonism in the Twentieth Century.* Provo, Utah: Brigham Young University Extension Publications, 1964.

Allen, James B., and Glen M. Leonard. *The Story of the Latter-day Saints.* Salt Lake City: Deseret Book, 1976.

Arrington, Leonard J. *Great Basin Kingdom: An Economic History of the Latter-day Saints, 1830–1900.* Cambridge: Harvard University Press, 1958.

Arrington, Leonard J., and Davis Bitton. *The Mormon Experience: A History of the Latter-day Saints.* New York: Alfred A. Knopf, 1979.

Atkin, Dennis H. "A History of Iosepa, the Utah Polynesian Colony." M.A. thesis, Brigham Young University, 1958.

Bailey, Paul. *Hawaii's Royal Prime Minister: The Life and Times of Walter Murray Gibson.* New York: Hastings House, 1980.

Baldridge, Kenneth W. "Search for a Site: Selection of the CCH Campus." In *Proceedings of the Fourth Annual Conference of the Mormon Pacific Historical Society.* Laie, Hawaii: Brigham Young University—Hawaii Campus, 1983.

Beck, Raymond Clyde. "Palawai Basin: Hawaii's Mormon Zion." M.A. thesis, University of Hawaii, 1972.

Barrett, Gwynn. "Walter Murray Gibson: The Shepherd Saint of Lanai Revisited." *Utah Historical Quarterly* 40 (1972): 142–162.

Bock, Margaret Comfort. "The Church of Jesus Christ of Latter-day Saints in the Hawaiian Islands." M.A. thesis, University of Hawaii, 1941.

Britsch, R. Lanier. "Another Visit with Walter Murray Gibson." *Utah Historical Quarterly* 46 (1978): 65–78.

———. "The Closing of the Early Japanese Mission." *BYU Studies* 15 (1975): 171–190.

———. "The Lanai Colony: A Hawaiian Extension of the Mormon Colonial Idea." *Hawaiian Journal of History* 12 (1978): 68–83.

———. *Unto the Islands of the Sea: A History of the Latter-day Saints in the Pacific.* Salt Lake City: Deseret Book, 1986.

Building Missionaries in Hawaii. N.p., n.d.

Campbell, Eugene E. "The Mormon Gold-Mining Mission of 1849." *BYU Studies* 1 & 2 (1959–1960): 19–31.

Cannon, George Q. *My First Mission.* 2d ed. Salt Lake City: Juvenile Instructor Office, 1882.

Chase, Lance D. "Character as Destiny: The Hawaiian Mission Crisis of 1874." In *Proceedings of the First Annual Conference of the Mormon Pacific Historical Society.* Laie, Hawaii: Brigham Young University—Hawaii Campus, 1980.

———. "Life in Early Laie, 1850–80." In *Proceedings of the Second Annual Conference of the Mormon Pacific Historical Society.* Laie, Hawaii: Brigham Young University—Hawaii Campus, 1981.

Clark, J. Reuben, Jr. "The Outpost in Mid-Pacific." *The Improvement Era* 38 (September 1935): 532–535.

Clement, Russell T., and Sheng-Luen Tsai. "East Wind to Hawaii: Contributions of Chinese and Japanese Mormons in Hawaii." In *Proceedings of the Second Annual Conference of the Mormon Pacific Historical Society.* Laie, Hawaii: Brigham Young University—Hawaii Campus, 1981.

Clissold, Edward L. "Address." Dedication of the Church College of Hawaii, 17 December 1958. Typescript in Church Archives.

———. "Assignment Kona, 1921." In *Proceedings of the Third Annual Conference of the Mormon Pacific Historical Society*. Laie, Hawaii: Brigham Young University—Hawaii Campus, 1982.

———. "Missionary Work Among the Japanese in the Hawaiian Islands." Unpublished typescript in Central Pacific Mission Historical Records, 1937–1950. Church Archives.

Cockett, J. Pia. "Visit of President David O. McKay in 1921." Typescript, n.d., in Church Archives, CR 3695 1, Box 1.

Conkling, J. Christopher. "Members Without a Church: Japanese Mormons in Japan from 1924 to 1948." *BYU Studies* 15 (1975): 191–214.

Cox, Roscoe E. "Religious Education in Hawaii." *The Improvement Era* 44 (December 1941): 728.

Cummings, David W. *Centennial History of Laie*. N.p.: Laie Centennial Committee, [1965].

———. *Mighty Missionary in the Pacific: The Building Program of the Church*. Salt Lake City: Bookcraft, 1961.

Daws, Gavan. *Shoal of Time: A History of the Hawaiian Islands*. Honolulu: University of Hawaii Press, 1968.

Deseret News 1983 Church Almanac. "Stakes of the Church by Geographical Location." Salt Lake City: Deseret News, 1983.

Deseret News 1989–1990 Church Almanac. Salt Lake City: Deseret News, 1988.

Directory: Church of Jesus Christ of Latter-day Saints, Hawaiian Mission. Honolulu: n.p., 1934.

Doctrine and Covenants. Salt Lake City: The Church of Jesus Christ of Latter-day Saints, 1981.

Grant, Heber J. "The Dedicatory Prayer in the Hawaiian Temple." *The Improvement Era* 23 (February 1920): 284.

Hartshorn, Leon R. "Mormon Education in the Bold Years." Ed.D. diss., Stanford University, 1965.

Harvey, Richard C. "The Development of The Church of Jesus Christ of Latter-day Saints in Hawaii." M.A. thesis, Brigham Young University, 1974.

Ivins, Antoine R. "Laie Plantation." Typescript, n.d., Church Archives.

Jenson, Andrew, comp. *Church Chronology*. 2d ed. Salt Lake City: Deseret News Press, 1899.

Johnson, Benjamin F. *My Life's Review*. Independence, Missouri: Zion's Printing and Publishing Company, 1947.

Judd, Gerrit P., IV. *Hawaii: An Informal History*. New York: Collier Macmillan, 1961.

Kuykendall, Ralph S. *The Hawaiian Kingdom*. 3 vols. Honolulu: University of Hawaii Press, 1947, 1953, and 1967.

Law, Reuben D. *The Founding and Early Development of the Church College of Hawaii*. St. George, Utah: Dixie College Press, 1972.

Loveland, Jerry K. "Dedication of the Old Laie Chapel." Typed copy, n.d., in possession of R. Lanier Britsch.

McConkie, Bruce R. *Mormon Doctrine.* 2d ed. Salt Lake City: Bookcraft Publishers, 1966.

McGhie, Frank W. "The Life and Intrigues of Walter Murray Gibson." M.A. thesis, Brigham Young University, 1958.

———. "Religious Education in the Hawaiian Islands." Typescript, n.d., in possession of R. Lanier Britsch.

Michener, James A., and A. Grove Day. *Rascals in Paradise.* London: Secker and Warburg, 1957.

Morison, Samuel Eliot. *The Oxford History of the American People.* New York: Oxford University Press, 1965.

Murphy, Castle H. "A Brief Resume of the Beginning of the Work of Preaching the Gospel to the Chinese and the Japanese in Hawaii in 1932 and 1944." In "The First Stake in Hawaii (and) the Japanese and Chinese Missions." Unpublished scrapbook and manuscript, 1975. Church Archives.

———. *Castle of Zion—Hawaii.* Salt Lake City: Deseret Book, 1963.

Musser, Joseph B. "Laie—Home Place of the Church in Hawaii." Typescript, n.d., Church Archives.

———. "Walter Murray Gibson—Oceanic Adventurer." *U.S. Naval Institute Proceedings* 52 (1926): 1709–1732.

Noall, Matthew. *To My Children.* Salt Lake City: Utah Printing, n.d.

O'Brien, Robert. *Hands Across the Water: The Story of the Polynesian Cultural Center.* Laie, Hawaii: Polynesian Cultural Center, 1983.

Pearl of Great Price. Salt Lake City: The Church of Jesus Christ of Latter-day Saints, 1981.

Pierce, Bernard Francis. "Acculturation of Samoans in the Mormon Village of Laie, Hawaii." M.A. thesis, University of Hawaii, 1956.

Pratt, Parley P. *Autobiography of Parley P. Pratt.* Salt Lake City: Deseret Book, 1938.

Pratte, Alf. "The Gospel Moves to Micronesia." *Ensign* 8 (February 1978): 76–77.

———. "Message Is Taken to the Pacific Isles: Gospel Is Taught to the Micronesians." *Church News,* 24 March 1979, p. 3.

Roberts, Brigham H. *Comprehensive History of the Church.* 6 vols. Salt Lake City: Deseret Book, 1930.

Smith, Joseph. *History of The Church of Jesus Christ of Latter-day Saints.* 7 vols. Salt Lake City: Deseret Book, 1973.

Smith, Joseph Fielding, Jr. *The Life of Joseph F. Smith.* Salt Lake City: Deseret Book, 1938.

Snow, Eliza R. *Biography and Family Record of Lorenzo Snow.* Salt Lake City: Deseret News, 1884.

Sousa, Esther L. "Walter Murray Gibson's Rise to Power in Hawaii." M.A. thesis, University of Hawaii, 1942.

Spurrier, Joseph H. "Jonathon Napela: Quiet Hero of Hawaii." *Ensign* 8 (August 1978): 49–51.

Stanton, Max E. "Samoan Saints: Settlers and Sojourners." In *Proceedings of the*

Second Annual Conference of the Mormon Pacific Historical Society. Laie, Hawaii: Brigham Young University—Hawaii Campus, 1981.

———. "Samoan Saints: The Samoans in the Mormon Village of Laie, Hawaii." Ph.D. diss., University of Oregon, 1973.

Stewart, John J. *The Life of Joseph Fielding Smith.* Salt Lake City: Deseret Book, 1972.

Taylor, Harvey L. "The Story of L.D.S. Church Schools." 2 vols. Bound typescript, 1971. Church Archives.

Taylor, Samuel W. "Walter Murray Gibson: Great Mormon Rascal." *The American West* 1 (1964): 18–27, 77.

Thurston, Lorrin A. *Memoirs of the Hawaiian Revolution.* Honolulu: Advertiser Publishing, 1936.

Tudor, Judy, ed. *Pacific Islands Year Book.* 11th ed., Sydney: Pacific Publications, 1972.

Young, John R. *Memoirs of John R. Young.* Salt Lake City: Deseret Book, 1920.

INDEX

Boldface numbers indicate illustrations.